C000177646

The M
Fighters 2

More Lives and Times of
Liverpool's Boxing Heroes

Gary Shaw and Jim Jenkinson

First published in December 2007 by Gary Shaw

Copyright © 2007 Gary Shaw and Jim Jenkinson

Features by Frank Johnson © Birkenhead News

ISBN 978-0-9557283-0-3

Printed and bound by Biddles

Published privately by
Gary Shaw

Contents

Preface

As we did for the first volume we would like to start by explaining why some boxers are not included in *The Mersey Fighters 2*. Although we tried exceptionally hard, using our extensive boxing contacts, knowledge, and making numerous appeals in local radio and media, we were unable to contact all those we set out to. Likewise some of those we were able to speak to were, for a variety of reasons, unable to be included before time simply ran out. It is for these reasons only - not a lack of enthusiasm on our part - that some boxers are not included.

Although first contact with some was made as early as late-2004 - just as the first volume was being printed - it has taken us over three years to find, interview, write, research and then re-interview and re-write, the 64 biographies that are included. At times it was an exhausting undertaking, but what kept us going was the belief that not only should the stories we were being told be made available to a wider audience, but also the fact that many boxing and sports fans, both local and international, were keen to discover what a particular boxer thought of his career, and also what they did when they retired. With these issues in mind we were especially pleased to be able to contact Kevin Pritchard. John Farrell and Jimmy Price, three boxers who were as elusive to find outside the ring as they were inside! Their stories make for interesting reading. We were also pleased that we are able to include a host of boxers that were specifically mentioned in the preface of Volume 1 due to their original omission; Billy Aird, Robbie Davies, Ray and George Gilbody, Paul Hodkinson, Shea Neary and Andy Holligan. It was a pleasure and a privilege to interview them and to recall their exploits in the hardest of sports, when they thrilled not only local boxing crowds but fans all over the country, and abroad.

Merseyside has an exceptional, almost unsurpassed, boxing history and we have endeavoured to portray that history in as interesting a format as possible. We hope that you enjoy the biographies we have managed to include, encompassing every decade of the area's pugilistic history, from the 1910s to the present. A broad spectrum of local boxers and their stories are included and although fewer in number than the first volume, we feel that they are of greater depth and focus.

Gary Shaw & Jim Jenkinson - September 2007

Acknowledgements

Obviously we cannot fail to acknowledge the contribution made by the former fighters featured within the book itself. They have given us their time to talk over their careers and for this we are forever grateful. We would also like to thank the relatives of some of those included who are sadly no longer with us, for supplying us with information about their loved ones careers. Again, it is much appreciated.

We would also like to thank one of Britain's foremost boxing record compilers and historians, Harold Alderman. A great friend of the Merseyside Former Boxers' Association (MFBA), Harold was always ready and able to answer any queries which arose during the course of our research. His help and support was often illuminating and always given in good grace. Although many of the fights referred to, particularly for the older boxers, cannot be found on record sites such as *Boxrec.com*, no bouts were included that Harold could not independently verify, making the stories all the more complete.

We are also grateful to former Birkenhead boxing journalist Frank Johnson. Just as Syd Dye published a number of articles on former fighters in *The Liverpool Echo* during the 1970s, so too did Frank complete a similar series on former fighters from the Wirral for *The Birkenhead News*. We thank Frank for allowing us to use his articles as the base for some of those included and where applicable he has been credited with the original.

In any undertaking such as this one the work behind the scenes is often as important as the research and writing done at the forefront. With this in mind we would also like to thank Kirkby ABC coach John Lloyd for putting us in touch with a number of retired boxers who proved particularly difficult to trace. Jacqui Ward-Jones was again awarded a sneak preview of almost all the biographies virtue of her hard work in typing most of them up! Her methodical approach is also appreciated.

Whilst every effort has been taken to ensure that all information is up-to-date and correct, we are only human and a few factual errors may occur. We only hope that this does not detract from your enjoyment of the book.

Gary Shaw & Jim Jenkinson - September 2007

Introductions

It is with immense pleasure and pride that, together with Jim, I have been able to add another series of boxing biographies to those featured in the first volume. Such great local boxers as Nel Tarleton, Ernie Roderick, Joe Curran, Dick Tiger, Peter Kane, Wally Thom, Hogan 'Kid' Bassey, Ike Bradley and John Conteh were featured in our earlier book and, as many of the biographies were based on the outstanding historical work originally undertaken by Syd Dye in the early-1970s, the others were drawn mainly from a time and era that preceded my existence.

By contrast however, this volume is very different. True, a number of old-time boxing personalities are included, but the vast majority are from a time I remember well. Indeed, I even had the honour and pleasure of being in attendance when some, such as Paul Hodkinson, Alex Moon, Shea Neary, Andy Holligan, Joey Moffat, Tony Moran and Gary Thornhill were at their peak.

The atmosphere I witnessed at the famous Neary v Holligan world title fight for instance, has yet to be surpassed at any boxing show I have seen before or since (although Jimmy's second round KO of Terry Southerland came close!). The disappointment I felt at Paul Hodkinson's heartbreaking loss to Marcos Villisanna in his first world title challenge in June 1990, when, in the eighth round and with both eyes closed, 'Hoko' turned to the referee telling him that he couldn't carry on, was profound. I had never felt so down after watching a fighter lose, but this was soon forgotten the following year when Paul boxed superbly to gain the title everyone in Liverpool so badly wanted him to win.

To say it has been a pleasure to interview these boxers would be a gross understatement. It really has been an honour. It speaks volumes that, even though two sets of biographies have now been produced on Merseyside's boxing heroes, not all those worthy of inclusion have been covered. Who knows? If Liverpool continues to remain at the forefront of British boxing a while longer, another volume may be forthcoming in a few years!

Gary Shaw September 2007

For my Mum, Eileen, with love - things can only get better Mam.

Introductions

When Gary and I wrote the first volume of *The Mersey Fighters* in 2004 we hinted then that if it proved successful then we would consider putting together a second. We also said that doing so would not take as much work. How wrong we were! It really is incredible just how quickly time seems to pass. We started on this volume almost while the ink was still wet on the first but before you know it the months have flown by, as have the years, and you're facing a struggle to meet the publishing date!

We hope that we have put together an interesting collection of stories on former Merseyside fight favourites, with a mixture of former champions and contenders from the last 20 years to those from the 1970s, 1950s and earlier.

I am extremely grateful to all those former boxers I have interviewed regarding their careers. Not one proved reluctant or unwilling to talk openly and honestly about both their wins and losses. It greatly adds to the integrity of the book.

There is a tremendous history of boxing on Merseyside, which I hope you will both acknowledge and enjoy through the first volume, this volume and, who knows, perhaps another. In addition to these however, it is also worthwhile mentioning the work the MFBA has recently completed regarding the setting up of a permanent Merseyside Boxing Archive. With the help of the Heritage Lottery Fund, the Association has interviewed over 60 former fighters from the area, and is in the process of interviewing many more, all of whom will be included on a DVD to permanently record their contribution to the area's social history. We have also collected a truly amazing collection of photographs, programmes and memorabilia, all of which will be included in the Archive. A static display commemorating this rich history has already been shown, to much acclaim, at various functions, schools and colleges, throughout the area. If anyone has any such memorabilia they would wish to donate or loan to the Association please let us know.

Jim Jenkinson September 2007

For Richard, Amie and Freya with much love.

The Mersey Fighters 2

More Lives and Times of Liverpool's Boxing Heroes

Gary Shaw and Jim Jenkinson

A member of Liverpool's famous Golden Gloves ABC, Billy Aird, who admits he only took up the sport to keep himself out of trouble, enjoyed a successful amateur career with the South Liverpool club – winning three North West Counties titles – before turning professional in 1969. 46 contests in a 14-year career (two for the British title) followed for the likable London-based 'scouser' and although he never won the domestic crown he is remembered as a more than capable performer who always gave his best, no matter who the opponent. Billy's last contest was in 1983 and he became a top-class referee before reluctantly retiring a few years ago. Still living in London but a regular face at boxing shows and ex-boxers' meetings in both Liverpool and the capital, this article was based on interviews with Billy in 2006.

BILLY AIRD

Ten-year wait for British title chance

"I was getting on a bit in years when I first started to become properly involved in boxing. I was 19 when I first went to the Golden Gloves ABC. I took it up really just to keep myself out of trouble. I was a big lad and it was easy to get involved in street fights in my teens. Once I started taking cthe sport seriously however, I was never involved in another fight in the street. I enjoyed the discipline that boxing gave me as well as the training. So much so that I was good enough to win three North West Counties titles.

"Altogether I had around 50 amateur contests, and lost just 15. I was 23 when I decided to have a go as a professional and, as there didn't seem to be anyone in the North who could look after me, I went to London. In those days it was really only Mickey Duff and his firm that ran boxing, but I didn't like them so decided to manage myself. However, I did manage to get one of the best 'scouse' trainers in the business to help me out, Johnny Winters. We enjoyed a good relationship and I managed a total of 46 contests as a pro, winning 26 losing 15 and drawing the other five."

Billy's first paid outing was a fourth round stoppage over Paul Cassidy in London in June 1969. Three wins followed in the calendar year before his first loss, a strange and rare three rounds (yes – three rounds!) points defeat to another up-and-coming British heavyweight, "My old mate Richard Dunn." Dunn of course would later become British, Commonwealth and European champion himself before losing to the great Muhammad Ali for the world title in 1976.

Billy would get his revenge over Dunn just three months later when he won a much more normal eight rounds points decision. In September 1970 the two met for a third time for the Central Area title in Manchester, with Billy winning his only professional title courtesy of a fifth round stoppage. "I stopped Richard in five rounds. I remember I had him up and down like a yo-yo!" The pair met for a fourth time in May 1973 at Mayfair's Grosvenor House Hotel, this time in a British title eliminator, with Dunn winning on points after ten tough rounds.

With seven wins from his first eight contests Billy was on his way up the domestic ratings – making the top ten for the first time in 1970. Two defeats followed his Central Area title victory however, the first to the Birmingham-based Jamaican Bunny Johnson – like Dunn another regular opponent of Billy's and yet another who would go on to win the British and Commonwealth titles.

In December 1970 Billy had the first of many contests outside Britain, a ten rounds points defeat to Foster Bibron in Melbourne. "I wasn't afraid to travel, and I wasn't afraid to meet anyone, no matter who they were. I boxed a lot in London of course as I based myself there, but I also fought in Spain, South Africa, and Germany. I fought twice for the British heavyweight title. The first against John L Gardner at London's Albert Hall in October 1978. I was badly cut over both eyes in the early stages and decided to retire myself after five rounds.

"The second time I fought for the title I lost on points over 15 rounds to Gordon Ferris in Birmingham. That was March 1981. Gordon had a good start but I came back strong in the later rounds but just missed out. I also challenged Alfredo Evangelista for the European heavyweight title. This was in March 1978 – before I'd fought for the British title – in Leon in Spain. I lost on points over 15 rounds but think I put up a good show." In fact, most neutral observers felt Aird had done enough to win.

Besides fighting in his native country, Evangelista was the heavier and younger man but, as the *Boxing News* reported at the time, "old-fashioned British courage," coupled with skill and ability wasn't enough to get the decision. They also added that had the fight taken place in England Billy would surely have won. As Billy himself states, "I had him in trouble a couple of times and would have certainly stopped him over here. As many have found before me however, you hardly ever win on points abroad." Asked if it was a difficult contest after the fight, Evangelista himself said, "Difficult? I'll say it was. Aird knows it all...I just didn't know where or how to hit him."

Besides Dunn, Johnson and Evangelista, Billy also met the likes of fellow-Liverpudlian John Conteh, an eighth round stoppage loss in June 1972, Roger Tighe and Denton Ruddock. "I fought some of the heavyweight division's hardest men. I drew with Jimmy Young – not the DJ! – and just two years later Young would KO George Foreman, and you mustn't forget the Peralta brothers from Argentina. I fought them both and they were, without doubt, the dirtiest fighters you could ever wish to meet. Everything went as far as they were concerned; heads, thumbs, elbows, the lot."

Billy Aird in training c. 1975   Source: Gary Shaw

Billy lost to Greg Peralta in Hamburg in 1973 and four years later was disqualified in the fifth of a right brawl against older brother Avenmar in Luton. Billy admits however that, "although they were tough men the hardest opponent I ever faced was a fellow called Cliff Field. I boxed him twice and beat him each time *[W KO2 January 1971 and W KO7 July 1971 eds.]*, but he was as hard as nails."

Although free to decide who, when and where to fight, Billy's professional interests may not have been best served by managing himself as opposed to being managed by a major promoter. He had been ranked in the top 10 British heavyweights every year from 1970-82; was in the top three from 1974-82; and was the No. 1 challenger in 1976, 1977 and 1979, yet had to watch others ranked below him get the call from the Boxing Board of Control. "These days with the likes of Matchroom, Hennessy and other promoters, things are much easier and lots of boxers get a title chance relatively early in their careers. The fact that I was self-managed definitely worked against me though, and I had to wait nearly 10 years before I boxed for a British title."

Not that this means those given such a chance actually deserve it however. Like many of his generation Billy sees lots of room for improvement for many of today's pros. "In my opinion many have little or no idea of how to fight on the inside. They just throw punches, but they don't think about what's coming back. They aren't taught how to block, parry or catch shots the way we were in my day."

In Billy's day of course there were far more boxing shows held, and far more venues in which great fight atmospheres could be generated, not least his old home town Stadium. "It was a sad day when they knocked down the Liverpool Stadium. I never fought there as a professional, but I did as an amateur and I enjoyed it very much. I fought there eight times and never lost. It had a great atmosphere, which I am afraid to say you simply don't get in many of today's arenas."

Looking back at his career Billy has few regrets. "I became a professional referee when I finished boxing, but I'm no longer active in that role now. I can't say a bad word about the sport though. It builds character and discipline and it certainly kept me out of trouble. I live in London now but I still make as many trips back to Liverpool as I can. I always try and call in on my old friends in the Merseyside Former Boxers Association (MFBA). Its great to belong to an organisation like that – where we can meet up with old friends and talk over old times!"

One of a number of talented African boxers who settled in Liverpool in the 1950s, Ghana's Sani Armstrong may not be remembered by many today, but he was a welterweight to be reckoned with in the late-1950s and early- 1960s. In his eight-year British career he had at least 21 contests, meeting the likes of Sandy Manuel, Johnny Fish, Fortunato Manca, Johnny Melfah, Johnny Kramer, George Palin and Carmelo Bossi. Still living in Liverpool, this article was obtained through interview with Sani in 2006.

SANI ARMSTRONG

Hard to beat - met two future world champs

"I was 15 years old when I first became involved in boxing," remembers Ghana's Sani Armstrong. "Although my older brother boxed as an amateur I didn't join an amateur club, instead joining a gym my uncle set up in his house in Accra, Ghana. I liked fighting as a young boy and the discipline boxing gave me calmed me down a bit." Despite having no amateur experience Sani was boxing for pay in his late-teens and had a number of contests in Ghana, winning them all, before coming to Liverpool in 1955. "I was undefeated in Africa and lost only a few in Britain."

After seeking out a local manager and training with the likes of Sugar Gibiliru and Israel Boyle, Sani's first contest in Britain was a fine six rounds points win over Tipton's Jim Stimpson at Walsall Town Hall in February 1956. Another points win the next month was followed by his first loss in Britain, a creditable eight rounds points loss to a fellow African émigré, Nigeria's talented Sandy Manuel. There was no disgrace in losing to Sandy however, as the likable Nigerian had won 22 out of 34 contests when Sani met him in Hartlepool in May 1956, and he was ranked in the top 10 in the Empire at the time.

Sani lost just a handful of his next dozen contests, were he enjoyed wins over Edinburgh's experienced Eddie Phillips and Harlow's highly-rated Johnny Fish. In September 1958 he was matched with unbeaten Italian Fortunato Manca in Cagliari, Sardinia. Despite it being his first contest outside of England since his arrival in Britain some three years earlier, Sani took the tough Italian the distance but eventually lost on points over ten rounds. Manca would later challenge for the world light-middleweight title and was EBU welterweight champion in 1965. Although boxing at welterweight, Sani met many light-middleweights and admits that, "For most of my fights I always had weight problems."

Sani had a mixed 1959, although he scored a great win over his fellow countryman, the ever-dangerous Johnny Melfah, at the Liverpool Stadium in May. A draw against Irish prospect Fred Tiedt in Dublin in July 1956 is also worthy of mention. Losses against the famous Cardiff-based Greek welterweight Tanos Lambrianides and West Ham's talented and highly-rated Johnny Kramer – when Kramer was no. 5 in Britain – were followed by perhaps his biggest win to date; a fourth round stoppage win over Nigeria's Eddie Phillips in Preston.

Sani's win against Phillips seemed to galvanise the Ghanaian, and he went on a great run of form. In November 1961 he outpointed Crewe's George Palin over eight rounds at Leeds Town Hall, a victory he repeated at Newcastle's St. James' Hall some five months later. Palin was ranked the ninth best welterweight in Britain when Sani beat him the first time, and no. 4 at the time of his second win. An eight rounds points win over Camden Town's Tony Lewis in June 1962 was another fine win as Lewis would later win the Southern Area title.

In February 1964 Sani was asked to travel to Italy again, this time meeting hot prospect Carmelo Bossi at Milan's Lido Palace. Sani lost on points over eight rounds but like his compatriot Manca some six years earlier, Bossi was a man going places. Three years later he would win the EBU welterweight title *[a crown he successfully defended against Bootle's Johnny Cooke in August 1967 eds.]* and in 1970 he was crowned world light-middleweight champion courtesy of a points win over Freddie Little in Monza.

A pro for almost eight years in Britain, Sani's career was slowing down and in December 1964 he had his last contest, a sixth rounds points loss to Germany's Werner Mundt in Frankfurt. Mundt would win the German light-middleweight title in his next contest.

Although he met a host of highly-rated domestic and European fighters during his career, Sani is reluctant to pick one above the other and says simply, "There were lots of tough fights in my time." He does however, acknowledge that to succeed in the sport in the 1950s and 1960s was certainly tougher than today. "It is a lot easier than it was in my time. Boxers of today seem to make easy money."

Of his contests at the Liverpool Stadium and the crowd there, Sani acknowledges, "They appreciated a good fight." He also never regrets taking up boxing as a career, nor indeed in moving to Liverpool all those years ago. "I don't ever regret coming to England and boxing. I enjoyed the sport and would gladly do it again. It was hard to get fights at first as I did not know where any of the British managers lived but I worked at the same time as boxing and I made many friends here in Liverpool."

Sani Armstrong c. 1960   *Source: Gary Shaw*

Born in Belfast in 1914, Billy Beattie won a schoolboy bantamweight championship at 14 years of age in what was probably his only amateur bout. He turned professional at the age of 16 making his debut at the famous Ulster Hall, Belfast. His pro career saw him defeat the likes of John Kelly and Jim Brady as well as reversing a previous loss to Jimmy Warnock. Perhaps his greatest ring performance however, saw him fight a draw with the great Benny Lynch in Lynch's own backyard. This chapter is based on an article written by Frank Johnson that was first published in 1972.

BILLY BEATTIE

Held great Scot Benny Lynch to a draw

When first interviewed at his home on the Ford Estate in Birkenhead in 1972, Billy Beattie was a 58 year old boilermaker with the Mersey Docks and Harbour Company. Although he met all the leading fly and bantamweights of the day, when great fighters at those weights could be found in their dozens in every town and city in the country, he rated his draw with Scotland's Benny Lynch among the most memorable memories of his ring career.

Billy was born in Belfast in 1914 and, although there was no real history of boxing in his family, both he and his younger brother, also called Billy, loved the sport. So much so that both turned professional, the younger brother boxing as a welterweight under the name 'Kid Farlo'. Billy himself won a schoolboy bantamweight championship when he was 14, but this was really the sum total of his amateur boxing experience for he turned professional just two years later, having his first professional contest at Belfast's famous Ulster Hall, with a six rounds win over Martin Hart. Billy's purse for that contest was £3.

Billy was a southpaw and he used his unorthodox style to great effect, causing problems for many of his opponents. His hard-hitting also created havoc, with his great left hook proving too much for Young Scott, who went out in three rounds after a blistering opening two rounds in which both boys hammered away at each other incessantly. In his first eight-rounder, Billy boxed a draw with Young Donnelly. His reputation was being enhanced with every fight he won and it wasn't long before the opposition became increasingly stiffer.

In August 1931 Billy had a great fight with John Kelly before winning in the third round. In October the same year he was out-pointed by

Johnny 'Kid' Truesdale over eight rounds, but this was certainly no disgrace, as the winner was rated at that time as one of the cleverest fighters around. Truesdale's all-round skill and ring-craft not only earned him the verdict, but also taught the eager Beattie some hard lessons. Billy bounced back in great style with a points win over Joe Dale at Dundarey, and he followed this up with a two round win over Jackie Finn who, at that time, was a contender for the Irish title.

At the turn of the century, there was a great bantamweight of gypsy ancestry by the name of Pedlar Palmer, and although no relation but out of respect, a canny Irishman took the same name and earned a great reputation as a trial horse for any up and coming lad who thought that he knew all the tricks of the trade. Billy traded leather with this character in November 1931 and beat him over eight rounds. In round four of a bruising battle, Palmer sustained broken ribs but he refused to surrender and although beaten he somehow came storming back in the last two rounds to put Billy under considerable pressure. In February 1932 Billy recorded a fine win when he outpointed Jim Brady over ten rounds at Dundee. Brady later became the British Empire bantamweight champion, so it was obvious that Billy was really making an impression in fight circles.

The flyweight tradition has been carried by many great Scots and Irish fighters, and one of the greatest to come out of the Emerald Isle was Jimmy Warnock. This same Warnock licked Benny Lynch twice over 12 rounds, and again over the 15 rounds distance, so his pedigree was certainly no myth. Billy Beattie rated Jimmy Warnock as one of the greatest fighters that he had ever seen and he was one of Billy's ring idols. The time eventually came for them to face each other and they met in Belfast over eight rounds and, although Warnock won, Billy had him in serious trouble in the sixth.

A ten rounds points win over Minty Rose boosted Billy's stock even higher as Rose fought the great Midget Wolgast for the world title at Madison Square Garden in a later encounter. A further outstanding win for Billy was recorded against Sunderland's Tom Smith who later fought Nel Tarleton for the British featherweight title. Billy also reversed his earlier defeat by Jim Warnock and finished off his 1932 campaign with 19 straight wins, 12 of these coming via way of KO. He retained his unbeaten record in 1933 with 12 wins from 12 contests, one of which included an eight round draw with Jimmy James, the Ulster bantamweight champion. In 1934, Jimmy would lose again to

'Kid' Truesdale, but would go on to reverse that loss with a first round KO.

Billy recalled attending a Donkey Derby at Moreton during the great pre-war era, when he boxed an exhibition with Tom Smith. Also there that day were Peter Kane, Nel Tarleton, Ernie Roderick and the world featherweight champion Freddie Miller of the USA who was over here to defend his title against Tarleton. In October 1932 Billy met Benny Lynch in Hamilton, Scotland, and although he was past his best he managed to hold the dynamic Scotsman to a draw over six rounds. Lynch of course would go on to hold the world flyweight title.

Billy ended his professional career in 1937 and it was then that he moved to the Wirral where he married and worked throughout the war as a foreman blacksmith. He may have retired from the ring but he soon discovered that he had moved into an area which lived and breathed boxing, and Billy kept fit by joining Dick Staden's Club in Charing Cross along with Nat Stewart and Jimmy Moore.

In 1938 he went along to George Reynolds Club where he helped in the training of local boys Frankie Williams and Tony and Danny Goodall. During the war he found little time for boxing but, in addition to his long working hours, he also served in the Home Guard at Irby. In 1945 he moved to Warwick Street, Birkenhead and the following year he helped Alex Powell at the Kingsway Club in Price Street. He later had spells at the Kingsway Club with Johnny Campbell and helped to train Pat McAteer, Joe Bygraves and Jimmy Stubbs.

After a spell at the Birkenhead ABC under Tommy Murray, Billy formed the Oxton ABC, making the ring himself and cadging equipment from all corners of the town. The club had a powerful team with Northern Counties flyweight champion Danny Pollard the leading light. Tommy Wiggins, Billy Griffiths and Dave Beattie were also in the team but in 1969, Billy handed over the reigns of the club to Gerry Byrne.

Billy rated boxing the ideal sport for keeping boys out of mischief and in peak fitness. He said that the best fighter that he ever fought was Jimmy Warnock, the toughest was Fred Archer and the cleverest, if only in sparring, was without doubt, the great Peter Kane.

One of the most famous Liverpool boxing personalities of yester-year, Charlie Blackburn enjoyed a successful career at the turn of the twentieth century, winning Lancashire, North of England titles and a coveted Jem Mace belt in the process, before becoming a respected boxing referee and renowned trainer. Charlie also found time to run a boxing booth, a number of pubs in Liverpool City Centre and was President of the local branch of the Professional Boxer's Union for a number of years. One of the last links between the bare-knuckle days and legalised gloved boxing, Charlie died in 1950.

CHARLIE BLACKBURN

North of England champ who became famous referee and local sportsman

Born on St Patrick's Day 1872 in Liverpool, Charlie Blackburn's family moved to Crosby when he was 16 and it was whilst in the Liverpool suburb that he first visited a gym with the sole intention of keeping fit. After sparring with a number of fighters who trained at the gym Charlie, then aged just 16, was asked to appear on a pro show, much to the consternation of his grandmother as up until this time Charlie had always intimated that it was his intention to become a minister.

Charlie was hooked however, and one of his first opponents of note was Tom Meadows, an Australian featherweight of some repute. As was common in those days, Meadows placed a challenge to any fighter of his weight in the North of England. Charlie took the Australian up on his offer but was defeated. Despite his loss however, Charlie was far from discouraged and before long he met and defeated Harry Brown in a contest billed as being for the featherweight championship of North England.

The great Jem Mace was by then touring the country with his boxing booth. Jem put up a cash prize, a cup and a belt for all-comers at 9st. Charlie entered the competition and won the lot in Leeds. In 1892 he moved up to lightweight and, trained by Tommy Jones, he claimed the lightweight championship of Lancashire by again beating Harry Brown.

In great demand in Northern rings, Charlie went on to win around 25 out of 30 or so contests, meeting al the principal fighters at his weight in the North of England and becoming highly regarded by all connected with the sport. In November 1917, Charlie was referred to in the Football Express in the most glowing terms. "He is modest, unassuming, rarely quibbles over decisions and is determined to prove that he is the best lightweight in the country." The article even went as far as to compare Charlie with George Dixon, the great black Canadian featherweight from the 1890s and 1900s.

Like Mace, Charlie also ran a travelling boxing booth and he visited all the main towns, festivals and fairgrounds in the country. He ran this for around 10 years and his party of boxers, including 'Young Starlight the Black' of South Africa, and Pedlar McMahon of Swansea would take on all-comers at all weights, almost every night of the week. Should any ladies be interested in showing their skills in the ring then Charlie, who often appeared as the main fighter on his 'shows', could also offer the services of Miss Daisy Wallace of Birmingham, who also travelled with the booth. Charlie's booth was the last to appear at Aintree Racecourse and one time he ran a private show for the visiting owners, trainers and jockeys. Charlie always maintained that the booth was the best training ground a boxer could ever have.

Charlie also trained a number of boxers, amongst them Will Curley who Charlie took to America for his world featherweight title challenge against George Dixon – the very man who Charlie had been compared to in his local sporting press. Unfortunately for Charlie however, Dixon won over 25 rounds at Coney Island in December 1899, thus depriving him of being the trainer of a world champion. Charlie also gave private boxing tuition. Advertising himself as Professor C. Blackburn, Charlie was in great demand and offered his services with the statement, "How to learn the noble art of self-defence. Taught in a gentlemanly and scientific manner without fear of being abused. Lessons strictly private."

On retiring Charlie maintained his interest in the sport by becoming a renowned and above all, trusted referee. His integrity was never in question with the press again stimulated to admiration of the highest kind. One local report stated, "Like poets, your real referee is born not made, and when Charlie Blackburn was born the mould was broken. Cool in moments of stress and a rare judge of the game, C. Blackburn in my opinion, stands in the forefront of modern day referees." Another reference stated, "In the years before World War One, the late John Murray, editor of *Boxing*, appointed Mr. Charles Blackburn of Liverpool to act as 'Third Man' in the ring for the many money matches for which that journal held side stakes. For he was not only a good judge, but also 'sea green' honest"

In later years Charlie and his wife Elizabeth became proprietors of a number of public houses in Liverpool, among them The Farmers Arms in Great Newton Street and The Stags Head at 40 Pembroke Place. They remained at the latter for almost 60 years and many of the fighters, trainers, managers and officials who had business at the Pudsey Street Stadium (now the Odeon Cinema in London Road) would lodge there during their stay. It was also at The Stags Head that the Liverpool branch of the Boxers Union would meet, with Charlie as local President.

Among the fighters that Charlie met during his career of over 100 contests were Jock Pearson, Henry Thompson, Jack Bancroft, Jack Culkin, Harry Blundell and the Liverpool pair of 'Punch' and George Vaughan. All were top rated fighters. He passed away on 2 August 1950, thus bringing an end to the link between the old prize-ring era of Jem Mace and the modern game. In August 2005 a number of Charlie's trophies and mementos were placed on view in the Museum of Liverpool Life.

An especially awkward southpaw who won two National Schoolboys titles as an amateur with Litherland ABC before turning pro with Chris Moorcroft in 1982, Bootle's Tony Brown enjoyed a fine 13-year career, amassing 20 wins from 36 contests. He won two Central Area titles, at light-welterweight and welterweight, and met the likes of Ian Chantler, Walter Clayton, Joseph Lala, Kostas Petrou, Rocky Kelly - in an eliminator for the British title, Derek Wormald and George Collins. Still living and working in Liverpool, this article was compiled after interviews with Tony in 2007.

TONY BROWN

Tricky southpaw won Central Area belt

One of 13 children, seven girls and six boys, Tony Brown's father was especially keen for the boys to learn to box and as such Tony found himself, "in the gym from around the age of seven or eight although I first started boxing proper with the Maple Leaf ABC when I was 11." A move to Netherton ABC, "with Bobby Mason and Benny Crispin," was followed by Tony joining Litherland ABC, where he enjoyed the training and discipline that boxing provided and was good enough to win National Schoolboy titles in 1976 and 77. He also won a Junior ABA title in 1977 and made the final of the 1981 West Lancs and Cheshire championships at the Stadium where he met Olympic bronze medallist Tony Willis. "It was a great fight between us," remembers Tony. "I honestly felt I'd won but Tony got the nod. The crowd didn't like the result either and made their feelings known as only a Stadium crowd could but the judges decision is final, you just have to accept it.

The disappointment of losing that final convinced Tony to turn professional and, "aged 20 and as fit as a fiddle," he signed with local manager Chris Moorcroft, making a winning debut at the Holiday Inn on 23 March 1982 by outpointing Birmingham's Paul Murray over six rounds. Six wins and a draw from his next seven contests gave Tony a fantastic start to his pro career. In September 1982 he outpointed St. Helens' Ian Chantler over six rounds but lost a return over eight just two weeks later. "Ian was a very awkward opponent. He was extremely tall for a light-welter - about six foot, and a very good boxer. It was my first loss and as well as spoiling my unbeaten record I think I let it get to me a bit as I lost my next two as well."

Despite these losses, Tony's next contest was for the Central Area title against Sheffield's Walter Clayton, in Sheffield. "Jimmy Bunclark was fighting for the Area lightweight title on the same bill and we were determined to make it a Mersey double!" The Liverpool boxers did just that, with both winning on points. "I was delighted," remembers Tony. "I'd beaten Clayton in his own backyard to win my first pro title. All I could think was that I was on the way up. He was a good boxer and I boxed really well to beat him." As Tony was still growing however, he never defended the title he had won so admirably, and from then on he boxed as a fully fledged welterweight. He does however, add a twist to his win over Clayton. "I never received a belt for my Area win. The Boxing Board said they didn't have one to give me but Chris had one made for me and I still have it. It's special because it's so unique."

Four wins and two losses from his next six followed before, in August 1984, Tony was matched with a South African Free State welterweight champion Joseph Lala in Sebokeng, South Africa. Despite Lala outpointing tough Birkenhead-born Kostas Petrou over eight rounds two months previously however, Tony wasn't over-awed. "I got the usual reception from his supporters but I gave as good as I got." Although he won a bruising encounter on points over ten rounds, Lala later admitted that it was a tough test for him and that Tony had been, "no push-over."

Two months later Tony met Petrou in Birmingham but was adjudged the loser over eight rounds. "I was certain I'd beaten him, but what made it worse was that the fight was televised." Six months later Tony had a chance to fight for another title, this time the Central Area welterweight crown. His opponent at Everton Park Sports Centre was local rival Cliff Domville, who Tony sensationally stopped in the first round. "I fought really well here. I had Cliff down three times in total before referee Harry Warner stopped it."

A six round points win over Cardiff light-middleweight Billy Ahearne was followed by a surprise win over Leeds welterweight Phil Duckworth. "I wasn't scheduled to fight Duckworth," explains Tony. "The morning of the fight I'd gone to work after doing my roadwork. I came home and went to the gym as normal and then went to Manchester to watch the fights. Duckworth was down to meet Lee Hartshorne, but Lee failed a medical. I said I'd box - talk about short notice - and I even wore Lee's shorts and boots! I got into the ring but had to climb out again after Nat Basso told me I couldn't box as I hadn't passed the doctor. I saw the doctor were I was told I could box despite them finding a heart murmur." Despite this unorthodox approach to getting fights, Tony stopped Duckworth in five rounds.

Despite the heart murmur, Tony was allowed to continue his career. Wins over Ian Chantler, in a defence of his Central Area title, and Kostras Petrou followed. "Like the first, the second Petrou fight was also on TV. I was made up after watching it as Jim Watt said that he thought I had won the first fight as well." Tony, who relinquished the Central Area title after his defence against Chantler, had now won 18 out of 26 pro bouts and was ranked high in the British ratings. His next contest, an eliminator for the British title against London-based 'scouser' Rocky Kelly in Wandsworth, would prove to be his toughest test to date.

"I still get headaches when I think about this fight," says Tony. In a contest later voted Fight of the Year by *Boxing News*, Tony gave everything in an all-action, non-stop encounter but was ultimately stopped in the eleventh round after being down in the sixth. Such was the ferocity of the fight that a full 12 years later, Claude Abrams, editor of *Boxing News* still described it as one of the most thrilling he had ever seen. He wrote, "The exchanges were bitter, but educated. The pendulum swung first one way, then the other, neither man, both utterly courageous, gaining much of an advantage until the later round's when Rocky's superior fitness and determination won the day. Involuntarily, my hands would go up, and I'd shift position as punches crashed home, with one man, then the other, appearing to weaken before thrashing back dramatically. Unforgettable."

Tony remains proud that a fight he was involved in was described in such a way, however he does admit that the contest took something out of him. "Although you don't realise it at the time, you are probably never quite the same fighter again." This seemed to be the case as Tony, who at one time was ranked in the world's top 10, lost six of his next nine, two of which however, came against talented operators Derek Wormald and George Collins. He also lost to Hull's Kevin Toomey in December 1994 but won a rematch two months later with the Central Area title again on the line. It was his last contest. "I knew it would be my last fight but I was determined to go out a winner. I had a bad cut over my eye and George Scholfield was thinking about pulling me out, but I carried on and stopped Kevin in the last round."

Tony recalls the Stadium with more than affection. "It was a unique place. The ring was huge and well sprung but the crowd made the place. The noise when they saw you leaving the dressing room was awesome and probably frightened the life out of some fighters. They were also very knowledgeable. I'm grateful I had the opportunity to box there."

Looking back on his career today, Tony has few regrets. "I won a few titles and enjoyed every minute of it. I'd do it all again but would probably concentrate more on my boxing skills. Then again I really enjoyed the occasional war!" I have a 20 year old son who has no interest on boxing and two 16-year old twin daughters who are keen dancers, but Paddy, who is seven, is mad keen on boxing - even though I've never pushed him into it. He can't wait to get to a gym and, if he feels the same in a few years time, I'll certainly give him all the encouragement and advice he wants."

Netherton lightweight Jimmy Bunclark won a National Schools title with his local club before turning pro with local manager Bobby Mason in 1980. Always popular wherever he appeared, southpaw Jimmy built up a fine 28 fight pro career, the highlight being his reign as Central Area lightweight champion in 1983. In a five-year career he amassed 13 victories (eight by KO), 14 losses with one draw, and met the likes of Glyn Rhodes, Brian Snagg, Lloyd Christie, Ray Hood, Gary Lucas, Vince Vahey, Mike Durvan and Steve Boyle. Still living in Netherton this article was compiled through interviews with Jimmy in 2006/07.

JIMMY BUNCLARK

Central Area title the highlight for Jimmy

Like many former fighters, Netherton lightweight Jimmy Bunclark's interest in boxing was first stirred by his family. "My father had boxed in the Army and my two older brothers also boxed for Litherland ABC so you could say I followed them into the sport," recalls Jimmy. "It was my brothers who took me along to Netherton one night and I enjoyed it so much I stayed!" Eight years old at the time, Jimmy enjoyed it so much that he stayed with the North Liverpool club for the next ten years, amassing around 65 fights in total and winning a National Schools title.

In 1979, aged just 18, Jimmy turned pro with local manager and former-pro Bobby Mason. Over the next five years he proved to be a popular and more than capable southpaw, and he met many of the top stars of the day, winning 13 of his 28 professional fights. His debut came in March 1980, a first round stoppage victory over Nottingham's Kevin Sheehan. Just two days before their meeting at the Liverpool Stadium in May 1980, Sheehan had sensationally KO'd Sheffield's Glyn Rhodes to record his sixth win from 13 contests, so it was a fantastic start to his pro career for the young Liverpool lightweight.

Jimmy had little time to celebrate his debut in the paid ranks however, as just five days later he was in the ring again, this time in Manchester, to face Rotherham's Robert Wakefield. Again Jimmy forced an early victory, the referee stopping the contest in his favour in the fourth round. Two months later Jimmy suffered his first defeat as a pro, an eight round points loss to Hull's former amateur star Jackie Turner in London. This was no disgrace however, as Turner had been a sensation in the unpaid ranks before crossing over to forge a successful pro career, winning not only a National Schools title in 1973 but also a

18

junior ABA title in 1976, NABC titles 1977-78 and senior ABA titles 1977-78. As if these weren't enough however, Turner had also found time to win a fantastic European junior bronze medal in Dublin in 1978. "It took me all day to get to this fight," remembers Jimmy. "Everything went wrong, the car broke down and I only got there about an hour before the show was due to start. I weighed in, saw the doctor and then they asked me if I minded going on top of the bill as the main bout had fell through. I said yes and ended up boxing eight three minute rounds with Jackie rather than the original six twos that I had prepared for. I thought I'd won it though. I cut him to bits, but in the end he got it by just half a point."

Three wins from his next five contests, including a seventh round stoppage victory over the ever-dangerous Glyn Rhodes and a points win over Wolverhampton's Lloyd Christie – a future British title contender, meant that Jimmy ended his first full year as a pro with five wins from eight contests. Just two contests followed in 1981, an eighth round stoppage loss against fellow scouse lightweight Brian Snagg, and a sensational fifth round stoppage victory over Nottingham's Gerry Beard at the Stadium. Jimmy remembers his contest against Snagg vividly. "It was a great fight that had the crowd on their feet throughout. They threw in a lot of 'nobbins' afterwards. I boxed well and must have been a few rounds up at least when the referee stopped it with just 20 seconds to go after Brian put me down late on. I was gutted at being so close to a good win but in the changing rooms afterwards the referee came in and said, 'Brian wants you to have this,' and gave me a white towel full of all the 'nobbins' the crowd had thrown in."

Jimmy's next fight, a top of the bill contest on a Liver Sporting Club show in February 1982, saw another early stoppage victory over another Nottingham fighter, Steve Parker. The following month however, Jimmy's fine run came to an end when another local lightweight in the form of Ray Hood continued his own winning streak by stopping Jimmy inside six minutes. In April Jimmy met Brian Snagg again but was unable to avenge his earlier defeat, the referee stopping the contest in Snagg's favour in the third round. "Brian had been away to the States for a few months and when he came back he was a different fighter," recalls Jimmy. "I said yes to a return but he was a different class then and he beat me fair and square." It was the first time Jimmy had suffered two reverses in a row and it was to be another five months before he stepped into a ring again.

With eight wins from 15 contests Jimmy's record was solid if not spectacular but he was good enough to end 1982 with two wins from four contests; six round points wins over the experienced former Golden Gloves amateur Gary Lucas, who was coming off a first round stoppage loss to Barry McGuigan, and Manchester's Les Remickie. An eight round points loss to Bradford-based Ghanaian Rocky Mensah was a gallant effort as Mensah was a tough opponent, whilst a fifth round stoppage loss to Belfast's Damien Fryers was understandable as Fryers, a protégé of Barney Eastwood, was fighting in his home town, the first time Jimmy had fought outside England.

Jimmy Bunclark (right) with Tony Brown c. 1983   Source: *Jimmy Bunclark*

A draw and a win from his next two contests progressed Jimmy's record to 10 wins from 19 contests and he was named as challenger for the Central Area lightweight title, a crown that Glyn Rhodes had won by stopping Kirkby's Kevin Pritchard in November 1982. Even though the contest was at Sheffield's City Hall, Jimmy was confident he could beat the local man. He had afterall stopped him in their contest in Liverpool two and a half years previously but he admits that this was his toughest fight as a pro. "My toughest opponent and fight was definitely Glyn Rhodes, the time I fought him for the Central Area title. I'd already stopped him a few years before at the Stadium but the second time we met, with the title on the line, was in his home town in March 1983. He was always a difficult, durable fighter, but this was really tough. It was toe-to-toe for every second of the ten three-minute rounds."

Jimmy's first title fight didn't pay as well as he hoped however, although he did receive more for his first defence. "I got just £650 for the Rhodes title fight but I managed to get £300 more for my first defence, also in Sheffield, just two months later. I had it easier than my first title fight though as I KO'd Vince Vahey in the first with a good right hand."

Weight problems forced Jimmy to relinquish his Central Area crown and move up to light-welter, but despite stopping Hartlepool's Keith Foreman in his next contest in September 1983, fights were getting harder to come by. Indeed, the Foreman win was to be Jimmy's last victory and with five early stoppages in his next six contests, one a second round TKO against Eltham's Gunther Roomes at almost light-middle, "when I broke my hand," he decided to call it a day in February 1985 aged just 23. "My heart hadn't been in it for a while and this is probably explains most of my later losses. I was just fighting for fightings sake and just couldn't find the motivation anymore."

Jimmy has no regrets at choosing boxing as a career. "I would gladly do it all again," he says. "In fact I wish I was starting over again today as I think some of today's fighters don't deserve the money or the position they're in. It was a lot tougher in my day, there were simply more quality fighters around and there weren't as many 'titles' to win either. Saying that however, I would wait until I was a few years older, maybe around 24 or so, before turning pro." Jimmy cites his Central Area win as the highlight but he also has many fond stories of the Liverpool Stadium. "I remember going to the Stadium as a spectator to see the Conteh v Hutchins world title fight, but I also fought there a few times as well, once as an amateur and five times as a pro. The atmosphere was always good but it was especially so whenever two local lads met. There would be a real buzz about the place then. The crowd were always appreciative though and there was never any trouble."

Since retiring Jimmy has had a few jobs and has just celebrated his 25th wedding anniversary to Janet. They have three daughters; Jemma 26, Stacie 22 and Elysia 13, "Janet and I recently renewed our vows in Mexico - taking the girls with us," and still live in Netherton, the area where it began for Jimmy all those years ago.

After a handful of fights as an amateur, Birkenhead's Jerry Burns soon realised that he was more suited to the training side of the sport. Starting in a small, shabby club that had no heating or hot water, Jerry became one of this country's top trainers, with the likes of Joe Byrgraves, Pat McAteer and Wally Thom listed among his charges. Through these Jerry, who died some years ago, put Birkenhead firmly on the boxing map. This chapter is based on an article written by Frank Johnson that was was first published in 1973.

JERRY BURNS

Tiny gym in Conway Place where it all began for Jerry

To step inside the lounge of Jerry Burns' home is to take a peep into a glorious chapter of local boxing history. Adorning the walls are large pictures of former champions Joe Bygraves, Pat McAteer and Wally Thom - the brilliant trio that, under the management of Johnny Campbell, put Birkenhead boxing firmly on the sporting map in the 1950s. That all three were as successful as they were in the ring was largely due to the dedication and expertise of their trainer.

In his youth Jerry spent time at a number of local boxing clubs and although he was never a top fighter, he did don the gloves several times before deciding that training boxers was more to his liking. Jerry was no ordinary sponge man capable only of wafting a towel into the face of a pressurised fighter. He picked up every trick in the book and never shirked the issue of telling one of his boxers, no matter who they were, exactly what they were doing wrong, and what they should do in order to improve their situation.

Fighters respected Jerry's straightforward manner, even if it hurt sometimes, as they knew that this was the only way to earn lasting respect. Boxing is not the sport to curry false favours, for when the bell goes, the moment of truth is close at hand and it is only then that a fighter knows if he has put the maximum into his preparation. Jerry always did his utmost to make sure that every one of his fighters was fit, and one of his proud boasts was that no fighter under his care ever had to shed weight when facing the scales before a fight.

Boxing always held a fascination for Jerry and having finally decided that he lacked the skills necessary to scale the heights within the ring, he turned his attention to the training side of the sport. He accompanied the highly respected local pro George Boyce to a club in Conway Place in 1930, that at the time was run by Fred Snell and Dick Staden. Situated in a loft, the tiny gym was lit by an oil lamp, whilst above the coal fire grate there was always a bucket of water heating so that the boxers could have a hot wash after their workout. Soon, Jerry and George persuaded Dick Staden to allow them to run their own classes on Tuesday and Thursday evening and even when Fred Snell left, they carried on and formed an ever growing stable of local stars.

Jerry often accompanied the late Bob Foster and George Boyce to Sam Barton's Booth at Seaforth and it was in this arduous arena that they learned fitness was vital. Four or five fights a night against some real hard cases isn't everybody's idea of a decent night out, particularly when a weight difference of stones not pounds was a common occurrence. 'Barton's Booth' became a mecca for Birkenhead boxers such as heavyweight Arthur Holsgrove, Young 'Kid' Fogo, Charlie Smith and Teddy Tierney. Class boxers were numerous at that time and it was only the best and fittest who could command regular employment.

Jerry remembers Birkenhead KO expert Charlie Smith challenging Ernie Roderick but the Liverpool star was having none of Charlie's sleep producing right hand. Roderick however, did meet Bob Nelson (Birkenhead), and Jerry was in Bob's corner on that memorable night when the Birkenhead welterweight outpointed Roderick by acting on Jerry's advice to crowd Roderick's powerful right hand. 'Boy' McCann was another local favourite to come under the expert eye of the Staden-Burns duo. It was McCann's punching power that forced promoter Johnny Best to put the blocks on a proposed fight between McCann and the great Goldborne flyweight, Peter Kane - then a firm favourite with the Liverpool Stadium crowds. Mr. Best just couldn't afford to have one of his drawing cards beaten at the time. Subsequently of course, Kane won the world flyweight title at Anfield with a great win over the clever Californian, Jackie Jurich.

In 1940 Jerry joined the RAF where he became a Physical Training Instructor (PTI). A short spell in Tenby was followed by a posting to North Africa where Jerry took charge of a boxing team at Oran. He dropped a points verdict to a rugged American soldier before moving on to Biskra where, in addition to his boxing activities, he also took charge of the station football team.

Demobbed in 1945, Jerry resumed his employment with Birkenhead Corporation Cleansing Department and he had a spell training lads at the Birkenhead Boys Club where he soon put together a fine team. Tommy Skillen and Teddy Ryan joined Jerry at the Boys Club and this experienced trio played a major part in launching the career of the great Pat McAteer, whose amateur debut at Byrne Avenue Baths ended in a fourth round KO defeat against Ronnie Doyle. Despite this initial setback Jerry had seen enough in Pat to realise his potential as a champion in the making.

Jerry's long association with Birkenhead manager Johnny Campbell first began at the Provincial ABC in Price Street, Birkenhead. Jerry took along half a dozen lads, including Pat McAteer, Pat Ellis - who later emigrated to New Zealand, Joe Bygraves and Leo Molloy. In these, Johnny had the makings of a great professional stable and when he did take the plunge into the paid ranks, it soon became obvious that not only was Birkenhead entering a boom time in boxing, but also that Jerry Burns was the man destined to steer their fitness to new peaks. After the club moved to Whetstone Lane, Wally Thom and Joe Bygraves also joined. Together with Pat McAteer they set the boxing world alight with their success whilst Leo Molloy was another who carved out a great name for himself.

Jerry held all of the boxers at the club in the highest regard but he always said that he rated Pat McAteer the cleverest boxer of his time. His immaculate left hand, skill on the ropes and ability to counter quickly when under pressure, stamped him as a great champion. Jerry was in Pat Mac's corner for all of his contents, from his two round KO debut win at Liverpool Stadium against Art Lewis, to his nine round Empire middleweight title KO defeat against Dick Tiger at the same venue. Powerful heavyweight Joe Bygraves, the man with the lethal left hook to the body, who KO'd Henry Cooper in nine to successfully defend the title, was another fighter Jerry had a high regard for, as well as Wally Thom who Jerry always said had the all-round skill which was to make him British, Empire and European champion.

The names and memories reeled from Jerry as he reflected upon his long career and, even as he approached his 70th year, he was looking forward to passing on his knowledge to some of the young hopefuls at the Oxton ABC.

A former amateur with the Provincial ABC in Birkenhead, Jamaican-born Joe Bygraves won Northern Counties titles at both light-heavy and heavyweight, a West Lancs and Cheshire heavyweight championship and also represented England. A beaten ABA semi-finalist in 1952, Joe turned professional with the famous Johnny Campbell stable the following year and enjoyed enormous success and popularity, winning the Empire heavyweight title in 1956. In his 14-year, 72 fight career (42 wins, 22 by KO), Joe met almost all the leading domestic and European heavyweights of the day including Henry Cooper, Peter Bates, Ingemar Johansson, Johnny Williams, Dick Richardson, Kitione Lave, Joe Erskine, and George Chuvalo. Information on Joe has been difficult to find in the past few years but it is assumed he is still alive and currently residing in Portugal.

JOE BYGRAVES

More than a handful - even for 'Enry

One of 12 children to a Jamaican Police Seargent, Joe Bygraves was born in Kingston on 26 May 1931. Only 15 when he came to England in the hope of studying for a trade – in his case an electrician - three of Joe's brothers also accompanied him; two settling in London, with Joe and another deciding on Merseyside. It was whilst living in Birkenhead that Joe first became interested in boxing, so much so that he joined the Provincial ABC aged 17 with his aim being a simple and modest one - to win an Olympic title! It was thought that prior to joining the Provincial, Joe had never put a glove on in his life, however subsequent enquiries have revealed that he did indeed have a number of schoolboy bouts in Jamaica although the results aren't known.

Such lofty aspirations didn't seem out of place for Joe however, as it wasn't long before he began to show great promise in the amateur game. He won Northern Counties titles at both light-heavyweight and heavyweight, and a West Lancs and Cheshire light-heavyweight championship – all between 1949 and 1952. He also represented England, along with Henry Cooper – a future opponent, Pete Waterman and his fellow club member Pat McAteer, against Wales in May 1952. Unfortunately Joe lost this bout as well as his ABA semi-final the same year and soon after he decided to turn professional. It was an amateur referee who was the cause of Joe turning professional and taking his great friend, Pat McAteer with him. Following an alleged disagreement Joe became disillusioned with the amateur game. He talked Pat into the same frame of mind and together they joined Johnny Campbell's stable in Birkenhead.

Joe, who whilst not boxing was a ship's painter, made his professional debut at the Liverpool Stadium on 12 February 1953 stopping Nottingham's Don Maxwell in the first round. He followed this victory with six straight wins, including a first round stoppage over his fellow townsman, and former ABA champion, Peter McCann. Joe was rapidly becoming a firm favourite of the knowledgeable Liverpool Stadium crowd. Despite his chosen profession, Joe was a deeply religious man and together with his good friend Hogan 'Kid' Bassey, another Liverpool fight favourite, he was a staunch supporter of the Princes Gate Baptist Church in Liverpool.

Any boxer winning their first seven contests would make a name for themselves, especially in the heavyweight division, and Joe was no exception. He was beginning to get noticed and for his next contest he was asked to travel to London's White City to take on Stepney's Joe Crickmar. It was a step up in class for Joe and he suffered his first reversal – a fifth round stoppage. Despite losing to Crickmar in a quick return just a month later, Joe gained his revenge at the Liverpool Stadium in March the following year when he scored an eight rounds points victory.

Further wins over the highly rated Paddy Slavin, Frank Bell, Peter Bates and Bermuda's Ed Polly Smith saw Joe continue his rise up the British rankings. Like Joe, another young heavyweight was rising fast

Joe Bygraves (right) KOs Aldo Pellegrini in the first round.
Pallazzo dello Sport, Milan, Italy. 17 December 1955　　　　　　*Source: Gary Shaw*

in the rankings - Bellingham's Henry Cooper, and the exciting young prospect was Joe's next opponent at Manor Place Baths in April 1955. Joe was adjudged the loser over eight rounds but just two weeks later he got back to winning ways with a fourth round KO over Battersea's Eddie Hearn at the Liverpool Stadium. A win over the dangerous Tongan sensation Kitione Lave, always a star attraction wherever he appeared in Britain in the 1950s, followed in Birmingham.

Joe's services were now being sought by European promoters and in October 1955 he travelled to Bologna, Italy only to be disqualified against Franco Cavicci. He returned to Italy six weeks later however, to spectacularly KO the highly rated Aldo Pellegrini in just 50 seconds! Earlier in the year Pellegrini had decked Ingemar Johansson before being disqualified himself.

Although a big man, with a bodybuilders physique, Joe was a clever, fast fighter. He did suffer from a stamina problem however, due in no small way to his training methods. By his own admission Joe disliked training, especially road-work. It was this lack of dedication to training that led to a split between Joe and Johnny Campbell. Joe was also running his own nightclub at the time on Liverpool's Upper Parliament Street, and this may have been a contributory factor in his failing to train fully. Joe may have felt however that he didn't need to train as hard as he should because if there was one thing he could do it was punch. There was no doubt that if he managed to hit you – you stayed 'hit'!

In January 1956 Joe returned to Italy and beat local boy Uber Bacilieri on points over ten rounds. A remarkable achievement. Indeed it was said that a foreign boxer often needed to KO the home fighter just to gain a draw in Italy at the time! The following month Joe had another trip abroad, this time to Gothenburg. Again he was adjudged a points loser over ten rounds but there was no shame in this as his opponent was non other than the 'Hammer of Thor' himself, Ingemar Johannsen of Sweden. Johannsen had KO'd seven of his 12 opponents as a professional previous to his meeting with Joe and he would win the European title just two fights later. The Swede would of course go on to win the world title in 1959.

Joe got back to winning ways with an eight round stoppage win over tough Belgian Marcel Limage in Cardiff. This was in May 1965 and a month later Joe was matched with previous opponent Kitione Lave for the vacant British Empire heavyweight title. After 15 hard fought rounds at Wembley Pool, the referee raised Joe's hand to declare him the winner on points. The big Jamaican, a champion at last, was scared of no-one and over the next 12 months he met all of the leading British contenders.

Following a disappointing retirement loss against Wayne Bethea in New York, Joe was matched against former British, British Empire and European champion Johnny Williams of Rugby for the first defence of his Empire title. This contest saw him back to his brilliant best and he stopped Williams in the sixth round at Belle Vue, Manchester. Next up was another old opponent; Henry Cooper. It was Cooper's first title shot, but Joe was again on superb form, and he sensationally KO'd the future champion in the ninth round at Earls Court. A further defence followed, this time against another future champion in the shape of Newport's Dick Richardson. Their May 1957 meeting in Cardiff resulted in a draw, which of course meant Joe kept his title. A disputed 15 rounds loss to Joe Erskine in Leicester in November 1957 saw Joe relinquish the crown and although he boxed on for a further 10 years he never fought for a title again.

In his 72 professional contests Joe met some of the country's, and indeed the world's, top heavyweights. Not only did he meet the likes of Cooper, Erskine, Richardson and Johannsen, but he also fought such men as Zora Folley, Karl Mildenberger, Jack Gardner, Billy Walker and Willie Pastrano. He had a total of 19 bouts in Liverpool, the last a fifth round disqualification against Ray Shiel in August 1963, whilst his final contest came at the Anglo-Sporting Club at the Hilton Hotel, London in March 1967; a ten rounds points defeat to Edwardo Corletti of Argentina.

After retiring, it is believed Joe purchased a farm in the South of England, where he bred pigs. As well as raising animals, Joe built a training camp for boxers, and would often let old-time fighters stay at a Portuguese villa he had acquired during his boxing days. Although Joe's post-boxing career is difficult to ascertain, it is believed he now lives in Portugal, although not in the best of health.

Billy Connor had over 100 amateur contests with just one club – Lowe House Boys in St Helens. After a successful amateur career, the highlights of which were representing England and the 1951 ABA light-welterweight title, and following a dispute with the club, Billy turned pro not long after with Tom Hearst. He notched up 14 wins and seven losses from 22 contests before retiring in 1955. He continues to live in St Helens and is a member, and regular at the monthly meetings of the MFBA. This article was compiled following interviews with Billy during 2006.

BILLY CONNOR

Talented Billy - ABA Champ 1951

"My only amateur club was Lowe House Boys' Club. I first started boxing there when I was 11 years old. This was in 1943. There was no history of the sport in my family, although my father obviously took an interest once I started. Unfortunately he died in 1945 before I won my first championship. The main reason I became interested in the sport was because I was friendly with a boy by the name of Wilf Kelly who at the time was a very talented schoolboy boxer. We are still friends today.

"The Lowe House Boys' Club wasn't just a boxing club. It was a flourishing social and games club – all of a high standard. The boxers trained on Tuesday and Thursday evenings and it was well organised. If you were conscientious enough, every minute of your time could be taken up with training. A conservative estimate of the number of fights I had would be around 100 and about 75 of those were wins, although the championships I won are much easier to recall!

"In 1944 I made the final of the Northern Counties Schoolboys championships. This was at 6st. The following year I won the Great Britain Schoolboys championship at 6st 7lbs. In 1947 I was a National Boys Clubs finalist at 7st 7lbs and in 1949 I won the NABC title at 8st 7lbs. In 1951 I won the ABA light-welterweight title *[A year before Frank Hope became Merseyside's first ABA champion – St Helens not being part of Merseyside at the time. eds.]* and the same year I also represented England for the first time beating D Budge in a match against Wales – he had been my opponent in the ABA final as well.

"I was 19 when I turned professional with Tom Hearst. It should be noted however, that I hadn't intended to turn professional so soon. With my amateur success and experience I had set my sights on representing Britain in the Helsinki Olympics in 1952. However, destiny seemed to play a part.

"Throughout my amateur career I had always been plagued with hand injuries. The reason being that although I could use bandages in training you weren't allowed to use them for contests at that time. I was receiving treatment for my injuries before the ABA Championships at St. Helens Hospital. I agreed with them that once the Championships were over I would rest for the summer. All was going well. I had won an ABA title and gained my first international vest. I thought that things couldn't get any better, but then I was selected to represent the ABA against an American team, the first to visit Britain since the end of the war. When I went to the club to inform them about my selection I was told that if I was going to box again it shouldn't be for the ABA but for a friend of one of the trainers to whom they had promised my services for a charity show. Of course I wasn't happy and told them so, but two days later I read in a newspaper that my club had withdrawn me from the English team due to my hand injuries. I was very disappointed with my treatment by the club and didn't go back for a while.

"On returning from work one day soon after this, who should be waiting for me at my home but Tom Hearst, a prominent local manager of the day who also managed Johnny Molloy and Wilf Glynn. I knew both boxers very well and had sparred with them many times. Suffice to say I fell for Hearst's patter and duly turned pro."

Billy's debut in the paid ranks was in November 1951 at Liverpool Stadium – a six rounds points win over Doncaster's Harold Palmer. Five victories followed before Billy was caught cold in the first against tough Manchester lightweight Dick Ashcroft. This was 8 May 1952 but just two weeks later Billy avenged this defeat with a solid points win at Manchester's Kings Hall. A win over former European amateur champion Paddy Dowdall in Belfast in September 1953 meant that Billy had won nine of his first 11 pro contests, form that today could generate talk of a title contest. Six losses from his next ten contests followed however, and Billy retired in 1955.

"I did not have quite the success as a pro that I had enjoyed in the amateur game," recalls Billy. "I won 14 out of 22 contests, with seven losses and one draw, but there were no championship fights. The hardest fight I had was probably against Willie Lloyd. This was in

November 1954 at the Liverpool Stadium. The winner was due to be matched with Dave Charnley. Unfortunately for me Willie won on points over eight rounds. Another tough fight was against Roy Bennet. This was at Newcastle's St James' Hall in November 1952, the winner to meet Joe Lucy. It was a draw, but it was only after the contest that I realised I had fought with a broken jaw.

Billy Connor c. 1951   *Source: Billy Connor*

"On the Friday night prior to the fight on the Monday next, I was sparring with Emmett Kenny. During the session I felt a distinct crack in my jaw but found that it was only really painful when I moved it from side to side. On my way home from the gym I called on a masseur who I knew quite well - Billy Helm. Curiously for a masseur Billy only had one arm! He thought it was possibly a ruptured masseter muscle and recommended I eat only soft food until the Monday and it should be all right to fight. After the contest however, I was still in pain and the fight doctor advised I attend my local hospital once I returned home.

"I presented myself at the A&E the next morning. A young doctor warmed to me. He was a boxing fan and told me he had read the report on my fight. He had a good idea who he was talking to because apart from a badly swollen jaw I also had a cut eye that also required treatment! The doctor informed me that he thought the consultant would send me to Broadgreen Hospital for further examination. This didn't happen however, as a few weeks later I received a large envelope containing my X-rays, and a letter telling me that an appointment had been made for me to see a dentist in St. Helens. It was he who made me aware of what had really happened.

"It seems that the roots of a wisdom tooth had impacted on the jaw bone causing pressure. A blow to the jaw had caused it to crack and the roots of the tooth had slipped into the crack. Consequently the jaw wouldn't heal until the tooth had been removed. It was the swelling caused by this that had ensured the consultant couldn't determine the problem earlier. To the dentist's credit my jaw healed perfectly.

"Looking back on my career today I do have a few regrets. The manner in which I left Lowe House Boys' Club wasn't the best nor with hindsight was my choice of manager. Once I realised my mistake I decided to treat the rest of my time as a pro as a useful experience. This isn't a flippant statement. As anyone who has been devoted to boxing for years will know, it's not easy to lose interest in the sport or to call it day. I endured quite a long weaning off period I can tell you.

"Would I do it all again? The game has changed so much since my day and although I still have an interest in the sport and like a good contest, I couldn't see myself part of it now. The amateur game however suited me. I enjoyed it. I know boxing isn't for everyone and I never promoted it to my boys. Indeed they attended the Boys' Club but found that boxing wasn't for them. My only concern was that they took up some kind of sport.

"With regards to my opinion of the sport and boxers today, I think that the general improvement of the economy and the overall increase in the standard of living since my day has determined the general lack of interest in youths participating competitively, particularly in the professional game. Whilst there are a number of very good boxers in the pro game, they do not get their skills honed to the same extent as the boxers of yesteryear, when every fight was an examination. On the other hand, modern boxers do not fight anywhere near as often as we used to, and the rewards seem to be much greater, which can only be a good thing.

"The boxing game doesn't bear any resemblance to the game I remember in the 1950s and, five decades on, why should it? Since its inception, it has gone through an almost constant overhaul of its rules in order to make it safer for the boxers. Television has brought money to the game but little seems to have been done to replace the likes of the Liverpool Stadium - small but popular venues that produced weekly shows, all of a high standard. The Stadium itself was a good venue, the fans there knew their boxing, as did the fans at St. James Hall, Leeds Town Hall and Blackpool Tower.

"After serving my time as an electrician at a local colliery I left at 28 to go into the licensed trade. After 17 successful years as a licensee I left to become a social worker working with the mentally ill, and I retired at the age of 62 following the death of my wife."

Born in 1921, Frank Cotgrave visited the professional Haymarket gym when he was only eight years old and was one of the first boxers to join the Birkenhead ABC when it opened at the same venue a few years later. He enjoyed modest amateur success, making the junior ABA finals and having his first paid fight aged 13, before joining the RAF and serving abroad during the Second World War. Frank boxed often whilst in the forces and captained the RAF team on a number of occasions. This chapter is based on an article written by Frank Johnson that was first published in 1973.

FRANK COTGRAVE

Amateur star who boxed in Alexandria

Born in Oakfield View, Birkenhead in 1921 Frank was one of six boys and a girl and, although times were hard in his early days, he enjoyed a happy childhood. It wasn't long before he made his mark at St. Hugh's School through his sporting abilities. At the age of eight, Frank visited the famous Haymarket gym - solely a professional gym in those days - and, encouraged by his father, he was soon learning the rudiments of boxing under the guidance of Tommy McKeown and Joe Nolan. Frank was the first youngster to attend the gym and he did so three or four nights a week. Before long, several of his friends accompanied him including Tommy Carey, Mickey Carey, Tommy and Larry Murray, Dave Parnell, Frankie and Jackie Williams, Albert Price and Dennis Goodall. Even though none were yet ten years old, the Haymarket pros gave them every encouragement.

Schoolteacher Jack Peel, whose main sporting interest at the time was in speedway racing, went along and soon he too became a boxing fanatic. The pros in the gym at the time included Johnny McAteer, Martin Shinnicks, Jimmy Fallone, Joe and Teddy Breeze and a host of other fighters who were making their name on the local boxing scene. It wasn't long before Jack conceived the idea of starting the Birkenhead ABC at the Haymarket with Tommy Murray. With such a fine set of lads to get the club off the ground they could hardly fail.

Frank was one of these lads. Boxing brilliantly behind an immaculate left hand and, with such natural ability, it came as no surprise when he won a Birkenhead Schoolboy Championship. He recalled going along to watch a pro show, but when a flyweight failed to appear he stepped in at the age of 13, and boxed a draw for a 7/- 6d purse. That little excursion into the paid ranks had to be kept quiet but his heroes of those days, Jimmy Fallone and Martin Shinnicks, were on the same bill and they kept his secret. Frank didn't need any assistance in the ring however, and his rapid improvement soon placed him in the front rank of juniors.

In 1936 Frank won the Northern Counties Junior ABA 6st 7lbs title. The following year he made it a double against some tough opposition. This was the same year he reached the Junior ABA finals and to get to that exalted stage he had to have nine fights, five of which came in one afternoon. The finals took place at the Holborn Stadium, London and in Frank's corner was local fighter, Frank Price. Despite giving his all, young Frank was adjudged to have lost but the decision so riled his chief second, that he flung the stool into the centre of the ring and, amidst tumultuous applause from the packed arena, carried Frank shoulder high to the changing rooms. With at least a bout a week, Frank boxed regularly on the Merseyside circuit. He was beaten in the West Lancs and Cheshire finals by E. Larkin of Knotty Ash, after having beaten Jimmy Molloy in the semi-final. In January 1939, aged 17, Frank joined the RAF as an aircraft fitter and was stationed in Gloucester to do his basic training. Whilst there he won a recruits welterweight championship before transferring to St. Athan, South Wales for his trade training.

Boxing was never far away however, and Frank soon forced his way into the station team and represented them against the Metropolitan Police. He was honoured by being selected as Captain for the combined RAF, Army and Royal Navy team. In 1940 Frank boxed in the RAF championships at RAF Uxbridge. This was a major step as, due to the war, the services now had their ranks flooded with top class men from 'civvy street'. Seconded by the great Ted 'Kid' Lewis, Frank won all of his four fights in the afternoon but fell at the fifth hurdle. Disappointed but certainly undaunted, Frank had a 48-hour weekend pass and, after borrowing ten shillings from Lewis, he set off for the West End to 'do the town'. He went to the Palladium and saw a variety show featuring Pat Kirkwood, Vic Oliver and the famous xylophonist, Teddy Brown. He had two glasses of bitter at former heavyweight champion, Jack Bloomfield's pub, still had enough for bed and breakfast at the Union Jack Club, at a cost of 1/- 3d, and was able to pay his way back to camp. An adventurous 48 hours and one recalled, not only with nostalgia, but also with a great deal of envy at what you could do for a mere ten shillings.

Frank joined the famous 222 Squadron at Duxford and it was here that he saw bravery at its highest, with the pilots hardly taking time to refuel, as they flew back to the Dunkirk beaches to give the fleeing British Army what cover they could. One of the acting Pilot Officers with the squadron was none other than Douglas Bader, whose wartime exploits have become legend. Bader asked Frank to become his personal flight rigger and the Birkenhead man performed this duty for 12 months. It was while he was stationed at RAF Hornchurch that Frank recalled being in charge of the moving of personal baggage and aircraft spares. Two planes were allocated but somehow they became mixed up the outcome being that Bader's spare pair of artificial legs were in the plane that went astray. A hurried search next morning, and one or two timely telephone calls, brought the mishap to light and Bader's legs were restored to their rightful owner, thus preventing the great flyer from being grounded.

In March 1941, Frank was posted abroad, serving in Egypt, Dar-es-Salaam, India and Burma. He boxed at every opportunity during this period however, once appearing on a pro show at the Alhambra in Alexandria under the name of Frank Cotty. He outpointed a Greek whose name he can't recall, but remembered that boxing on the same bill were well known pros, Bert Chambers from Widnes and Joey Dixon. In Columbo, Frank won a Service Championship at welterweight, but the more serious fighting was hotting up in that area and he joined aircrew in Burma as a flight mechanic on Sunderland flying boats. This meant trips into the Burmese interior to bring out wounded and other personnel but he came through unscathed and returned to the UK in 1945. Frank hung up his gloves but he did have one or two spars with Les Langford while home on leave.

Demobbed in 1946, Frank worked for the Blue Funnel Line as a fitter's labourer. He married in 1948 and became the proud father of two boys, Peter and Paul. Boxing was never far away though, as his brother-in-law is Jack Foster 'Young Fogo' and he was also uncle to the late Don Rice. His wife's father was also a well known former professional who boxed as 'Young Gorton'. Frank maintained his love for boxing, watching and reading about the sport, and it was always his intention to try and form a boxing Club to encourage youngsters to take up the sport. He and several friends did once attempt to start such a club at the Woodchurch Community Centre but the support was not forthcoming, and Frank was never able to fulfil his dream.

Without doubt one of the most exciting local fighters to watch, both as an amateur and also during his short professional career, Birkenhead's Robbie Davies knew only one way to fight and that was to go after his opponent from the very first bell. A late starter in the amateur ranks, Robbie soon made a name for himself in the newly formed light-middleweight division and won Northern Counties championships before adding the ABA light-middleweight title in 1977. He also represented England at international level and was a member of the 1976 Olympic Games squad. Turning pro in September 1977 Robbie had a total of 15 contests in three years, winning 11 (nine by KO). A staunch supporter of the Wirral and Merseyside Former Boxers Associations Robbie still lives and works in Birkenhead and this article was compiled through interviews with him in 2006/07.

ROBBIE DAVIES

Exciting Robbie always a popular draw

So exciting a fighter was Birkenhead's Robbie Davies to watch during the 1970s that, at either a professional or amateur show, his inclusion on a bill would be guaranteed to pack the venue to capacity. It wasn't that Robbie couldn't box - he could - but he liked nothing better than a right good tear-up. More often than not Robbie would leap from his corner and test his opponents chin with a cracker of a punch early on. On occasion his opponent would be of a similar style and, if this was the case, then the fight audience would be treated to a slam-bang affair that had little in the way of boxing artistry, but plenty of courage and determination.

Coming into the amateur game later than most, Robbie joined the Birkenhead ABC in 1972. It wasn't long before the club realised they had found something special. Robbie won a Northern Counties title in 1973 and was a losing ABA finalist, to the Army's Roger Maxwell, in the newly formed light-middleweight division the same year. Success followed success, and Robbie was beginning to collect a huge following on both sides of the Mersey. Despite being crowned Northern Counties champion once again the following year, it seemed as though Robbie was destined to go so far but no further in the pursuit of an ABA title, as he missed out again at the semi-final stage.

Robbie's disappointment at not winning an ABA title was offset however, by his selection for the 1974 Commonwealth Games in Hamilton, New Zealand. Robbie showed he could rise to the occasion by winning a fantastic bronze medal. Thinking that a change of club might change his fortunes in the ABAs, Robbie joined the Golden Gloves ABC in 1975. He collected another Northern Counties championship but the change of clubs didn't change his luck however, as once more he returned home from the senior ABA championships a losing finalist, being beaten by Denbeath ABC's A. Harrison. These losses certainly didn't affect Robbie's chances as far as international appearances were concerned however, for he was chosen to represent the ABA in 1973 against France and West Germany. More vests followed; in 1974 against Bulgaria; 1975 against Scotland, Hungary and West Germany; and against Scotland and Ireland in 1976. Of those eight appearances, Robbie won five and lost three.

Following on from his Commonwealth Games bronze medal two years previously, Robbie was also chosen to represent Great Britain at the 1976 Montreal Olympics. Although he KO'd Australian Wayne Devlin in the first series however, Robbie was outpointed by Venezuela's Alfredo Lemus in the second round. By 1977, Robbie had not only returned to Birkenhead ABC but he had also moved up to middleweight. Again, he won the Northern Counties title and once more headed for the ABA finals full of confidence, if not expectation. Robbie needn't have worried this time however, as he stopped Clay ABC's Michen Shone in the first round to win the title. Having at last succeeded in winning an ABA title, Robbie now felt it was time for him to turn to the professional ranks. The middleweight division has traditionally provided some of the ring's best fighters, and with his all-action, crowd pleasing style, Robbie was sure he would prove to be a popular addition to the paid ranks.

Robbie made his pro debut at the Liverpool Stadium on 8 September. He carried on where he had left off in the amateur ranks by stopping Shrewsbury's Joe Hannaford in the fourth round. An immediate Stadium favourite, Robbie returned to the Stadium a month later stopping Spaniard Francisco Carmona, in two. A return with Hannaford a month later saw the Shrewsbury man last half as long as their first encounter, the referee coming to his rescue in the second round. Yet another early stoppage win meant that Robbie finished 1977 with a Northern Counties amateur title; a senior ABA championship; and four inside the distance pro wins. It certainly looked like he was destined for a glittering career.

On 2 March 1978 Robbie returned to Liverpool Stadium to face a different class of opponent in Johnny Heard of the USA. Heard was a ring veteran who had been in with some of America's best and he demonstrated to the Stadium crowd the way to beat Robbie – box him. He gave a classy exhibition over eight rounds and was rightly declared a points winner. Robbie recalls, "I spoke to Johnny as he came out of the shower and he told me that he couldn't believe that he, a black fighter, had been given a points verdict over a local white favourite. I explained to him that the colour of a fighter's skin meant nothing to a Liverpool Stadium fight crowd. What they were interested in was whether or not you could fight, and if they felt you deserved the verdict over the local fighter, then they would support you fully." Heard left for home stating that the Liverpool Stadium and the stadium crowd 'were the best' in his eyes.

Robbie Davies (left) v Johnny Heard, 2 March 1978, Liverpool Stadium
Source: John Farrell

How would Robbie handle his first defeat? The answer came just three weeks later when he faced Frenchman Marcel Giordanella at the Stadium. If anyone felt that Robbie's loss to Heard had affected his confidence then they were soon mistaken as Robbie tore from his corner and knocked the brave but outgunned Giordanella all over the ring, forcing the referee to rush in and save him inside the first minute. Robbie was back on the winning trail. A win over John Smith was followed by Robbie's first appearance in his hometown; a fourth round stoppage win over Clapham middleweight Mal Nicholson. Another early stoppage win just two weeks later meant Robbie ended 1978 with a fantastic record of eight wins from nine fights, all his wins coming early.

Robbie didn't fight again for six months but when he returned to the Stadium in March 1979 it was the fight every local fight fan had been waiting for – a Birkenhead v Liverpool contest against local Liverpool favourite Joe Lally. Both had similar styles and both could bang so the crowd who filled the Stadium that night came expecting fireworks – and that's exactly what they got. The contest lasted just four rounds but those rounds had everything. First one man hit the deck, then it was his opponents turn. "The noise inside the Stadium was deafening," remembers Robbie. It couldn't last at this pace and in the fourth round Robbie produced the punch that finally counted and it was all over. Lally was counted out and the Birkenhead supporters in the stadium, "went home feeling as though they'd won the pools."

Robbie was now looking towards a British title fight and his next contest at the Stadium provides him with just that opportunity. Billed as an eliminator for the British light-middleweight title, Robbie's opponent was the cagey Pat Thomas of Cardiff, the Welsh light-middleweight champion and former British welterweight champion. Again, the Stadium was packed to the rafters with Robbie's supporters. It was a 12-rounds contest, but if anyone thought that Robbie would not be able to last the distance they were proved wrong. Robbie realised that he was just one fight away from a lucrative British title contest and he put everything into it. The Welshman from St. Kitts had been over this distance before however, and he paced himself better to rightly take the decision - a verdict that was magnanimously accepted by the Stadium crowd.

Disappointed but not disillusioned, Robbie returned to winning ways at Blackpool in October 1979 with an eight round points win over

Peckham's Jamaican born Oscar Angus. The following January he stopped Cardiff's Errol McKenzie in the fourth round at Bradford, before a return with Johnny Heard at a packed Stadium in February. The tough American proved that his first win was no fluke however, by again beating Robbie, although this time the end came in the seventh round. With a life outside the ring that was even more colourful than inside, Robbie was perhaps beginning to lose interest in the sport. He was KO'd in six by Jamaican Glen McEwan in Blackpool in April 1980 and announced his retirement soon after.

Characters like Robbie Davies are good for boxing. He would be guaranteed to fill any hall he was appearing at and is still an interesting character to engage in conversation today.

One of Birkenhead's great boxing characters of yesteryear, Jack Elliot fitted out the top room of his home as a gym and won an all-comers competition at a travelling boxing booth when he was 13. It was as a boxing trainer that Jack became more famous however, taking Johnny Bee to London to meet Ted 'Kid' Lewis for the British title. He was also lucky enough to see the likes of the most famous heavyweight champion of them all, Jack Johnson, in exhibitions as well as Roland Todd, the great French boxer Jean Bernard and Buffalo Bill. This chapter is based on an article written by Frank Johnson that was first published in 1972.

JACK ELLIOT

When Jack Johnson and Buffalo Bill came to town

Former Birkenhead boxing trainer and manager, Jack Elliot, was born in Oak Street during 1882, the year that John L. Sullivan won the world heavyweight championship by knocking out Paddy Ryan in nine rounds in a bare-knuckle fight in Mississippi. That was the era of Gentleman James J. Corbett, Tom Sharkey, Bob Fitzsimmons and Jim Jeffries.

When he was just nine years old, Jack used to dash home from school, go down to the Liverpool Echo offices at Bridge Street, collect six bundles from the manager Mr. Nags and then race through the streets selling them to the local office workers. When he was 13 he fitted out the top room of his home as a gymnasium and soon the sound of leather being traded became a common disruption within the household. Jack won an all-comers competition as a welterweight at a travelling boxing booth sited at the Court Field in Price Street and it wasn't long before he began to take a more active interest in the fight game.

Jack left St. Laurence's School, Meadow Street and started work on the docks, retiring when he was a 'youngster' of 79. That is the calibre of the man and it was an outlook that stood him in good stead throughout his long life, for he was 91 years of age when first interviewed. By his own admission Jack, "was always active and never sat back to await the outcome of events."

At 17 Jack bluffed his age to become an infantryman in the Cheshire Regiment at Market Street and he received the princely sum of 2/- for his trouble. His two pals who had the idea first, were not accepted, but undeterred, all three trooped off to the Theatre Royal and entered the gallery door in Henry Street for 4d.

At the age of 20 Jack gave up the gloves to take up a new career as a trainer and manager with several local Birkenhead boys coming under his keen and expert eye. One of those lads was Johnny Bee who, with Jack in his corner, fought the great Ted 'Kid' Lewis at the Albert Hall for the British middleweight title in 1920. Lewis won by fourth round KO with Bee receiving £50 for his troubles, a not inconsiderable sum in those days. Lewis of course, was an all-time great in boxing annals and he later fought the brilliant French ace George Carpentier for the world light-heavyweight championship. Featured on the Lewis v Bee bill was the great American heavyweight Fred Fulton, who sparred three rounds apiece with Birkenhead stalwarts Ike Clark and Dick Morris.

Jack rates Johnny Bee as the most accomplished boxer he handled. Bee fought Roland Todd twice, who later won the British title from Lewis. He also held a decision over Tom Berry, who went on to win the title after a terrific 20 round battle with Sid Pape in 1925. Jack also managed local lightweight Jimmy Dawson, an all-action ten-rounder who was one of the few men in his day to hold a verdict over the Liverpool tearaway 'Butcher' Moore.

In the days before the Great War, Jack recalls seeing the great black world heavyweight champion Jack Johnson in an exhibition at the Hippodrome (later the Co-op) in Grange Road, Birkenhead. Local welterweights, Berk Williams a butcher from Bentink Street and Billy 'Snowball' Jones, each sparred three rounds with Johnson. Jack also remembers going to the Theatre Royal (later the ABC Cinema) in Argyle Street to see Buffalo Bill Cody of legendary wild west fame, and his gallery seat cost 4d.

Jack recalled the outstanding figure in Birkenhead boxing at this time, Dan Whelligan, who in 1886 was promoting shows at a hall in Priory Street off Hamilton Street. He featured Pedlar Palmer against the hammer-fisted local Lairage Slaughterman, Jimmy Green. Whelligan later refereed a contest in which 'Peerless' Jim Driscoll fought. Jack's memories come flooding back, when purse money of £6 for six rounds, and £10 for ten rounds was common. Boxers abounded and only the best kept active as promoters could afford to be choosy.

In 1892 Jack recalls a famous circus came to Birkenhead and set up their wooden construction on the site which later became the Hippodrome. Needless to say, Jack and his friends saw the show free after slipping through a convenient open tent flap. In the circus at that time was a clown who drew great crowds to the Birkenhead streets to watch him race a horse tram from Woodside to the Park gates - wearing stilts!

The best middleweight that Jack ever saw was the Frenchman, Jean Bernard, who had a memorable fight with the 'Fighting Fisherman' Gerry Thomas at Liverpool. Thomas later beat Curly Davies of Birkenhead.

Jack always felt a hankering for the sea but, after a trip as a trimmer to Canada and a voyage to Norway in a cruising ship with the Prince of Wales (later King Edward VII) aboard, Jack swallowed the anchor. At 20 he remembers stowing away on a liner bound for the USA but, after soon being discovered, was put aboard the pilot boat at Point Lynas for return to Liverpool. As the ship drew alongside the quay however, Jack scampered ashore to avoid any official action.

At the turn of the century Jack remembers that boxing was regularly held in Old Hall Street, Liverpool. The entrance money here was 2/-6d ringside, 1/-6d, 1/- and 6d. Out of this, the boxers earned 30/- for a win and a pound for a defeat. Jack met many personalities of his day including showbiz impresario, CB Cochran. When Jack and Johnny Bee were in London for a fight, Cochran gave them two tickets for his theatre show.

A talented bantamweight with first Kirkby, Knowsley Vale and finally Holy Name ABC, John Farrell won the vast majority of his amateur fights, that included numerous England appearances and a multi-nations gold in Greece, before turning pro with Manny Goodall in 1982. In a seven-year career John won 12 out of 21 contests winning the Central Area title in the process and meeting his great rival at the time, St Helens' Ray Gilbody, for the British title in 1985. Never one to refuse a tough contest, no matter where it was held, John also met tough Australian Jeff Fenech – when Fenech was world bantamweight champion, and the likes of Peter Harris, Valerio Nati, Anthony Brown, Jean Marc Renard and John Sichula. Still living and working in Kirkby this article was compiled through interviews with John during 2007.

JOHN FARRELL

One of the five 'fighting Farrells', John gave everyone a tough time, even Fenech!

Kirkby's John Farrell was 15 when he followed a younger brother and started boxing for his local club. "Tommy went originally, did OK and my Dad asked him to take the rest of us us with him to see if we liked it. In the end we all went; Tommy, me, Jimmy, Chris and Gordon. We were called the 'five fighting Farrells'. Tommy later turned pro, beating a Frank Warren boxer called Khalid on an afternoon show the day I got married, as did Chris."

John took to the sport easily and soon developed into a top class amateur, winning the North West Counties flyweight title in 1977 and 78; the Northern Counties bantamweight title the following year; representing England on a number of occasions; and winning a gold medal at the 1981 Acropolis Cup in Athens, Greece. "I remember boxing four times in a week once. Monday, Tuesday, Wednesday, took Thursday off, and then again on the Friday. I won them all as well!"

Although undoubtedly proud at representing his country as an amateur, John has mixed feelings when recalling his international career. "When I was 18 I boxed for Young England at light-flyweight and this was the first time I experienced something that would later affect my pro career. I remember struggling to make the light-fly limit and no matter that I didn't eat anything for days I still couldn't make the weight."

John won the majority of his amateur fights although like many it is his losses he remembers the most. "Ray Gilbody beat me a few times. They were always hard battles against Ray. I also lost to an Irish lad called Ray Webb in a representative match in Ireland. He was a big name at the time. I also remember my first championship fight as an amateur. I was only 17 and I met Terry Wenton who was at least ten years older than me – a proper man. I beat him in a tough fight but it was a great experience.

"The first time I boxed for England at Wembley I was given an England tracksuit to wear. I was well pleased with it but was amazed when I was told that, as boxers only got to keep them after they'd made two or three England appearances, I had to give it back at the end of the night! Not long after this Ray Gilbody and I had a great fight at the Liverpool Stadium in the ABAs. We were great local rivals, even as amateurs, and we put on a great show. People were talking about the fight for days afterwards. A week later I turned up at the Stadium to see the rest of the championships but was refused free entry – even though boxers who had competed in them usually got in for nothing. I'd had enough of being treated that way and so I turned pro soon after with Manchester manager Manny Goodall."

John made his pro debut at the Yorkshire Executive Sporting Club in Bradford in April 1982, outpointing South Shields featherweight Ray Plant over six rounds. A month later at the same venue he was matched with experienced local man Steve Enright, the reigning Central Area bantamweight champion. Enright was ranked No. 6 in Britain at the time but John boxed brilliantly to take a unanimous decision. It was a great win for the Kirkby man but, as many in the pro game discover to their cost, you can be too good for your own good sometimes. "After my win over Enright, Manny found it much tougher to get fights for me. I suppose I'd shown my true worth too early in my career and, as I needed contests to earn money, I had to take fights when I knew that even if I won, my opponents would be paid more than me."

A six rounds points win over Glasgow's Jim Harvey a month later maintained John's unbeaten start to his pro career, whilst in September he enjoyed another points win at the Yorkshire SC against the experienced Manchester featherweight Ian Murray. John remembers this contest, his first eight-rounder, in particular as, "One of my heroes, George Best, was guest of honour at this show but, despite the organisers delaying the start, he never turned up. I remember being made up that I'd won my fight on the night, but also being disappointed that I wouldn't meet Best."

A further win over Murray in October at Blackpool set John up for a return with Enright, with the Central Area title up for grabs. John discovered however, that not everything in boxing turns out as expected. "I trained for 10 tough three minute rounds against Enright but the fight fell through late on. Instead I was matched with Hartlepool's Keith Foreman, who was really a lightweight, over eight-twos. The difference in weight, styles and tactics meant I was never really in the fight and I lost on points but I had to take it, as I was married, had a baby, and was working in a wood-yard at the time."

Disappointed at losing both his unbeaten record, and his chance at a title, John returned to action in February 1983 with a fourth round stoppage over Hull's Stuart Carmichael at the Stadium. Two months later John was in action at his local venue again as he dominated every round against Bradford's George Bailey to force a stoppage in the seventh round. This contest was for the vacant Central Area title. "It was getting harder and harder for Manny to get me fights and George, whose style was made for me really, probably wouldn't have taken the fight if it hadn't been for the title and therefore more money."

So difficult was it for John to get fights that he didn't appear in a ring again for another eight months. This time however, he knew it would be his toughest test to date as in the opposite corner would be his old rival from the amateur ranks, Ray Gilbody, who had turned pro in March 1983 with Micky Duff. John admits it was a tough defence of his Central Area title. "Ray seemed to have a knack of boxing well against south-paws, and even though I thought I'd done enough to win he did have a good last round and I think that earned him the draw, which meant of course that I kept the title." It was the first time John had been ten rounds whilst he also recalls the weigh-in in particular. "Both Ray and I were pretty sure we'd be either on or just under the 118lb bantamweight limit, that's what my gym's scales told me anyway. But we were surprised when we both came in around 4lb under! To this day I'm sure the scales they used were well out!"

Despite his draw with Ray Gilbody, John ended the year ranked No. 3 in Britain. Logically this meant he should either be granted a British title shot soon, or that an up-and-coming star would try to gain his prized scalp to show their quality. Unfortunately for John however, his chosen career was professional boxing, a place where such logic is rare in the extreme. Neither of these events happened and it was a full ten months before he fought again.

John Farrell c. 1985   *Source: John Farrell*

Domestically, few boxers were prepared to meet John and he was forced to take a contest in an open-air football ground in Sekunda, South Africa. "I took the fight straight away," remembers John. "I didn't care where it was as I needed the money. I remember arriving at Johannesburg Airport and walking into the arrivals' hall. There were quite a few photographers and reporters milling around and when they saw me they all came rushing over. I turned around thinking that someone famous was behind me but there was no-one there. I couldn't believe it when it turned out they wanted to photograph and interview me. It seemed to be big news that a man from Britain was coming to fight over there."

Although he decked local hero Jeremiah Mbitse, the reigning South African featherweight champion, three times enroute to a fine eight rounds points win, it was events post-fight that amused John. "After I'd got changed my trainer, Franny Hands, and I went back into the stadium to meet our driver - the man who was meant to take us to the airport, which was two hours away, only to find it empty! For a minute we thought we'd be stuck there but another man volunteered to drive us, even though he lived two hours in the opposite direction!"

Despite a fine points win over Swansea's ever dangerous Peter Harris two months later, "he walked onto the best left hand I've ever thrown and went down for an eight count in the first round, but the ref gave him time to recover," John was becoming increasingly disillusioned with his lack of bouts. "It wasn't Manny's fault," says John, "but he was only a provincial manager and in order to fight often, and for the titles that I knew I was good enough to win, you really had to be a big name."

It was for this reason that around this time John held talks with Frank Warren. "I had a family and kids and needed to know how many fights a manager could guarantee me a year. How much I was going to get paid and so on, but all Frank ever said was, 'I'll get you a British title shot.' I replied that I was No.1 in the country by then anyway and that I'd have to get a shot sooner or later and so I decided against joining him and went with Brendan Ingle instead."

It was a full eight months before John boxed again, in which time Ray Gilbody had outpointed the champion, John Feeney, in Hartlepool to win the British title. "It didn't look like I'd get a shot at the title anytime soon and I was desperate for a fight," says John. "When they offered me the chance to go to Australia to fight some Australian I took it straight away. It was only three days later I was told the man I was to face was Jeff Fenech – who'd won the world title in his last fight! His backers were looking for him to meet a top European and I was ranked in the top 10 in Europe at the time."

The youngest son of Maltese parents, Fenech was a rough, hard punching whirlwind of a fighter, a product of his tough upbringing in Marrickville, Sydney. He had won the WBC title in only his eighth professional contest, a ninth round KO of Japan's Satoshi Shingaki. In a 12-year career he would go on to become one of the biggest boxing stars of the 1980s beating the likes of Daniel Zaragoza, Carlos Zarate, Victor Callejas, Marcos Villasana and holding the great Azumah Nelson to a draw at super-featherweight in 1991. He was certainly a force to be reckoned with, although even with just three weeks notice John was unperturbed.

"I arrived in Australia about 10 days before the fight. There was lots of interest and I was interviewed by the newspapers, radio and TV. I remember watching the TV one night in the house we were staying in and an advertisement for the fight came on. First came Fenech's picture with a dramatic voice saying something like, 'Australia's hero – Jeff Fenech, versus,' followed by a pause and then, after a picture of me flashed up, the voice said - 'the Pom!' It was funny but at the same time surreal seeing myself on TV like that! Later on the fight was previewed on the main news programme and I remember them saying that it had finally been confirmed – I was a bantamweight. They thought I was too big to only be 8st 6lbs."

To show the Australian press that he wasn't over-awed by the challenge ahead, John decided to do something different at the weigh-in. "Rather than wear a tracksuit, or training gear, I turned up for the weigh-in wearing a double-breasted, three-piece suit. It went down a storm and everyone loved it. I'd had breakfast that morning and our scales said I was OK but the official one said I was 2lb over, but I got that off in a few hours and there were no further problems. I'd been laughing and joking with the press and officials, but when I saw Fenech stripped off I knew it was going to be tough. I hadn't seen any tapes of him at all, but in the flesh you could see he was a big lad."

Although John rates Fenech the toughest of his 21 professional opponents, "his punches weren't devastating in a knock-out type of way. It was just that there were so many of them! He swarmed all over you and never seemed to stop throwing punches. He was super-fit and really strong. I think I gave him a tough fight though, probably one of the hardest of his career so far, and I managed to catch him a few times but despite giving him a small cut under his eye he seemed to walk right through my punches."

It was certainly no disgrace for John to be stopped in the ninth round and his view that he gave the Australian a tough contest is echoed in Fenech's official biography. Author's Grantlee Kieza and Peter Muszkat wrote in 1988 that John was, "a gritty little bruiser in the tradition of the British bulldog and his refusal to give in against Fenech typified the harsh environment in which his fighting instincts had been nurtured in Kirkby...There he was something of a working-class hero... a 27 year old southpaw with a wife, a kid, 10 wins and a draw in 12 fights, and plenty of 'bottle' – he had the heart to go with his overflow of self-confidence." Kind words indeed, but perhaps the best compliment they could pay John was when they say he, "gave Fenech a far tougher test than Shingaki," the man from whom the Australian had won his world title just three months previously.

John returned to England with his reputation enhanced even further. So much so that he was named official challenger for the British title held by Ray Gilbody, with the fight set for November 1985 at the York Hall, Bethnal Green. It had been nearly two years since their last meeting for the Central Area title however, and John admits that time had taken its toll on his ability to make the weight. "I really struggled to make the weight for this fight. The night before I was 4lbs over and this was despite the fact I'd hardly eaten a thing for about four days beforehand. If you look at a video of the fight you can see I look really drawn. This isn't to take anything away from Ray though. We had a bit of history as regards to our local and national rivalry but he won fair and square. There were no real tactics involved in this fight – we just tried to wear each other down. Although it was stopped in the eighth due to a cut over my right eye I was still surprised when the referee stepped in."

Five months later, John shook off his disappointment at losing to Ray – who fought for the European title just three months after their meeting – by packing his bag once more and heading for Lucca, Italy. Here, on the Gary Hinton v Reyes Antonio Cruz IBF world light-welterweight title show, he lost on points to the top class former European champion,Valerio Nati. Nati would later win the European featherweight title and challenged Daniel Zaragoza for the WBC title just two years later.

The decision still frustrates John however, as, "I boxed brilliantly in this fight. Everything seemed to go right. To be honest I boxed his head off. I couldn't believe it when he got the decision and by the look on his face, neither could he. Then again it was against an Italian fighter, in Italy, and it was well known that they were much more biased towards their own fighters than most other countries. The crowd were fantastic though. They cheered and clapped me whilst I did my lap of honour, and did so again when Brendan Ingle made me go round for another."

Any satisfaction John got from his performance in this contest however, was completely over-shadowed by a poor performance in his next – an eight round points loss to Manchester's Muhammad Lovelock in Manchester in December 1986. There was a heartbreaking reason for this however, as John poignantly explains. "The fight was on a Monday. I'd already signed for it and training had gone well. On the Saturday before though my younger brother Christopher, who had had a couple of fights himself at light-welter before retiring in 1984, was killed when his car was hit by a train at a level crossing in Eastbourne, not far from his home.

"I didn't really want to fight but my manager and trainer persuaded me to carry on, saying it might be good for me to take my mind off things. I believed them for a while but as soon as the bell went for the first round I thought to myself, 'What the hell am I doing here?' I just wanted to take my gloves off and go home. I just didn't want to be there at all but my corner persuaded me to carry on. After the fight the MC informed the crowd of what had happened and they gave me a great reception, but with hindsight I should never have boxed."

The Lovelock fight was made at, a much more comfortable for John, 130lbs and in future he would campaign at the featherweight limit of 9st. A month later, John was matched with his former sparring partner from the Gilbody British title fight, Anthony Brown from St Helens, who had carved out a useful 14 wins from 20 contests. Despite his record he had yet to meet someone of John's standard and the Kirkby man knocked him down with a vicious uppercut in the first round on his way to not only a sixth round stoppage victory, but also his second Central Area title, this time at featherweight.

Some things remained the same for John however, and fights were as hard to come by as they had always been. Eight months later he lost a tough 12-rounder to Swansea's durable Peter Harris in Sollihul. With few wanting to meet him in Britain next up for John was a trip to Izegem, Belgium, to meet reigning European super-featherweight champion Jean Marc Renard. Renard had lost only three times in his 37 fights to date, and these were against Barry McGuigan, Steve Sims and Pat Cowdell, and he was highly rated by all the major governing bodies at the time. John more than held his own for seven rounds however, before his corner retired him in the eighth due to an arm injury. Renard would later challenge for the WBA world featherweight title.

It was to be more than 12 months until John's next contest. A ten rounds points win over local man Les Walsh in Manchester in February 1989 was followed by another points win over Kid Sumaila just two months later. The following month, on the Barry McGuigan v Jim McDonnell bill at Manchester's G-Mex (McGuigan's last fight), John got a crack at the Commonwealth super-featherweight title held by 34-year old Zambian John Sichula. John decked the champion in the fifth round, and had him hurt and bleeding at times, but couldn't finish the game African off. John took some punishment in the eighth though, and the referee stepped in to save him, and thus brought the curtain down on his fine seven-year career. "I felt that if I couldn't beat Sichula then I shouldn't really be carrying on, and I decided to retire."

After retiring John had his own cab for 10 years and now works for MDA Rail. He has been married to Debbie for 23 years and has three daughters, Jade, Chelsea and Christie. "The birth of Maya Jade has recently made me a Grandad, whilst Chelsea is an actress who has been on TV a few times. Christie is our youngest and she trains at Kirkby ABC, where I am helping out before taking the ABA Assistant Coaches Course." On boxing today John says that the time he spends at Kirkby shows that, "there are still loads of kids interested in boxing. I suppose it will always be that way in Liverpool." He admits though, that the scoring system has changed a lot since his amateur days. "It seems to go against body shots, which the judges are meant to score but don't seem to in many of the fights I've seen." The professional game too has changed since John gave local fight fans plenty to shout about in the 1980s. "There seems to be more titles these days, which can only be a good thing for the boxers really as it means that TV are more likely to show them and therefore they are more likely to get good money. It's a shame they knocked the old Stadium down though. I had some great memories from there."

Born in 1911, and despite his mother being against two of her sons becoming fighters, Jack Foster followed his elder brother Bob into the ring and had a total of over 80 professional contests, with many more in the various boxing booths of that time. He met a host of local fighters and characters during his career, the first five years of which were spent living in the Conway Boxing Club where the likes of Charlie Smith and Charlie Tonner were fellow members. This chapter is based on an article written by Frank Johnson that was first published in 1973.

JACK FOSTER

Changed his name to 'Young Fogo' and began throwing punches

In the thrill-packed annals of boxing, there have been many strange names assumed by pugilists. In that category is Birkenhead bantamweight Jack Foster, who took the name of 'Young Fogo' when he turned professional at the age of 16 in the pre-depression year of 1927. Jack's elder brother Bob was a well known Birkenhead pro who tragically died as the result of a motor cycle accident in 1932. It was natural that Jack would follow in his brother's footsteps as a boxer, particularly with his future father-in-law, Peter Edwards 'Young Gorton', encouraging him.

One of four sons and two daughters, Jack was born at St. Mary's Gate in 1911. He left St. Paul's School when he was 13 years old to contribute to the family income, his first job being a helper to a local milkman, and two years later joining Cammell Lairds. Boxing was a key sport in those days, with Birkenhead overflowing with talented performers, and the boxing bug was gradually biting Jack. He met with major opposition from his mother however, who thought that with Bob making the ring his career, one fighter was quite enough for one family. Unknown to his mother however, Jack used to slip away to the Conway Boxing Club and at the age of 16, he had his first fight under the management of Fred Snell, with Dick Staden his trainer.

Having tasted the thrill of combat in an unofficial backyard fight against his schoolmate Vic Scott, Jack signed up for his first professional contest but the first snag to be overcome was to select a name in order to keep the fact away from his mother that he was about to embark on a fighting career. Fred Snell came up with the name

'Young Fogo' and Jack was billed under that name when he had his first fight - a six-rounder against Ellesmere Port's Albert Harvey. Jack lost this first encounter but he put up such a good show that the promoter engaged him for a return. This time he held Harvey to a draw over eight rounds at Little Ness, with his purse money 7/- 6d for the first fight and 10/- for the return contest, with no additional expenses forthcoming.

Fred Snell liked what he saw of 'Young Fogo' and he arranged a series of build-up contests at various venues. Jack boxed Harry Horrocks at Chester in a three fight series ending all square with a win, a draw and a defeat. Jack recalled that Horrocks was a tearaway fighter who, owing to his short stature, had to get inside to pummel away to the body. The Birkenhead man didn't carry a KO punch but he had an immaculate left hand, and this was a real crowd pleaser with the clash of styles.

It wasn't long before Jack's secret was out and this led to him leaving home and taking up residence at the Conway Boxing Club, sleeping rough with a punch-bag as a pillow. Fred Snell allowed Jack to stay for nothing provided that he acted as caretaker and general handyman and Jack lived like this for five years from the age of 16 until he was 21. He had a total of 30 contests under Fred Snell but when his manager became a full time referee, it was Bob Foster who took over Jack's affairs, despite the fact he was still an active boxer at that time. Frank Price, Charlie Smith, Charlie Tonner and Nipper Hughes were Jack's companions at the Conway BC in those tough days. In addition to boxing, Jack was also playing centre forward for the Shaftsbury BC with Tich Pearson, Bobby Tongue, Mutt Robinson, Frankie Wilson and Jim McKay - all of whom eventually played soccer professionally.

Jack crossed gloves with some tough customers including Peter Clarke, an all-action butcher's assistant who used to build up his reserves of stamina by drinking an ample supply of animal blood whilst doing his cutting up. Life was tough enough without those sort of aids, and even when he left the sport for two years following the death of Bob Foster in 1932, he knew he would return one day.

Jack remembers being KO'd in seven rounds by George Stevens at Wigan in a scheduled ten-rounder, whilst he also recalls arriving for an open-air show at Southport to see the publicity hand-out blaring to all concerned that his opponent was a hammer-fisted gentleman known as Dyke Archer, who had supposedly rattled up 150 wins, including over 100 by the KO route! Jack gave Archer a good fight however - until the lights went out in the eighth round. He was brought round in the dressing room afterwards by the well-known Southport cruiserweight, Kid Moose, who had been in his corner. The fight earned Jack a neat collection of ten stitches and the princely sum of 35/-, and he had to run for the train afterwards!

The boxing booths were thriving in the 1930s and Jack went to Len Barton's booth at Seaforth to take on all-comers on Friday and Saturday nights. This meant having an average of five fights a night, often giving stones away and he had to win to earn his money. Occasionally, the promoter made sure that a man from the crowd won in order to bring in greater crowds for a natural return, when a very different result would be forthcoming before a 'Full House'.

Jack had over 80 professional fights plus many more in the booths. Among his opponents were Nobby Clarke, George Davies, Ossie Parry, Young Mack, Chucky Scoles, Harry Oxton, Billy Jones and Young Cooper. He also met that great local fighter Billy Morris, who gained the nod at the Central Hall in Hoylake. Jack also conceded two stones to a great Wirral character 'Bill the Boatie' and received a hiding for his trouble against the Ellesmere Port docker. Jack retired from boxing in 1939 and was called up in 1940 for war service with the RAOC. He was a keen member of the Wirral Former Boxers Association until his death some years ago.

One of the city's most talented amateur stars, Liverpool's Joey Frost had almost 290 amateur contests for Lee Jones ABC, the Rotunda and the old Bronte ABC, losing less than 20. An England regular in the late-1970s and early-1980s, Joey won a senior ABA title in sensational fashion in 1979 courtesy of an amazing KO in the first 20 seconds! Selected for the 1980 Olympic Games in Moscow, where he was unlucky not to win a medal, Joey had a host of podium finishes in numerous multi-nations events at the time and turned pro with Manny Goodall in 1981. In a three-year career cut short by eye problems, Joey won nine out of 11 pro contests, winning the Central Area welterweight title in the process. Still living in Liverpool this article was compiled through interviews with Joey during 2007.

JOEY FROST

Top amateur star lost just 18 out of 287!

Joey Frost was around 10 years old when he first took up boxing, firstly with the old Lee Jones ABC, "with Georgie Vaughan and Jimmy Albertina as trainers," before following both to the Rotunda. "George then went to the Bronte and I went there too," says Joey. Although there was some history of boxing in his family, Joey didn't follow anyone into the sport for that reason. "My Dad had boxed in the Army, 'to get better food,' he used to say, and my older brother Tommy also boxed for the Lee Jones and the Rotunda – he was quite good – but I went simply to stay out of trouble really."

Joey's amateur career is almost peerless, with an amazing 269 wins from 287 contests. He won a National Schoolboy title and a Junior ABA crown in 1976 with Lee Jones. The following year, with the same club, he added an NABC title – outpointing future world champion Lloyd Honeyghan enroute to the final - and another Junior ABA crown. He won the first of a host of England vests in an U19 match against Hungary – with Tony Willis and Ray Gilbody also in the team - in Szekszard, Hungary in August 1978, Joey winning his bout as the ABA lost 6-5. The same year he was selected for matches in Essen, West Germany; Rostock and Wismar, East Germany; Dieppe, France; and London against the USA. Joey won all his fights except those against America and West Germany, where reigning European champion Ernst Muller forced him to retire in the second round.

In 1979 Joey scored another points win over Lloyd Honeyghan in the ABA semi-finals in Gloucester, before going on to record a sensational win in the final - his 15 seconds win over Lochaber's Alan Mann is probably an ABA finals record. A fantastic gold in the Tampere multi-nations tournament in Finland in October 1979 was achieved by beating the highly rated Bulgarian Plamen Yankov, a 1974 world, and 1977 European, bronze medallist. "Yankov gave me a hard fight," says Joey. "He gave me a standing count in the first round, another one in the second round but then I KO'd him in the third." Joey also won 'Best Fighter' in the same tournament.

Joey was selected for the 1980 Olympic Games in Moscow, but despite two first round KO wins in the early rounds he came up against East Germany's Karl Heinz Kruger in the quarter-final. "I got robbed in this fight. Everyone thought I'd won and I couldn't believe it when he got the decision. I boxed his head off. He was a southpaw and all he did was block my shots. I don't think he caught me once." Kruger, a European silver medallist in 1977 and 1979 and a world bronze medallist in 1978, went on to win a bronze in Moscow.

A move to the Bronte ABC with Georgie Vaughan saw Joey move up to light-middleweight. He made the semi-finals of the ABAs that year, eventually losing to Standard Triumph's talented Errol Christie. "This was a great fight," remembers Joey. "We were both down twice but Errol got the nod. The Lord Mayor of Gloucester sent my Mum flowers and chocolates afterwards, saying that it was the best fight he'd ever seen!" Christie would win a European junior gold medal at 75kgs the following year before turning pro soon after.

With such a fantastic amateur record, it was no wonder that Joey got offers to turn pro from all quarters. "Everyone wanted me to sign for them. Local promoters and managers, London managers, everyone. I even got offers to turn pro in the USA but it was a big step to take at the time. I'd just had my first child, Kelsie, and so I went with whoever offered me the most money and that was Manny Goodall." Joey's pro debut at welterweight came on 24 September 1981 at the Stadium – a first round KO win over Manchester's Kevin Walsh. Joey didn't have long to enjoy his victory however, as just four days later he was in action again, this time in Bradford. Although the location was different the result wasn't and Joey scored another first round stoppage win, this time over Swansea's Jeff Aspell. Two wins from his next two contests, one a fine eight rounds points win over experienced Manchester middleweight Chris Coady, ensured Joey ended 1981 with four wins from his first four contests.

A great points win over Cardiff-based Jamaican Horace McKenzie in Preston in March 1982 was followed by another exciting victory in May. Future Scottish light-middleweight champion Tommy McCallum was dispatched inside three minutes by Joey at Preston's Guild Hall. "McCallum had me down in the first few seconds and hit me while I was on the floor. I went after him straight away and KO'd him soon after. His legs completely went and they had to carry him out of the ring."

Joey Frost c. 1980   *Source: Joey Frost*

In June 1982 Joey suffered his first reverse, a fourth round stoppage to Scottish welterweight champion Dave Douglas, but this didn't prevent him from being named as challenger for the vacant Central Area title against Sheffield's Peter Bennett. In the unusual surroundings, for a Central Area title at least, of Morley Town Hall in London on 24 June, Joey forced a stoppage in the fourth round and was declared champion. Despite a record of seven wins from eight however, Joey had just two contests in 1983, a surprise fourth round stoppage loss to Wolverhampton's talented Lloyd Christie (a future British champion and European title challenger) in January and a successful defence of his Area title against Manchester's Lee Hartshorn the following month. Managerial issues and problems with his eyesight ensured that Joey had just one fight in 1984, a sixth round KO over another Mancunian Phil O'Hare for Billy Aird. It turned out to be his last contest.

Joey has few regrets when asked about his career today. He is thankful for the opportunity amateur boxing gave him to literally travel the world but admits he, "should probably have turned pro with another manager – maybe one of the big London promoters at the time." Although Joey thinks, "it seems a lot easier for boxers today – there were simply better and classier fighters years ago," he does admit that," boxing is the hardest game in the world and you still have to be good to get to the top. You may not walk to the top but certainly the journey is a bit easier these days."

When asked to name his toughest opponent Joey finds it difficult to separate Errol Christie, "he was a great amateur, he didn't lose many," Plamen Yankov and local man Dave Jennings. "I met Dave twice and they were both really tough fights. He was a cracking man outside the ring as well."

Being a favourite of the Liverpool fight crowd, especially as an amateur, Joey has fond memories of the legendary local venue. "The atmosphere there was great. I boxed all over the world but the Stadium was the best. As you left the dressing room and walked up the tunnel to the ring and then entered the hall - it was amazing. The whole place would cheer when they saw you. It really got your adrenaline going."

Although the Stadium could generate tremendous excitement for a local boxer, Joey jokingly stresses the negative side of the St Paul's Square venue. "I never got a single bye or walk-over the whole time I boxed in championships at the Stadium! I nearly always had to box two or even three times a night. I remember doing just that one Thursday evening and, because you weren't allowed to box four times in a day, having to go to Manchester on the Monday to finish up. I won this as well. First round KO!" Although the name of his opponent escapes him now, Joey also remembers boxing an Irish boy in the NABC's. "I saw his trainers trying to get two right hand gloves on him – they must have brought the wrong ones – and then asking other trainers for a left-handed one!"

After retiring Joey had a number of jobs in Liverpool but, due to a rebuilt knee that required four operations, he no longer works. He has four children, Kelsie 26, "who has given me three grandchildren – Kieran, Faye and Luke," Jayde 21, Lois 17 and Joel 8. Still seen at boxing shows in the city Joey was, and remains, a great favourite in Liverpool boxing circles.

A top class boxer before he left Barbados for Liverpool in 1949, Ivor 'Kid' Germain was just one of the many African and West Indian boxers who settled in Liverpool during the 1950s. A firm favourite of the Liverpool Stadium fight crowd due to his all-action style and never-say-die attitude, Ivor won the majority of at least 55 fights in his 16-year career, the highlight being his reign as Empire lightweight champion for three months in 1954. Ivor's last contest came in 1957 but his post-fight career details have been difficult to discover.

IVOR "KID" GERMAIN

Overcame hand injuries and five-year wait to become Empire champion

The late 1940s and early 1950s saw an enormous influx of fighters arriving on these shores from Africa and the West Indies. Many were given a lot of help and assistance by the then Labour MP for Liverpool Exchange, Bessie Braddock. One of that group of fighters was a young man from Barbados, Ivor 'Kid' Germain. Born in Barbados in 1923, Germain was no young hopeful travelling to this country to try and earn a living with his fists, as he was already an accomplished fighter at the time of his arrival who held no fewer than three professional boxing titles in his native country. The reigning bantamweight, featherweight and lightweight champion of Barbados, Ivor was a married man with a six-year old daughter and the owner of a thriving taxi business on the Caribbean island. He always maintained that he came to Britain for one purpose only - to win the British Empire lightweight championship.

The fifth child in a family of six, with four brothers and a sister, Ivor was always destined to be a fighter. He started boxing at a young age and when he was only 16 years old he turned professional, making his paid debut at the Yankee Stadium in Barbados. His first year as a pro proved so successful that he was soon matched with 'Lightfoot Kid' for the bantamweight Championship of Barbados. Ivor was a points winner so at 16 years of age he found himself champion of his country. In addition, his all-action style of fighting made him a favourite with his local fight crowds.

Following his defeat the 'Lightfoot Kid' moved up to featherweight and in 1941 he and Ivor met once more, again with the national title on the line. After a thrilling battle that saw Lightfoot on the floor for two long counts, Ivor was adjudged the winner on points, thus becoming a dual champion.

Ivor's stock was rising and he was in great demand by local promoters. After several more wins, Ivor matched with Barbados' Al Brown, the current lightweight champion. Their March 1942 contest proved to be one of the most ferocious battles ever seen on the island. It was a non-title contest and Brown, a strong and courageous fighter, soon discovered that this young opponent was a deadly puncher with rocks in each glove. They went at each other like young lions, each man belting the other for round after round. The champion took two long counts and at the end of a pulsating and thrilling contest, Ivor was declared a points winner. The fight public screamed for a return with the title at stake but instead, Ivor took a boat journey to neighbouring Trinidad to meet their lightweight champion, Al Tunny.

Like his contest with Brown, this too proved to be a terrific contest with the crowd treated to a non-stop punching spectacle. At the close, Ivor was declared a points winner and he returned home to Barbados to meet Al Brown again, this time with the title at stake. At the finish of their long awaited return, Ivor was the proud holder of three Barbados ring titles, the feather, bantam and lightweight championships. Ivor returned to Trinidad for a return with Tunny and, once again, he proved the master. In the summer of 1944, he returned to Barbados to meet Victor Moreno, the lightweight champion of Venezuela, winning on points after another terrific contest. Moreno demanded a return but their second contest went the same way as the first with Ivor a clear points winner.

In November 1946 Ivor was matched with Young Tanner (brother of Kid Tanner) the reigning lightweight champion of British Guyana and, once again, he proved the master winning on points. 1947 saw Ivor take a break from boxing while he concentrated on starting a business. He formed a taxi company in Barbados which soon developed into a highly successful business. Soon however, he began to miss the roped square. He realised that the British Empire lightweight title was vacant and that he had what it took to add that belt to his growing collection.

Ivor set sail for Liverpool, arriving in February 1948. He immediately sought out local promoter Johnny Best who matched him with Belfast's Gerry Smythe at the Stadium the following month, a fight the

Barbadian won on points over eight rounds. As well as the stress of making his debut in a world famous arena in a foreign country however, Ivor also had to struggle against the handicap of a carbuncle on his wrist. His win impressed the knowledgeable Liverpool fight crowd however, and they immediately took to him, remaining loyal supporters throughout his subsequent ring career in this country. Ivor never looked for an easy fight and most of the men he fought were champions of one country or another.

Next up was Harry Hughes, the lightweight champion of Scotland. This was not an easy contest for Ivor but the Barbadian southpaw went after Hughes immediately, peppering him with lefts and rights, putting him down for a count of nine early on. Hughes got to his feet and squared up only for a terrific left to the heart to put him on the canvas again - this time for a count of eight. The second round was similar to the first in that Hughes attempted to nail Ivor with a hard right to the body, but the Barbadian walked straight in to smash a terrific left hook to Hughes' jaw. The atmosphere inside the packed hall was electric and the crowd were going wild as Hughes, game to the end, once again struggled to his feet. Ivor however, was in no mood to hang around. A huge right to the jaw was followed by a left to the stomach and Hughes was down once more - this time for good. 'Kid' Germain was now the darling of the Liverpool Stadium fight crowd, but this contest was not without its drawbacks for Ivor had broken his left thumb and this kept him out of the ring until June 1948, when he faced another champion in the shape of Josef Preys, lightweight champion of Belgium.

Ivor found Preys a master of defence, hard to hit and despite a good seventh round he lost his first fight in Britain. Just two weeks later, Ivor was back in action against former European amateur champion, Paddy Dowdall. Ivor KO'd the Irishman in two rounds but his fierce punching style again damaged his thumb, the injury keeping him out for five months. His eventual return saw him travel to Abergavenny where former British champion Cliff Curvis stopped him in five.

Ivor's former opponent, Scottish lightweight champion Harry Hughes, had meanwhile fought his way to a British title fight with champion, Billy Thompson. First however, Hughes wanted a return with the only man who had handed him a KO defeat, and exactly a year to the day after their first contest, Hughes and Ivor faced each other once more, this time in Manchester. The Scotsman would be sorry he insisted upon a return, as again Ivor proved his master, winning clearly on points over ten rounds. This victory, over a top-ten rated lightweight, was not without complication however, as once again Ivor's ferocious punching resulted in damage to his hand. Victory in his next contest was followed by a visit to hospital for extensive treatment.

His ring successes saw Ivor talked about as a possible contender for championship honours and he took a huge step towards realising this ambition when, on 18 August 1949, he went in against South Africa's Jimmy Toweel at Liverpool Stadium. Recognised as an eliminating contest for the Empire crown, a full house saw Ivor emerge victorious when Toweel was disqualified for an alleged low blow in the eighth round. There was almost a sensational ending to the contest in the first round when Toweel came rushing in only to be caught with a tremendous left hook which spun the South African completely round. Toweel came back fighting but Ivor caught him again with a further left hook to the head and a powerful right to the jaw, which put him on the canvas. He regained his feet and the contest was continued in this furious manner until the unfortunate ending in the eighth round following warnings in the second and fourth rounds to keep his punches up. Following this great win, Ivor returned home to Barbados for a short holiday whilst six wins from his next nine contests included two great wins over Laurie Buxton.

Johnny Best knew that all he had to do to ensure a full house at the Liverpool Stadium was to put 'Kid' Germain at the top of the bill and this proved to be true once again on 29 March 1951, when Ivor faced yet another champion, this time the welterweight champion of Holland, Giel de Roode. As well as having to concede eight pounds in weight to the Dutch champion, Ivor also burst his thumb in the very first round which meant he could only use his left hand sparingly. Although he, unsurprisingly, lost a ten rounds points decision, Ivor received a standing ovation from both the crowd and de Roode, when they were informed of his injury at the end of the contest.

Ivor was finding that his all-action, hard punching style was causing fighters to give him a wide berth unless he conceded weight and just four weeks later he met top class Italian *welterweight* Luigi Coluzzi, winning on points. Another points win over Liverpool favourite, Jimmy Molloy at the Stadium, followed, although again Ivor was forced to concede near 10lbs in weight.

Finding fights difficult to come by in the UK, Ivor travelled to Australia but found that his reputation had preceded him and few were prepared to face him. So frustrated was Ivor that he even contemplated returning home, but the offer of a contest against Spanish lightweight champion Agustin Argote in Melbourne in January 1954 persuaded him to stay. The Spaniard, fresh from a KO victory over Australian Pat Ford, was strongly favoured to beat Ivor who, by now, was 30 years of age. Ivor however, had other ideas and after almost being out on his feet at the end of the first round he hung on to win a ten rounds points decision.

Ivor 'Kid' Germain c. 1951   *Source: Gary Shaw*

Ivor had won an eliminating contest for the right to challenge for the Empire title in August 1949. Such is boxing politics however, that it was now January 1954, and he still hadn't fought for the title. He had been in Australia since July 1952 and by the time he finally left he had fought there thirteen times, winning seven and drawing one. Most of his five losses were against welterweights. He had beaten George Barnes, the Australian welter champion, Agustin Argote and had taken the New Zealand welterweight title holder Barry Brown the distance. Was he now, at long last, going to get his deserved crack at the Empire lightweight crown?

On 9 April 1954 in Melbourne, Ivor "Kid" Germain's dream came true, for he challenged the Australian holder of the title, Pat Ford. Although the Australian was ahead on points at the end of the sixth round, Ivor had fought back and was on level terms by the tenth round. He concentrated on the champion's body and, after taking a breather in the eleventh and twelfth rounds, both of which were won by Ford, he finished strongly and took the last three rounds to win - and take the title.

Ivor had set sail for Liverpool in 1949 and now, at last, in April 1954, he had achieved his dream of becoming British Empire lightweight champion. An all-action fighter, who never failed to give the crowd full value for their money, Ivor 'Kid' Germain remains a great favourite with the Liverpool fight fraternity. Always well dressed out of the ring, it is believed Ivor had a photography business in the Kensington area of Liverpool in the 1950s but, despite extensive efforts to ascertain what happened to him once he retired little is known of his post-fight career.

Yet another example of famous boxing brothers from Merseyside (the Green brothers from Warrington, McAteers from Birkenhead, and the Mason family from Bootle were all featured in the first volume), George and Ray Gilbody of St Helens dominated amateur boxing between 1974 –1981, winning a staggering eight ABA titles between them in this period. Ray turned professional after winning three ABA titles and a Commonwealth Games bronze medal in 1982, going on to win the British title and challenge for the European crown, whilst older brother George remained a stalwart of the amateur code. In a 17-year career he became one of the most successful amateur boxers the British Isles has ever produced. Still resident in Cheshire articles were obtained via personal interviews with the brothers in 2006.

GEORGE GILBODY

11 National titles made history

A mainstay of ABA teams throughout the late 1970s and early 80s, winning gold at the 1974 Amsterdam Multi-Nations, another gold at the 1979 Acropolis Cup in Athens, and a bronze medal at the European U21 championships, a notoriously difficult tournament in which to succeed, in Kiev in 1974, George Gilbody's amateur record is simply impeccable. Indeed, George's 11 national titles (many forget to include his 1972 ATC national title) make him the most successful English amateur to date.

Such success seemed a world away when George first began to take an interest in the sport when he was just five years old. It didn't surprise his parents however, as they had long been interested in boxing. "My Dad – also named George - had boxed as an amateur when he was 16 and continued to do so whilst he was in the forces," says George. "He turned professional and had three pro fights – one of which was against Syd Greb at Liverpool Stadium when he broke his hand and lost on points. He was a coach at Lowe House for a time and had also been former pro Ray Shiel's coach and sparring partner."

Like any proud father, George snr followed his sons' careers with relish, although as George recalls this could sometimes lead to some amusing incidents. "My father was enthusiastic to say the least. During my schoolboy days, at a North-West Counties match in Ellesmere Port, he was made to leave the building because he was shouting in disagreement with the referee. He had to watch from outside on his tiptoes through the window - I'm sure it was raining as well! At

Meadowbank in the 1974 England v Scotland international match, this was actually on TV, he got over-excited again and was carried out of the building by a bunch of Scots! Luckily I didn't find out about the incidents until after my contests! Together with my Mum, who was a big boxing fan herself – she used to go with her father to watch boxing all over the country – I received full support and encouragement from my parents when I decided to take the sport seriously." A glance at George's record certainly shows how serious he took boxing, amassing an incredible 180 wins from 195 amateur contests, the majority with St Helens Star ABC, drawing one and losing only 14.

George's first national crown was a junior Schoolboy title in 1970. He added the senior Schoolboy title the following year, as well as a junior ABA crown. As a senior he won nine West Lancs/Cheshire titles; nine North West Counties titles; eight Northern Counties and an amazing five ABA titles. The first of these was at featherweight in 1974 when, representing the Golden Gloves ABC in Liverpool, he outpointed New Tredegar's J Pritchard. The following year George lost in a preliminary round to the eventual champion Ricky Beaumont and in 1976, now boxing at lightweight, fate dealt him a cruel blow when the '28 day rule', that prevented KO'd boxers from fighting again within 28 days, forced him to sit out that years' championships. George had been sensationally stopped in the first round against Scotland's Tommy McCallum whilst representing the ABA in January.

In George's absence Repton's Sylvester Mittee won the ABA title that year and it was the London man the ABA turned to to represent Britain at that year's Montreal Olympics. However, this was only after George dropped a split decision, highly disputed at the time by fans and journalists alike, at a pre-Olympic tournament at Wembley.

As part of the build up to the Games, a Great Britain team was selected to box America. Despite not being the reigning ABA champion George was picked for the tournament. He had already represented the ABA nine times (seven wins) at various levels in the previous three years, whilst he also won a multi-nation tournament gold in Holland (1974) and a bronze at the European U21 Championships. The Europeans took place in the Ukrainian capital Kiev, and it was no surprise that with East-Europeans winning gold in all weight divisions (the USSR won seven out of 11 golds) medals were hard to come by. However, joining George on the rostrum that fortnight were Charlie Magri, who won a silver, and Kirkland Laing who also won a bronze.

The team selected for the match against the USA in June 1976 was a strong one, containing the likes of Magri, Pat Cowdell, Cornelius Boza-Edwards*, Clinton McKenzie and Colin Jones, all of whom went on to either win or challenge for world titles as professionals. Most observers felt that all George had to do was win this match and he would be picked for the Olympics. As it was however, George lost to an up-and-coming 17-year old by the name of Thomas Hearns, a future world champion at five different weights! His chance at Olympic selection was gone - the ABA sending Sylvester Mittee instead, but George would get another chance at Olympic glory four years later.

[*Despite boxing for England on a number of occasions, Boza-Edwards was selected by his native Uganda for the 1976 Olympics, only for the country to boycott Montreal due to the inclusion of New Zealand whose rugby union team had earlier toured apartheid South Africa eds.]

George Gilbody (left) v Tommy Hearns, 5 June 1976, Wembley   Source: George Gilbody

Not letting the disappointment of his non-selection for the Olympics deter him however, George was back with a vengeance in 1977 winning the ABA lightweight title courtesy of a semi-final win over Terry Marsh - yet another future world champion - and a points decision over Lochaber's Alan Mann in the final. That year he was selected (in a four-man team that also included Birkenhead's Robbie

Davies) for the European Senior Championships in Halle, East Germany, but no English boxers won medals. Again, East Europeans dominated, winning all gold medals and the USSR winning five.

George boxed for the ABA on only two occasions in 1977. In January he met his first round conqueror from the year before, Scotland's Tommy McCallum, in Dundee, and in November he found himself up against a formidable Romanian at Liverpool Stadium. Both bouts were memorable for different reasons however, the first resulting in another loss – this time on points, the second a victory over D Ilie. George's victory here was the only one for the home boxers, who lost 10-1, thus ensuring that the ABA did not suffer a whitewash for the first time in its history.

Illness ensured George missed the 1978 ABA championships after winning the West Lancs & Cheshire Title, but he was selected for the team that went to Edmonton for the Commonwealth Games. This turned out to be a poor tournament for England however, with only four boxers winning medals and only one gold, George being stopped with a cut requiring four stitches after a head collision with Kenya's Patrick Waweru, whom George beat over in Kenya the following year.

1979 was a different story however, and George returned to win the first of three consecutive ABA titles. His 1979 and 1980 title wins, over Fisher's Mickey O'Sullivan and Repton's Tony Bowden respectively, are particularly memorable as it was during these championships that younger brother Ray also won ABA titles – the Gilbody's thus becoming the first brothers to win ABA titles on the same night since the Hair brothers in 1887. The brothers' fantastic run of form in 1980 ensured they were both selected, together with fellow Merseysider's Keith Wallace, Tony Willis (who was GB's only medal winner – a bronze) and Joey Frost, for the Moscow Olympics. George however lost to Richard Nowakowski, the reigning European champion and a previous Olympic silver medallist at featherweight – this was one of a total of eight points decisions which George still believes he shouldn't have lost.

With a record that includes contests against all the world's leading amateurs of his day, including Terry Marsh, Pat Cowdell, Tony Willis, Johnny Verderosa, Simion Cutov, John Trainor, Jeff Decker and George Feeney, not forgetting his split decision loss to Tommy Hearns, it is not surprising that George takes his time when asked who was his toughest opponent. "It's difficult to say which was my hardest fight. I won against many greats, perhaps the most memorable being my two victories over Terry Marsh, a win over Pat Cowdell and Johnny Verderosa. Similarly my wins over Tomczech and Tzvetkov where tough fights but if I had to name one I'd probably say Tsacho Andriokovsky, a Bulgarian who stopped me in the first round in an ABA representative match at the Royal Albert Hall in December 1974." Andriokovsky had won gold at bantamweight in the 1974 European U21 Championships in Kiev, the same tournament where George had won a bronze, and was a beaten finalist in the senior Europeans a year later in Katowice.

Like many ex-boxers looking back at their careers it is the losses George focuses on the most. "Although I loved my career and am grateful for all my successes, my eight points defeats were in my opinion all unjust and to a certain extent they lessened the impact of my career. I'd love to go back and do it all again and get the decisions I think I deserved, but you only get one chance don't you?"

The amateur code has changed a lot since George's day and in his opinion not always for the better. "I believe that the standard of amateur boxing has dropped since the 1980s. The ABAs are of course only English now, whereas in my day they included all of Britain, and this has lessened the prestige to a certain extent. This has had the result of reducing the number of top class boxers active today, and even though the top boxers earn good money to stay amateur now – I'd have been a wealthy man! – I still feel that too many still turn pro at too young an age. Technically of course we didn't have headguards when I boxed, and although these are good for reducing cuts and injuries I feel that they reduce the gap between good and top class boxers as it reduces chances for an average boxer who can punch but increases the size of the target when punches might not be on target.

As a top class international George boxed all over Britain, Europe and the world, but recalls Liverpool with affection. "I remember the Liverpool Stadium well. I must have boxed there around 30 times and I think I only lost once. Of course the crowd were partisan and wanted their own boxers to do well and I remember being booed going into the ring and out in an ABA preliminary contest, but once I won the West Lancs title I began to be called 'scouse' and they cheered me on. It was as good a venue as Belle Vue – where the ABA semi-finals were held in those days – and almost as good an atmosphere as the

Olympics, Commonwealths and Europeans. I can still see myself down in the changing rooms warming up, getting weighed-in, listening to the draw and hearing Joe McElhinney shouting to us to 'glove up'! Happy memories!"

Near the end of his amateur career, George found work in Leisure Management and has been Outdoor Facilities Manager for Salford Council for 14 years. "I'm the eldest of four brothers; Ray, Ian and Neil – all four of us boxed on the same night at Cronton Social Club in 1974! I have four sons; George jnr (27), Tony (25) and Matthew (21) from my first marriage, and Ben (5) with Beryl to whom I am now married. Mum and Dad (both 74) are well but my Dad snapped his achilles tendon in March 2006 – skipping with my old leather skipping rope in his back garden would you believe!

"I always felt blessed in my family life, education, sporting career and employment and in 2005 I became a born again Christian. Beryl and I were baptised on the same day in November 2005. I was always brought up to respect people and property and to help people whenever and wherever I could so following God was a natural thing for me."

Like elder brother George, Ray Gilbody was a top class amateur, winning three senior ABA titles. Unlike George however, Ray turned pro and went on to win a British title and challenge for the European crown. In a four-year career, Ray won 11 out of 16 pro contests, meeting the likes of John Farrell, John Feeney, Antoine Montero and Billy Hardy. Still living and working in Warrington, where he is a coach at Bridgefoot ABA, this article was obtained via interviews with Ray in 2006.

RAY GILBODY

Top class amateur and pro - robbed in Euro title bid

Although both domestically and internationally, Ray Gilbody's amateur career was exceptional, it didn't look like it would turn out that way when he made his debut, for the Warrington fighter managed to lose his first contest! "I gave a lot of weight away just to get the match", explains Ray. "It wouldn't be allowed these days - but then I won my next 36, so I must have been good!"

This is a gross understatement however, as Ray went on to become one of Britain's most successful amateur stars winning three national schoolboy titles (Junior B in 1974, Intermediate in 1975 and Senior in 1976); a junior ABA title (1976); an NABC title (1976); and three senior ABA titles (1979 at flyweight, 1980 and 1982 at bantam).

It was a family double in 1979 with older brother George outpointing Mickey O'Sullivan for his second senior ABA crown at lightweight. Ray won the flyweight title by defeating Kelvin Smart by the same route. As if this remarkable achievement wasn't enough for the Gilbody brothers they repeated the feat in 1980 when George won a third title and Ray his second by stopping Jim McDonnell in two rounds. This was a good year for Merseyside amateur boxing in general - and St Helens in particular - as clubmate Keith Wallace also won the flyweight title, with Lowe House's John Lyon making the light-flyweight final and Tony Willis (Rotunda) and Jimmy Price (Holy Name) also winning senior titles. Ray's third ABA title in 1982 came virtue of a points win over Alan Coveley.

Although Ray admits it was elder brother George's involvement in boxing that first got him hooked on the sport, he acknowledges that another family member is also worthy of a mention in this regard. "I first became interested in boxing when I was about seven or eight years old, mainly through my brother George, who was five years older than me and who was already involved, but also because of my father. He boxed himself when he was younger. He reckoned that what he achieved didn't amount to much but he deserves some credit for all the time he devoted in this respect to his four sons. Our two younger brothers, Ian and Neil, also boxed but they didn't really continue much after they'd left school."

Young Ray boxed for a variety of clubs but, "as far as I can remember I trained at Lowe House in St. Helens. I also boxed for the Golden Gloves in Liverpool although I spent most of my career with the St Helens Star in Clock Face. "I had my first amateur contest when I was 11 and my amateur career lasted until I was 23. I had 108 contests in total losing only eight. Some of these losses were in my opinion bad decisions, although I did lose to some top class boxers. In 1978 I lost to Richard Sandoval in a Young England (U19) match v USA in London *[Sandoval later becoming WBA bantamweight champion. eds]*. I also lost to Daniel Zaragoza in the 1980 Moscow Olympics – a very close call. *[Zaragoza went on to become a three-time world champion at both bantam and super-bantamweight. eds]*

"I boxed for Young England a number of times;- v USA (lost), v Hungary (won and lost), v East Germany (won and lost), v West Germany (won twice in 10 days), and v France (won). The win v Hungary came against top flyweight James Varadi in 1978. Varadi went on to win Olympic bronze in Moscow in 1980."

Ray's amateur career is dotted with appearances and medals at all the top boxing tournaments of the day. At the famous Tampere multi-nations in Finland in 1979 he won a gold medal at flyweight – with Joey Frost and Tony Willis also winning gold. The same year Ray also tasted victory at the Acropolis Cup in Greece. "This was a fantastic tournament as we boxed at the old Olympic Stadium – George also won gold at the same tournament." In 1981 Ray won a gold at the Ankara multi-nations beating the Turkish number one in the semi-final. "I remember being booed going in and out of the ring!"

"One incident I remember fondly occurred on a senior tour of Kenya in 1979. We boxed first in Nairobi (lost 6-5) where, although I had him down for the first time in his career, I was stopped in the first round by their top star at the time - Michael Irungu *[Irungu won gold at the 1978 Edmonton Commonwealth and in this contest Ray was down twice, the Kenyan once. eds.]* We then all packed our bags, my brother George and Liverpool's Tony Willis were also in the team, and headed for the second set of fights in Lake Nakuru. We left the hotel and climbed onto the coach, but for some reason were left waiting for a good 40 minutes without anything happening. At the time we didn't know why but when we were asked to unload our bags and return all 'mislaid items' we figured it out! Soaps, shampoos, pillowcases and even a quilt – I can't remember who had 'borrowed' that - were handed over and only then were we allowed to leave! Happy memories and great times. Incidentally we won the second match 8-2."

Ray's domestic dominance at bantamweight, together with his international experience, ensured he was selected to go to the 1980 Moscow Olympics, but the luck of the draw put paid to any medal hopes he may have had. "At the larger tournaments such as Olympic Games, the draw can be cruel. I won one fight then in the next round lost a disputed decision to a young Mexican flyweight called Daniel Zaragoza. We all know how good he turned out to be!"

Two years later Ray was part of arguably the strongest English boxing team to attend a Commonwealth Games. "I won a bronze at Brisbane in 1982. This was a really great trip as all the English boxers won medals. Chris Pyatt and Jimmy Price won gold, with five silver – including John Lyon and Jim McDonnell - and two bronze. I beat a Kenyan in the quarter-finals but then lost a disputed decision in the semis to the eventual winner J Orewa of Nigeria." *[Both Kenya and Nigeria were extremely strong at the time and both countries won three gold medals each at the games. eds]*

Not long after the Commonwealth Games Ray surprised many by turning pro at the relatively old age of 23 with Mike Barrett and Mickey Duff. His first contest after 'turning over' was a second round stoppage win against Bradford's George Bailey at the Albert Hall, London in March 1983. Bailey was a seasoned campaigner but like many were to discover, he had no answer to Ray's potent right hand, being dropped for a count of eight in the second round with the referee calling a halt soon after.

Welshman Steve Cleak, a full featherweight with a lot of experience, was Ray's second opponent at the same venue just five weeks later. On paper it looked a tough assignment for Ray yet he was clearly in front when the referee ruled Cleak out in the sixth for 'persistent fouling'. Five weeks later Dutchman Roy Somer managed to last the full eight rounds at Wembley but could manage a share of only two sessions – and he too was floored by a right, this time to the body, in the sixth.

Ray's biggest test to date came in his fourth contest, when Luis de la Sagra of Spain found himself in the opposite corner. De la Sagra had twice challenged for the European bantamweight title;- a 12 round points loss to Italian Valerio Nati in Italy in 1981, with a similar outcome the following year against another Italian Guiseppe Fossati, also in Italy, so the Spaniard was rated highly. Again however, Ray's skill and strength were to the fore, the Spaniard being stopped on cuts in the eighth and last round with Ray the proverbial street ahead on points at the time.

In December 1981, in a contest between two highly-rated prospects that boxing fans rarely see these days, Ray was paired with Bootle's John Farrell (seven wins from eight at the time) for the Central Area title at the Liverpool Stadium. It was only Ray's fifth contest as a pro. "The result was a draw but after the fight many spectators reckoned I had won. John was my toughest opponent as a professional; a southpaw and an extremely good hit-and-run type of fighter. I boxed him five times in all, three of those in the ABAs, but he still didn't beat me!" Although Ray kept his unbeaten record, and by virtue of the draw Farrell kept his title, it showed that he could go 10 rounds without too much bother, whilst he also managed to deck the champion in the last round.

Ray remembers his next contest well - an eliminator to meet John Feeney for the British title. "It was one of my best wins. I stopped Dave George of Wales in two rounds at the Grosvenor Hotel in Park Lane, London. I was expecting a really tough 12 rounds but it was a great win for me. Mike Barrett thought I should have let the fight go for a few more rounds! I wonder why?" It was certainly a good win for Ray. In his previous contest George had scored a lop-sided win over Southern Area champion Johnny Dorey, dropping him twice and not losing a single round. Ray however was simply far too good for the proud Welsh champion. He was shaken to his boots everytime Ray connected with his right, the ref calling it off in the second after George had taken three long counts.

Three wins out of four fights followed; early victories over Spain's Vicente Fernandez (RSC 2), New Yorker Felix Marquez (CO 6) and Ghanaian Kid Sumali (RSC 7). With Marquez having challenged for the IBF super flyweight title just five months before his October 1984 loss to Ray, and Sumali taking British champion Feeney all the way in a September 1982 contest in Mayfair, losing out by the then minimum half-point margin, it was clear Ray was improving all the time as a professional.

A shock reverse to Uganda's Sandy Odanga followed for Ray, although this was a seventh round retirement courtesy of a dislocated right wrist. The February 1985 contest had been jinxed from the beginning. Originally the date had been pencilled in for Ray's long anticipated British title challenge against John Feeney. However, the Hartlepool man withdrew following a training injury, with Ray's former amateur opponent Mike Irungu (the Commonwealth Games gold medallist from Kenya who had sensationally stopped him in the first round on the ABA tour of Kenya back in 1979) filling in instead.

Just 36 hours before the contest however Irungu pulled out and Odanga, who had never boxed as a pro before, agreed to step in and save the show. The African was a revelation however, and he managed to not only cut Ray and put him under the sort of pressure to which he was unaccustomed, but he also managed to floor the Warrington man for the first time in his pro career. The referee stopped the contest in the seventh and Ray, who was discovered later to have been suffering from a blood disorder at the time, had his first setback as a pro - and a few weeks rest courtesy of his hand injury.

The British title shot was guaranteed however, and Ray finally managed to meet Feeney, who had himself challenged for the European crown four times, in June 1985 – although it wasn't in front of his own fans in Warrington as he had hoped. "I outpointed Feeney to win the British title in his home town of Hartlepool. It was a hard fight but I definitely deserved the decision. I was in really great shape and won despite a cut left eye." The *Boxing News* reported that Ray was in superb physical condition and was a worthy winner due to the high work-rate that took the champion right out of his stride. "This was a great time in my career," remembers Ray. "I defended against John Farrell and stopped him on cuts in eight rounds at the York Hall, Bethnal Green. This was November 1985. Then in January the following year I was matched with the Italian Ciro de Leva for the

European title in Cosenza, Italy." Despite some close calls in the fourth, sixth and tenth rounds, Ray used his superior height and reach to good advantage, and seemed to many impartial observers to have done enough, especially behind his stiff left jab, to have warranted the decision. As Ray points out however, "I was adjudged to have lost on points over 12 rounds but I was definitely robbed, but then again this was nothing new in Italy.

"They extended the rounds to suit the stronger Italian. I boxed 12 minutes extra on top of the stipulated 12 x three minute rounds. The eleventh round lasted a full four and a half minutes whilst the last round was just 10 seconds short of five minutes long!" Manager Mike Barrett complained to the EBU and they ordered an immediate rematch but de Leva vacated the title to box the Panamanian Bernardo Pinango, who had won a silver at the Moscow Olympics, for the WBA title. "Despite this contest also taking place in Italy *[Turin. eds.]* Pinango stopped de Leva in the tenth so I suppose justice was done."

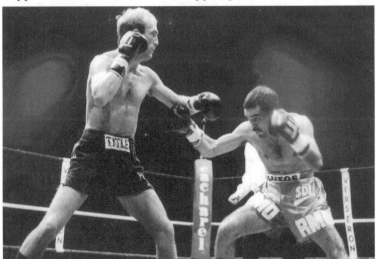

Ray Gilbody (left) v Antoine Montero, Paris, October, 1986   *Source: Gary Shaw*

Ray was then matched with the highly rated Madrid-born Frenchman Antoine Montero for the vacant title. Ray was again forced to travel to his opponent's country in order to get the match – the contest taking place at the Winter Circus in Paris in October 1986. Montero had been a European champion himself, at flyweight, and had ruined the unbeaten record of Keith Wallace with a shock KO. As if this wasn't enough to fill any opponent with dread, Montero had also challenged for the world crown, albeit at super-flyweight, just a month earlier. Ray recalls that, "Despite being gloved up and ready to go they kept me waiting in the changing room for over an hour while they sorted out the TV for the show. By the time I got to the ring all my interest and energy seemed to have gone and I was stopped inside a round." A southpaw left had caught Ray cold and he never recovered, the Belgian referee coming to his aid after being put down again soon after.

Next up for Ray was a tough British title defence against Sunderland's Billy Hardy - a former amateur opponent - at Sutton Leisure Centre, St. Helens. Despite home advantage Ray was dropped three times inside the first six minutes and was saved by the referee in the third. "Billy was just too young *[by four years. eds.]* and too strong for me at 8st 4lbs. I had been struggling to make 8st 6lbs and had lost over a stone in just five weeks in order to make the weight. I also tore the rotary cuff in my right shoulder and that was the end of my career."

Like many boxers Ray has no regrets over his choice of occupation. "My career was at its height in the late 1970s and early 80s and I got some good TV exposure. There are a few things I would like to change of course, but I can't do anything about it now and that's life! Looking back I think that myself and some of the British boxers I met could easily be world champions today. The introduction of Sky TV has ensured boxers get paid more – which is great for the lads involved, as is the proliferation of alphabet titles. A WBU, WBF or WBO title is still a world title to some people. If only I'd been fighting today! The amateur game has changed most I think. The introduction of head-guards and shorter rounds means it's a totally different sport from when I boxed amateur, although if it is to reduce the risk of injuries for the boxers then they have to be a good thing. Computer scoring is different though. I was at the final of the junior ABAs in Barnsley recently and some of the scoring amazed me. How can a kid not register a single point in six minutes of boxing? It must be so demoralising.

"Although the atmosphere at the old Liverpool Stadium – and the Kings Hall at Belle Vue – was electric, and I enjoyed it immensely, I preferred to box abroad as there was less pressure. Out of my six tournaments abroad I won four gold and a bronze – only an Olympic medal eluded me."

On retiring Ray started his own painting and decorating business and ran this successfully for 15 years before gaining a maintenance position at the National Epilepsy Centre just outside Knutsford, Cheshire. He met Sallyann in 1983 and they married in 1988. "We have been married 18 years now and have two great boys – Ryan 15 and Liam 13 - both have their Dad's good looks!" Ray recently passed the ABA Assistant Coaches course and works with former amateur and pro Derek Groarke at Warrington's Bridgefoot ABC. "I knew Derek as a teenager and it's strange that we spent 20 years apart and now meet up again at the gym. Derek and his wife Amanda have done a fantastic job with the club. It's always full and we have just had our first champion in Lee Ward – junior ABA champ at 48kgs. I hope this success continues."

One of Birkenhead's most popular boxers, middle/cruiserweight Vic Harrison was a formidable puncher, with an all-action style that appealed to 1950s fight fans up and down the country. A great amateur as a junior and senior with both the Birkenhead ABC and the the Royal Marines, Vic made the 1950 light-heavyweight final before turning professional with local manager Tommy Murray soon after. A bus driver with Birkenhead Corporation Vic collapsed and died at the wheel of his bus some years ago. An extremely popular member of the Wirral Ex-Boxers' Association at the time of his death, this chapter is based on an article by Frank Johnson that was first published in July 1972.

VIC HARRISON

Rare for Vic to be caught with his pants down!

With Foreign Minister Mr Ernie Bevin ringside at a packed Wembley Pool, Birkenhead middleweight Vic Harrison had the fans roaring their approval as he endeavoured to force an England win against a powerful Belgian team. The newsreel cameramen were catching the action when suddenly Vic's shorts split from top to bottom and he found himself standing in the middle of the ring bereft of cover with the crowd hooting and whistling their amusement! That was the only time Vic was caught with his pants down as his all-action, hard-hitting style kept him to the forefront of 1950s boxing.

Small in stature but possessing great strength and the ability to move inside to hook powerfully with both hands, opponents certainly found Vic a formidable opponent. Born in 1928, Vic attended Laird Street and Brassey Street schools but he never boxed as a youngster. After leaving school Vic gained an interest in the sport and, with Wally Thom as his idol in those days, he regularly watched the Saturday afternoon amateur shows at the Liverpool Stadium. Watching however, was not good enough for Vic and he soon joined the Birkenhead ABC at the Haymarket, soon making his mark in that great club line-up. At 15 years of age he was a bantamweight and as a member of the famous 400 ATC squadron he won the Northern Area title. Later the same year Vic won the Great Britain ATC junior welterweight championship at the Albert Hall with Herbie Arthur, another fine member of the Birkenhead club, also winning the flyweight title.

In the junior ABA Northern Counties Championships Vic was outpointed by Jackie Dillon of Lowe House but increasing weight meant that, by 1945, he was boxing as a middleweight. In the 1945 junior ABA Northern Counties championships, a then 16 year old Vic was outpointed over four rounds by none other than Randolph Turpin, the result meaning that Vic became the first boxer to take Randy the distance as an amateur. Vic then joined the Royal Marines to serve his National Service and he won the Marine Northern Command championship for two years running as a light-heavyweight, with Turpin the Royal Navy champion at the same time.

Demobbed in 1948 Vic resumed work at the Mobil Oil Plant at Bidston and he also restarted his boxing career with the Birkenhead ABC. He was good enough to be selected for England on four occasions, twice against Belgium, and once against Ireland, where he won on a second round KO in a match which England lost 8-2. He also KO'd Norie Anderson in the first round in a match against Scotland.

In 1951 Vic reached the ABA light-heavyweight semi-final and was sore at not getting the verdict over the Navy's Pete Messervy. This disappointment forced him to turn professional with Tommy Murray as his manager and, with the extra training needed for the tougher professional circuit he soon found himself back down at middleweight though this didn't neccesarily mean he would meet fellow middleweights as, in his pro debut, he outpointed Liverpool cruiserweight Gerry Nolan over six rounds, earning £25 for his efforts. Vic started his pro career in barn-storming style with 11 straight wins at the Stadium.

Vic always drew a large Birkenhead following to the Stadium on fight nights and in August 1950 he had them roaring their approval as he defeated Sheffield's light-heavyweight title contender Ron Crookes. He also beat the Welsh middleweight champion Ron Cooper, a win which earned him his biggest ever purse of £90. Vic's 12th fight was to prove his downfall however, as he was outpointed over ten rounds by future Midlands champion George Roe of Wolverhampton. A hernia operation put Vic on the sidelines for a spell and when he made his comeback with a first round KO over Belfast's Tom Meli, it was with Birkenhead's Johnny Campbell as his manager.

In his second fight for Campbell, Vic was stopped in nine rounds in a return against Roe, and he then suffered a first round KO defeat to the

Northern Area champion Rocco King. In his last fight Vic was stopped by Charlie Lake in the tenth round and although his professional career was only a short one of 17 contests Vic topped the bill on only his fifth pro outing. Indeed, he earned top billing seven times in total, all at the Liverpool Stadium.

It was always the amateur game that carried the greater appeal for Vic however, and it is that side of the sport that holds his fondest memories. Vic recalled one trip to Huddersfield when his selected opponent failed to put in an appearance. The show secretary offered a substitute of no supposed repute and Vic agreed. Near the end of the fourth however, this supposed no-hoper decked Vic with a tremendous right hand to the jaw and the bell sounded with Vic still on the deck. His seconds scrambled into the ring to carry him to his corner and rather conveniently his trainer Jimmy 'Custard' Murray tripped and emptied a full bucket of water onto the canvas. In the five minutes it took to clear up Vic regained his senses and went on to win. The opponent that night, Ken Milson, was so incensed at what appeared to be certain victory that he secured a return with Vic at the Harrowby Road Drill Hall. He needn't have bothered however, as he was KO'd by Vic in the first round.

Vic lived in Woodchurch with his wife Joan and five sons and five daughters. Barry was the only one of the family to follow in his father's footsteps and take up a boxing career and he won a West Lancs and Cheshire welterweight title in 1971. Vic was also a keen golfer, playing off a very respectable 10 handicap and enjoyed a spell as secretary of Woodchurch Golf Club

One of Merseyside's most famous amateur boxers, Thomas 'Tucker' Hetherington was first trained by his father, Thomas 'Tucker' Hetherington Snr, at the Litherland ABC then with Kirkby and Knowsley Vale. He won his first National Schoolboy title when he was 12 years old and continued to collect titles at North-West Counties Championships and the Junior ABAs. He also won the Territorial Army featherweight title, represented Young England, was a full English ABA International representative and he took part in a Multi-Nations tournament in East Berlin. At the age of 33 he took part in his last Championship against an opponent who wasn't even born when 'Tucker' won his first title!

THOMAS "TUCKER" HETHERINGTON

Tucker boxed until he was 33!

When your father is the renowned boxing coach, Thomas 'Tucker' Hetherington, then it is probably a foregone conclusion that you will also take up a ring career. Young Thomas, who naturally also became known as 'Tucker', not only took an interest in the ring from a young age, but he soon began collecting amateur titles on an almost annual basis.

'Tucker' started boxing when he was 11. Within 12 months, and aided by his father's as much as his coach's tuition, 'Tucker' developed into a skillful schoolboy, with his best punch, a left hook, already looking like it would bring him many early nights. As a 12 year old schoolboy, he entered the 1962 Schools Amateur Boxing Finals at the Albert Hall, Pudsey, returning home with the 5st 10lbs Championship. The date was 31 October 1962 and it marked the beginning of a string of title wins and championships for the young Litherland schoolboy. That same season 'Tucker' represented Lancashire against Middlesex in the Middlesex Schools Amateur Boxing Championships. Here he won his second title in the 6st 3lbs Junior class.

As well as further representative appearances for Lancashire, 'Tucker' was also showing his credentials at domestic level. In March 1963 he won his first National Schoolboy title - at 6st 2lbs. The following year, a growing 'Tucker' made the semi-finals at 7st 3lbs and in 1965 again a National semi-finalist - this time at 8st 9lbs. West Lancs and Cheshire and North West Counties titles followed at 8st 7lbs. Such continued progress meant it was only a matter of time before 'Tucker' added another domestic title to his collection of trophies and this duly came in March 1966, when he won another National title at 8st 9lbs. After adding another West Lancs and Cheshire title at featherweight, 'Tucker' representing Kirkby ABC, won his first junior ABA title at the same weight.

In 1967 'Tucker' had his first trip as an international when he was selected to represent Young England against West Germany, but although adjudged a points loser to the German Champion - Hamburg's Helmut Stock, the German press thought otherwise, stating that the local, "came through a somewhat fortunate if not unearned win," against, "an outstanding opponent." 'Tucker' was fast becoming a one-man title machine for Kirkby ABC. West Lancs and Cheshire and North West Counties titles followed again in 1969 and 1971, whilst his international career continued with vests against the USSR and Ireland - both in 1972.

1974 saw 'Tucker' not only switch clubs, from Kirkby ABC to Knowsley Vale, but also drop down a weight, from feather to bantam. Both changes did little to stop 'Tucker's' dominance at local level however, as he won West Lancs and Cheshire bantamweight titles in 1975 and 76, and a North West Counties crown. He also boxed for the TA, winning two featherweight titles in succession.

By 1976, 'Tucker' was starting to ease off as far as active boxing was concerned. He was getting on in years and, apart from not winning a senior ABA title, he certainly had nothing to prove to anyone as far as his boxing skills were concerned. He still kept in training however, and in October 1981, he was suddenly called into action once again. The Chief Constable was running a Charity Show at the Centre Hotel between West Lancs and Cheshire (Merseyside) and Eastern Counties (Cambridgeshire). When the Eastern Counties team arrived with only eight boxers instead of 13 the show looked like being cancelled. Frantic calls were made to several stand-by fighters, one of whom was 'Tucker' who, despite having completed a heavy training session, didn't hesitate when asked to appear and he went straight to the venue to make only his his second ring appearance in four years. There was to be no fairy-tale ending however, for 'Tucker' dropped the tightest of points decisions to one of the rising prospects of the Eastern Counties, 19 year old Colin Rance.

The manager of a printing firm, 'Tucker' was now 32 years old but, despite this loss, he wasn't ready to quit the ring just yet. A married man with three young children, it was nearly 20 years since 'Tucker' had won his first championship as a young schoolboy but he was still fit and training religiously under the guidance of his father. Hetherington Snr. would have much preferred his son to retire from the sport altogether but on seeing his determination to go for one last title and knowing that he was still extremely fit, he gave young 'Tucker' his full support.

Tucker made a tremendous start in attempting to achieve this ambition when he won his way through to the following year's West Lancs and Cheshire finals with the quickest win of the evening at a packed Liverpool Stadium. In a six hour show, 'Tucker' proved that he was still a force to be reckoned with when he stopped Richie Mellor of St. Ambrose in only 58 seconds with some tremendous left-hooks. This meant that Tucker would face defending champion Dave Kenny of Holy Name ABC, a man who wasn't even born when 'Tucker' won his first Schoolboy title all those years ago. Kenny was also a product of the Kirkby ABC, the club that 'Tucker' and his father had served with such distinction. Tucker's quest to secure for himself one last title was to end in disappointment however, for young Kenny was adjudged a points winner after a hard fought contest.

This brought to an end one of Merseyside's finest amateur careers. Thanks to his dedication and, of course, the patience and teaching skills of his father, 'Tucker' Snr., one of the country's finest boxing coaches, young 'Tucker' enjoyed a long and distinguished amateur career. Having trained to championship level not only his eldest son, but also the likes of John Conteh, Joey Singleton, Tony Byrne, Alf Matthews and Paul Kinsella, 'Tucker' Hetherington snr. passed away in March 1984 following a short illness aged just 60. Young 'Tucker' has nothing but fond memories of his great career although his only regret is losing the medal he was awarded at the Multi-Nations tournament he boxed at in East Berlin in 1970. 'Tucker' left it behind when he moved house some years ago and although he has tried to recover it, he has been unsuccessful. It would be his greatest joy if this medal could be returned to him. 'Tucker' retains his interest in the sport through his membership of the MFBA, where he loves to talk over old times.

One of the outstanding British fighters of the 1990s, Paul Hodkinson's boyhood hero was John Conteh. Amazingly, if it wasn't for the ABA's decision to drop Paul from the 1986 Commonwealth Games squad, a decision that made his mind up to turn pro, Paul would surely have added a gold medal to his collection and thus mirrored fellow Kirkby ABC star Conteh's career almost exactly. After tasting senior ABA success in 1986 Paul turned pro with Belfast promoter Barney Eastwood and won his titles the old-fashioned way; British, then European and then WBC world featherweight crowns were his before he retired in 1992 with 23 wins (22 KOs) and one draw from 27 contests. A devastating body puncher, Paul beat the likes of Steve Sims, Peter Harris, Kevin Taylor, Eduardo Montoya, Steve Cruz and most famously Marcos Villasana in his six-year career. This article was compiled after interviews with Paul during 2006/07.

PAUL HODKINSON

From Kirkby ABC to world honours - 'Hoko' won his titles the 'old-fashioned' way

With 101 wins from 111 contests, to say that Kirkby's Paul 'Hoko' Hodkinson enjoyed an outstanding amateur career would be a gross understatement. His father's decision to take him to Kirkby ABC in 1975, "to keep me off the streets," certainly seems to have paid off with his first taste of success coming just a year later when he was 11 years old. This was the first of five straight North West Counties titles and more honours followed; an intermediate schoolboy title in 1981; a senior schoolboy title the following year; and a junior ABA title in 1982. Like his grandfather James Hodkinson, who had claimed the flyweight title of all-India whilst in the Army, and his great-grandfather before him, A. Fergus, who had won an ABA title in 1908, Paul seemed to be enjoying his time in the ring.

Such success did not go unnoticed by the selectors at the ABA and Paul won his first full England vest against Ireland at Milton Keynes in January 1984. Three months prior to this Paul had travelled to Podzdan in the old East Germany to represent the ABA in an U19 match. He emerged victorious on both occasions. In March and October 1984 he was on his travels again, to Venice, Italy and Tampere, Finland respectively to take part in multi-nations tournaments. Although he returned without medals the tournaments were excellent learning experiences and the following year he won a silver medal at the famous Acropolis Cup in Athens, Greece. In total Paul won seven full England vests, one of which he has donated to his old club Kirkby ABC where it is on permanent display, whilst he also won three England Schoolboy and four Young England vests.

1986 was an eventful year for Paul to say the least. As the leading amateur featherweight in the country it was perhaps surprising that he had not gained more international vests than he had done already. However, travelling to training camps at Crystal Palace – not always with the guarantee that your expenses would be paid – was always difficult for the young Kirkby boxer and in those days if you didn't train in London, no matter what your credentials, then you simply weren't picked. Matters came to a head later in the year despite Paul adding the senior ABA title to his amateur honours by stopping Bellahouston's David Anderson in the third round.

A trip to America as Belfast promoter Barney Eastwood's guest, to train with the best amateurs of the day, didn't go down well with the ABA. On his return to the UK Paul was unceremoniously dumped from the Edinburgh Commonwealth Games squad. "They booted me out of the team for not attending week-end training sessions," remembers Paul. "That was my reward for trying to get fitter and learn something. I was sick to the stomach when my Dad rang me with the news as I was confident of winning gold in Scotland." Paul was in good company however, as the ABA in their wisdom had also dropped Nigel Benn from the squad for the same reason!

The America trip did have its positives however, as the young Kirkby amateur turned more than a few heads as he engaged in some outstanding sparring sessions with the leading US amateurs and novice pros of the day. With a style that was seemingly made for the professional game; aggressive, with tremendous power in each hand, especially those numbing hooks to the body, Paul traded in his vest slightly earlier than he expected, and turned pro with Eastwood not long after his return to the UK.

Any thoughts that Paul may have turned pro too soon were quickly banished however, as he made his paid debut in style on the undercard of Frank Bruno's world heavyweight title challenge against Tim Witherspoon at Wembley Stadium in July 1986. "Barney and Mickey Duff got along well at the time and Barney asked if he could put me on just before the main bout. Duff agreed and I went on in front of almost 34,000." Despite some nerves in the initial stages, Paul KO'd Bournemouth's Mark Champney in two rounds and was on his way.

Just days after his 21st birthday Paul had his second paid outing; another second round victory, this time over Birmingham's Phil Lashley in Kensington, London. In an explosive start to his paid career, five straight stoppage victories followed, including a stunning fifth round KO in January 1987 over former British champion Steve Simms at Belfast's Kings Hall. Paul was beginning to be noticed in British fight circles and his ranking was moving ever upwards. Indeed 1986 ended with him winning the BBC Grandstand Young Prospect of the Year Award, an honour he shared with fellow Merseyside boxer Gary Stretch.

Paul travelled halfway around the world for his eighth contest, meeting Tomas Arguelles in a six-round contest in Panama City. This was on the undercard of South African Brian Mitchell's WBA world junior lightweight title contest against local favourite Francisco Fernandez. Over 36,000 spectators attended this contest, generating an atmosphere that Paul rates, "second only to the old Liverpool Stadium, where I boxed a number of times as an amateur." *[Mitchell won courtesy of a 14th round stoppage. eds.]*

A draw meant that Paul's winning streak had come to an end, but the old adage - that a draw for a British fighter in a foreign ring is as good as a home victory - was proved true when Arguelles was stopped inside six rounds in the return in Belfast just three months later. Two more early victories, over Marcus Smith (TKO 7) and Ritchie Foster (TKO 3), both in Belfast, set Paul up for a May 1988 British title challenge against Swansea's Peter Harris in Port Talbot, Wales.

Three years older than Paul, Harris had also been a pro for three years longer and had amassed a record of 13 wins, six losses and two draws from his 21 contests to date. Paul had won 11 of his first 12 pro fights but despite fighting away from home it was his workrate and punching power rather than his relative inexperience and youth that saw him stop the game Welshman in the 12th round. It was the first time Paul had gone beyond eight rounds in his career to date, although he insists it wasn't as tough as it first appeared. "He moved away from me for the first six rounds or so but then he began to tire. I got stronger and finally got to him late on." Harris simply had no answer to the relentless power of Paul's hooks, especially the energy sapping ones to the body, and it was testament to his toughness that the Welshman lasted as long as he did.

With this victory Paul won a Lonsdale Belt but planned defenses were cancelled due to injuries and withdrawals however, and it was a full six months before he was in the ring again, this time making his first professional appearance in Liverpool. Ever since he had seen his childhood hero John Conteh's world title bout against Len Hutchins at the Liverpool Stadium when he was 11 years old Paul had dreamt of topping the bill in front of his hometown supporters. "I hadn't fought at home since I was an amateur. Nothing excited me more and I couldn't wait for the training in Belfast to end."

Merseyside fight fans love nothing better than welcoming a local champion back to the city. They weren't disappointed as Kirkby Sports centre, just a stones throw from his old Kirkby ABC gym, was packed out on a bitterly cold 14 December evening to see the local hero give them an early Christmas present by stopping Rochdale's Kevin Taylor inside six minutes. Like many before him southpaw Taylor had no answer to Paul's tremendous punching power and he was sent crashing to the canvas three times in the first round. "He went down with more or less the first right hand I threw."

Paul kept busy by boxing again just five weeks later, in January 1989, in a non-title contest at the Royal Albert Hall against the American Johnny 'Showboat' Carter. There was no showboating for Carter however, as he was 'sunk' by Paul inside two minutes. Some clever matchmaking by Eastwood then saw Paul paired with Frenchman Raymond Armand for the vacant European title at Belfast's Ulster Hall in April 1989. Decked three times in the second round before the referee came to his rescue however, Armand felt the full force of Paul's punches and he was blown away inside six minutes.

It was a full five months before Paul boxed again, this time defending both his British and European titles against a familiar face – former opponent Peter Harris. Whereas Harris had taken Paul to the 12th round of their May 1988 British title fight before the end came, Paul stopped the game Welshman three rounds earlier in this contest courtesy again of some withering body shots. In so doing Paul won the Lonsdale belt outright but was forced to relinquish the British crown in order to concentrate on his European and world ambitions.

Just three months later Paul again delighted his adoring local fans by stopping another Frenchman Farid Bendredjeb in the eighth round at Kirkby Sports Centre. With victory in what was only his 17th pro contest to date, Paul not only successfully defended his European crown for the second time but also secured the promise of an official final eliminator for a world title. The eliminator was not long in coming, and in March 1990 Paul found himself facing Mexico's Eduardo Montoyo in an eliminator for the IBF version of the world title, then held by another Mexican Jorge Paez, at Manchester's recently opened G-Mex Arena. What world title aspirations the tough Mexican had however, were nothing compared to Paul's and he was blasted out inside three rounds, but not before giving Mersey fight fans a scare by decking Paul for the first time in his pro career. Three months later Paul was again top of the bill at the G-Mex, only rather than IBF champion Paez, the man Eastwood had managed to place in the opposite corner was the iron chinned Mexican Marcos Villasana. At stake was the vacant WBC world featherweight title.

Five years older than Paul, Villasana, from a poor farming family with five brothers and three sisters, had been a pro since 1978 and had amassed 49 wins (a quite staggering 43 by KO) from his 59 contests to date (seven losses). His first shot at a world title had been in 1986, the year Paul had turned pro, when he lost a points decision to the legendary Ghanaian Azumah Nelson. A rematch a year later saw the decision repeated. The Mexican had then drawn with WBA champion Antonio Esparagoza, only losing his chance at winning the title by the deduction of a point for a low blow. A year later Villasana had his fourth shot at a world title, taking the tough Australian Jeff Fenech to the judges in Sydney, but again emerging the loser. In addition to his experience and world class pedigree, not once in his career had the Mexican been decked. It was certainly a tough proposition for Paul although he came to the fight full of confidence.

Paul's game plan, "was to outbox," Villasana, using his swift jab and body punches to pile on the points. "I prepared really well for this fight and was sure that not only could I win, but that I would be the first to floor Villasana." With a cut eyelid in the second round however, Paul was forced to try and finish the tough Mexican off early. With an unrelenting and frenzied pace Paul set about the tough Mexican with everything he had from the third. By the start of the seventh Paul was well ahead on all three judge's scorecards but he had also been taking some punishment himself, particularly around his eyes. Fate took note and before long stepped in to cruelly snatch the title away from him. With both eyes closing due to rapid swelling Paul was decked mid-way through the eighth. Bravely getting up he turned to referee Arthur

Mercante jnr., shook his head and simply told him, "Ref, I can't see...I can't see." The fight was stopped and to the consternation of Paul's supporters Villasana was the new champion. "My eyes were bad but I still felt strong. I knew I'd beat him in a return. I could tell my punches were hurting him."

It was a full 24 hours before Paul could open his eyes properly and a full seven months before he had his next contest, a defence of his European title against Frenchman Guy Bellehigue at Wembley Arena. A third round KO eased the pain of the Villasana loss to a certain extent but for Paul all he wanted was another shot at the big one. In November 1991 he got his wish and Belfast's Kings' Hall was the venue for the world title rematch. Whereas everything seemed to go wrong for Paul in their first meeting, this time he made no mistakes. After a near perfect performance with all three judges giving him every round bar one, Paul was declared the winner. "I boxed really well here - even at the end I felt good." The Villasana fight was Paul's only contest in 1991 and he fought only twice in 1992. In April Steve Cruz, the man who had sensationally ended Barry McGuigan's world title reign in the Las Vegas sun in June 1986 was stopped inside three rounds, again in Belfast, while Frenchman Febrice Benichou was finally worn down after ten tough rounds in Biagnac, France in another successful defence of his world crown.

Although he had had some tough fights in his six-year pro career to date, most notably his first contest against Marcos Villasana, Paul rates his contest against Benichou as one of his hardest, "The first Villasana fight was really difficult, as was the second. I knew he would be tough but Benichou was tough *and* awkward. He was hard to hit cleanly. It was also one of the dirtiest fights I've ever had. Benichou used everything in that fight, his head, elbows, shoulders, everything!"

Paul made his London debut at a packed Earls Court in February 1993 when number one contender and former world title challenger Ricardo Cepeda was dispatched with relative ease in the fourth round. Just under three months later Paul was matched with Mexico's Gregario Vargas, in Dublin in his fourth world title defence. Vargas had lost just three of 31 fights since turning pro in 1988 and although rated highly it was still a major shock when he stopped Paul in the seventh. "I just couldn't get going against Vargas," remembers Paul. "Everything I did seemed difficult. I tried to step up a gear but there was nothing there."

Paul Hodkinson (right) v Ricardo Cepeda, 3 February 1993, Earls Cour
Source: Gary Shaw

Just a week or so before Paul's shock defeat to Vargas, a little known Welsh featherweight with a modest record of 13 wins from 23 contests, who wasn't even ranked in the WBO's top ten and who had just 48 hours notice of the fight, stepped in to outpoint local hero John Davison in Washington, Tyne and Wear to win the vacant WBO featherweight title. Two successful defenses of his crown followed, one an outstanding 12 round points win over Colin McMillan, before Steve Robinson was matched with Paul, in Cardiff, in March 1994 to defend his crown once more. With a performance that would underline his credentials as a truly world-class featherweight however, the Welshman KO'd Paul in the last round of what was later voted the British Fight of the Year.

It had been a full 11 months since his last contest, whereas Robinson had fought twice, and it was perhaps this that proved the difference with Paul unable to avoid Robinson's punches throughout. The Welshman built up a commanding lead before almost ending the contest in the eighth, forcing Paul to the ropes with a vicious assault. Paul recovered only to take a count of six in the 12th but although he bravely got back to his feet a three punch combination sent him to the canvas again. Unable to raise himself this time, Paul was counted out

95

with 1.40 of the round gone. The brave Kirkby lad knew his time was up and, unable to contemplate continuing unless it was at the level he had become accustomed too, Paul retired soon after. "Just like the Vargas fight there was nothing there when I needed it. I was gutted as I knew that at my best I should have won easy. I was also keen to meet Colin McMillan - that would have been a big fight at the time - but losing this meant I obviously couldn't. It seemed as good a time as any to retire."

With four sons; Kevin, Jason, Lewis and Dylan, Paul still lives in Kirkby and works all over North West England in the maintenance department of Network Rail. Looking back on his career Paul is grateful for the chances boxing gave him, "How many other kids would have got the chance to travel all over the world like I did at my age? Boxing, both amateur and professional, allowed me to do that."

Like many who boxed there though, Paul laments the passing of the old Liverpool Stadium. "I boxed there a few times as an amateur. It was the best in the world. There was nowhere like it anywhere that I boxed amateur or pro." With an outstanding career, that brought world titles and enjoyment to countless fans, it is unsurprising that Paul has no regrets about his chosen profession. "I'd certainly do it all over again no problem! In fact I think I'd probably do even better as it's much easier in my view to win a world title these days. There are far too many fringe titles." Most local boxing fans would agree with Paul in this regard, and many would surely agree that winning titles the so-called 'old-fashioned' way, as Paul famously did, is the only way such titles should be won. Alas however, it seems that such methods are considered far too risky for some of today's fighters, but it should be remembered with pride that in the 1980s and 90s one local lad did just that. From Kirkby ABC to world honours, Paul definitely won his titles the proper way.

Andy Holligan first boxed for the old Netherton ABC before moving to the Rotunda. It was with the Kirkdale club that he won an ABA title and a multinations bronze in 1987. Turning pro with Belfast promoter Barney Eastwood soon after, Andy went on to become one of the most exciting British stars of the late-1980s/early-1990s, winning British and Commonwealth light-welterweight titles and challenging for a world title on two occasions, once against Mexican legend Julio Cesar Chavez in Mexico, the other against his great domestic and city rival Shea Neary. In a fantastic ten and a half year pro career, Andy had 30 contests, winning 27 and losing only three – meeting the likes of Sugar Gibiliru, Tony Ekubia, Ross Hale, and Paul Ryan in the process. Currently living in New Brighton, this article was compiled through interviews with Andy in 2006/07.

ANDY HOLLIGAN

British champ fought Mexican boxing legend for world title - in Mexico

"There was no real history of the sport in my family," Andy recalls, "but once I joined the Netherton ABC (now Sefton ABC) I found that I enjoyed the training and the discipline that boxing required. In total I think I had about 70 amateur contests, winning around 60. I won a senior ABA title at light-welterweight in 1987 *[a points win over Fitzroy Lodge's A Bryan. eds.]*, and a bronze at the famous Acropolis Cup multinations tournament in Athens just a week or so after my twentieth birthday the same year. I turned pro with Belfast promoter Barney Eastwood soon after my ABA win. Barney had Barry McGuigan at the time of course, and several other good fighters and this meant there was always a high level of training and sparring in the gym."

It was in his promoter's hometown that Andy made his paid debut on 19 October 1987, a six-rounder against Sheffield's Glyn Rhodes. Rhodes was a tricky southpaw with 34 previous fights and a former Central Area lightweight champion. Despite this record however, Andy won 59-57. It was a good learning curve however, though even at this early stage of his career Andy showed signs of the power in both hands, especially his hooks to the body, that would be inflicted on many of his future opponents. Rhodes, who was rarely stopped, actually came close to being KO'd in the fourth round.

Indeed, none of Andy's next four contests went the distance, and only one, Welshman Andrew Morgan (undefeated in three prior to his January 1988 meeting with Andy) who was stopped in the fifth, lasted beyond the third round. Jimmy Thornton (Sheffield) and Nottingham's Tony Richards were both stopped in the second, while David Maw (Sunderland) was stopped in the first in Sheffield in June 1988 – Andy's first contest outside Belfast. Richards would later lose on points to Carl Crook in a British and Commonwealth lightweight title challenge.

Former Southern-Area light-welter champion Lenny Gloster, like Glyn Rhodes a wily and experienced boxer, took Andy the full eight rounds in his next contest in October 1988 – again in Belfast – and two months later another scouse fighter, Sugar Gibiliru, managed the same in Kirkby. The Holligan - Gibiliru fight was chief support to Kirkby featherweight Paul Hodkinson's British title defence against Rochdale's Kevin Taylor. Shown live on BBC's Sportsnight, 'Hoko' stopped Taylor inside two rounds and the producers chose the Holligan – Gibiliru contest to fill the remaining time. They couldn't have made a better decision for it was a fantastic scrap. Both boxers fought toe-to-toe and non-stop for the full eight rounds, with Andy edging it 79-77. "I suffered bad cuts in this fight," recalls Andy. "I'd been taking a skin treatment that really dried my skin out. It would crack even if I smiled! After the fight I was cut to bits."

So good was the fight that 'nobbins' were thrown into the ring after the contest. The exposure this gave Andy marked him out as a man to watch in the British rankings. Sugar would of course drop down the weight divisions and win a British title at super-featherweight in 1991. "I suppose you could say that I was an all-action type of fighter," says Andy. "That was certainly the way I was described. I liked to get in and get the job done. There's no point hanging around in the ring any longer than you have to!"

Andy boxed just three times in 1989, winning early on each occasion. Whitley Bay's Northern Area light-welterweight champion Jeff Connors was stopped at the Elephant and Castle in London in March; six months later Edinburgh's Billy Buchanan – a former British lightweight challenger – met the same fate in Belfast, and the following month Brixton's Tony Adams was also stopped at Wembley. Adams had been a star amateur himself, representing England on a number of occasions, winning an NABC title in 1980 and the senior ABA title at light-welter in 1982. Although he hadn't quite made a name for himself in the pro ranks, Adams had lost twice in eliminators for the British title, was a former Southern Area champion and like Andy, was a renowned puncher. Indeed, in his previous contest he had sensationally KO'd former British lightweight champion Alex Dickson. It was arguably the toughest test yet for Andy and few reckoned the contest would go the distance. The majority were proved right as Adams was decked in the fifth, the referee coming to his rescue soon after. An 11-month lay-off followed for Andy, during which time he changed management team from Barney Eastwood to Mickey Duff. Londoner Duff also managed the European 10st. champion Pat Barrett, and there was talk of Andy contesting this belt before the British one if Barrett vacated it for a shot at a world title.

Andy put such talk behind him however, and his first outing for his new manager was a first round KO over Mike Durvan, a former Southern Area lightweight champion, at the National Sporting Club in September 1990. A left hook to the body, by now one of Andy's most punishing shots, floored Durvan early on, then another dropped him for the full count. Two more early wins, against Frenchman Eric Corroyez at Wembley in October 1990 and Pat Ireland in Kensington in April the following year, reinforced Andy's position as No. 1 challenger to the British champion, Manchester's Tony Ekubia.

Indeed, just days after victory over Ireland the Board ruled that the Mancunian should defend against Andy within two months, and with Mickey Duff winning purse bids, the stage was set for a Liverpool v Manchester British title showdown at Everton Park Sports Centre in June. First up however, was a 'warm-up' fight against the experienced Simon Eubank at Everton Park. Again the contest finished early with Eubank, who was one of only three men to have taken Ekubia the distance, sensationally stopped with Andy's trademark left-hook to the ribs in the second. "I was glad I stopped Eubank early," says Andy. "He must have weighed about 11st 6lbs. He was massive - like a bodybuilder!"

Nigerian-born Ekubia was a good, solid champion. Although seven years older than Andy, with only 18 contests since turning pro late in 1986 he was certainly not ring weary. The Mancunian had won 16 of those 18 fights, 13 of which had come inside the distance so, like Andy, he possessed a decent punch. He also had championship experience whereas Andy had not once gone beyond eight rounds in his 14 fight unbeaten pro career. Undaunted however, the sell-out partisan crowd were witness to some frenzied action in what would later be voted by *Boxing News* as one of the top domestic fights of the year. Andy's

Andy Holligan c. 1992   *Source: Gary Shaw*

powerful body punches wearing the champion down in the later
rounds and securing a hard fought points win. "This was a tough fight.
Tony was a good champion but I think he struggled to make the
weight and would perhaps have been just as good at welterweight -
don't forget he'd beaten Eamon Loughran at welter the year before."
Andy was enjoying the following he now had, especially in his home
city. "I always had great support from the local fans." After the title win
against Ekubia he found himself ranked high in the world ratings, and
there was even talk of a world title contest in the future. He defended

his Commonwealth belt against Steve Larrimore of the Bahamas five months later at Liverpool's Central Hall, Renshaw Street – a former Methodist meeting hall. Although Larrimore had lost seven out of 24 paid outings at the time he had mixed with world class boxers, including Freddie Pendleton and Darryl Tyson. Undaunted however, Andy won by yet another stoppage, this time in the eighth.

Andy boxed just four times in 1992 but managed to win a Lonsdale Belt outright by successfully defending his British and Commonwealth titles against Leicester's former British champion Tony Mckenzie, "he was another tough, hard fighter," and then Tony Ekubia – this time courtesy of a seventh round KO. A left hook at the end of the sixth floored the former champion and a similar punch dropped him for the full count barely two minutes later. This was an indication of how much Andy had improved since their first encounter. Ekubia duly announced his retirement from the ring and was applauded by the Everton Park crowd after paying tribute to Andy's courage immediately afterwards.

1993 saw Andy ranked in the top ten in the world at light-welter and previous talk of him challenging for a version of the world title finally materialised this year. Andy had changed managers from Micky Duff to Frank Warren, and his new manager's connections with American Don King paid off when he was offered a fight for the world title. In his career to date Andy had boxed in Belfast, Sheffield, London, Mansfield, Kirkby and of course his hometown Liverpool. For his tilt at the world title however he would have to not only travel halfway around the world, but also challenge one of the legends of the sport in his own backyard; Julio Cesar Chavez in Puebla, Mexico!

Five years older than Andy, Chavez was that rarest of things in professional sport, a true living legend. He had had 89 fights since turning pro in February 1980 and had won all bar one - and that was a draw for the WBC title against 1984 Olympic gold medallist at lightweight, Pernell Whitaker. It was a daunting prospect for Andy and few expected him to last beyond the first few rounds let alone gain a shock victory.

"It was an offer too good to refuse," says Andy. "I was ranked No. 4 in the world by then anyway and Warren said he could get me a world title fight in my first fight for him so when my contract was up with Mickey I went with him. I couldn't believe it when they got Chavez."

So keen was Andy to take the fight with the Mexican legend that he admits, "I would have fought him for nothing really. I just wanted to say I'd been in the same ring as him."

In one of the most hostile environments you could ever imagine, Andy recalls, "There were thousands there – all Mexican of course, all screaming for their hero, and all wanting me to lose. I think the only supporters I had there were my corner and I don't think many British journalists travelled over for the fight." Andy did have one unexpected fan in the crowd though. "As I was climbing into the ring and they were announcing my name, the boos and taunts were deafening. Out of the screaming crowd however, I hear a lone voice, in a thick 'scouse' accent shouting towards me, 'Come on Andy lad, you can do it! Easy!' I couldn't believe it and wondered who it could be as I didn't recognise the voice at first. I looked around to see who it was and there, at ringside – God knows how he had got there! - was former fighter Robbie Davies from Birkenhead. I couldn't believe my eyes! It was a surreal moment and one I'll never forget. I still laugh when I think about it now!"

Andy admits that a win for him would have been one of the greatest shocks in boxing history. Despite his best efforts however, Chavez simply proved too good, Andy lasting five rounds before being forced to retire in his corner with a damaged nose and a cut right eye. "I gave it my best shot but Chavez was something special. Few people knew it at the time but a few weeks before the fight I broke my nose sparring with the tough Mexican light-middleweight Fidel Avendano. We thought about pulling out but knew I had to take it no matter what. In the end I used a mask for my last bits of sparring. Now although Chavez was good I was really up for the fight. I was sure I would catch him and he'd know that he was in a fight but the first shot he threw was a right uppercut which got me right on the nose. It wasn't as hard as I thought it would be but I knew my nose had gone again - and it definitely hurt - but then he got me with, what was my favourite shot as well, a left hook to the body. It was perfect. I thought to myself, 'What was that? Just don't get stopped in the first round', so I gritted my teeth and saw the round out."

Defeat comes hard in the ring for any fighter, especially so if you're fighting for a world title. "It's at times like these that you find out a lot about yourself. You can either go home and feel sorry for yourself, or you can put it out of your mind and concentrate on your next fight.

This is what I did and just two months later I stopped an Italian, Massimo Bertozzi *[still boxing in May 2007 eds.]* at Earls Court. It was great to get back in the ring again."

Andy then faced the number one challenger to his British and Commonwealth titles, Bristol's Ross Hale in his opponent's hometown. With 22 wins from 23 contests, 15 of which had come early, Hale was a dangerous opponent but it still came as something of a shock when he stopped Andy in the third to send his 2,000 fans delirious and thus become Bristol's first ever British champion. Many thought the loss to Chavez had perhaps taken more out of Andy than he may have realised but Andy has more plausible explanations. "I don't want it to sound like I'm making excuses for the loss to Hale. He stopped me fair and square, but my preparation for this fight was all over the place. Less than four weeks before the fight I was on holiday in Turkey and when I returned to the UK I was almost 13 stone! Try as I might I just couldn't get the near three stone I needed to lose off – in fact I was still four pound overweight on the day of the fight as the weigh-in was the same day. It was my own fault. You have to keep a tight watch on your weight at all times as a pro boxer but on this occasion I didn't. Come fight time I was 'knackered' and paid the price."

As an ex-champion, "something I really hated," Andy contemplated retiring from the ring but he returned 13 months later with a second round stoppage over Hull's Tony Foster at Everton Park Sports Centre. Five months later Darlington's Allan Hall fared no better. In March 1996 a sixth round points win over the solid Karl Taylor, showed that Andy was back to his best. Although Andy had met better boxers than Taylor he admits that the Birmingham man was his toughest opponent. "He was very small and could take all your best shots. He was in your face all the time with his head and he gave me a very bad cut over my left eye in this fight."

With three comeback victories under his belt Andy was on the right track again and was duly matched with the new champion Paul 'Scrap Iron' Ryan of Hackney in a British and Commonwealth title challenge in July 1996. Ryan had wrestled the titles in sensational fashion from Ross Hale courtesy of a stunning first round stoppage in December 1995. This took his record to 22 wins from 22 contests, a remarkable 20 inside the distance, so his defence against Andy wasn't expected to last long. In one of those rare 'blink and you'll miss it' contests Andy silenced the partisan Bethnal Green crowd by taking Ryan's best blows without flinching or emotion, then unleashed two left hooks to the head that sent the Londoner crashing to the canvas. He was counted out by referee Larry O'Connell with 2.09 gone in the opening round. It was an awesome performance by Andy to say the least. "I knew Ryan couldn't take my shots and that he'd go if I caught him right." Andy never defended his regained titles, opting to relinquish them in pursuit of European and world honours in June the following year. Despite his eagerness to fight regularly however, he fought just once in 1997, outpointing Lithuanian Rimvidas Bilius in Hull, and it was another 11 months before he fought again.

Three months after Andy's win over Ryan, Jimmy 'Shea' Neary, his great city rival, had won the fringe WBU world light-welterweight title by outpointing Darryl Tyson at Everton Park Sports Centre. A recent phenomenon, the WBU had only been in existence a few years but was rapidly gaining in importance in Britain, not least through a TV deal with ITV which ensured its top shows were seen throughout the UK. In Neary they had secured one of the most exciting boxers in the country and, with Andy unable to secure a European or more well-known world title shot, discussions were soon under way to make the fight that the city's fight fans craved. With interest in the March 1998 fight at levels unheard of since the days of the old Liverpool Stadium, Everton Park Sports Centre was simply too small to accommodate the 5,000 fans who eventually witnessed one of the domestic fights of the year and the contest eventually took place in a specially-built marquee in Liverpool's Stanley Park.

The unbeaten Neary, a body shot specialist like Andy, was unbeaten in his 18 pro contests to date and, such was his power, had required the judges to declare him a winner on just three of those occasions. No-one expected it to last the distance and so it transpired with Andy finally succumbing in the sixth round following his second knockdown of the fight.

With a proud record of 27 wins from 30 contests in his 11-year career, Andy finally called it a day and retired soon after. Asked if he would do it all again Andy is more reticent than most explaining that although he loved his career he, "would do it differently if given my time over. I would stay in the gym far longer than I did. I only trained in the weeks leading up to a fight but at the top level you need to really treat it like a day job and be there all the time. If that means five days a week then so be it." Although Andy acknowledges his preparation let him down at times, his roadwork never suffered. "My good friend Dave Taylor always made me do my road-work. Every morning, no matter what, he would knock at 5.30 and get me to go on a run with him. Sometimes he would literally be dragging me out of bed!"

Andy only boxed at the Liverpool Stadium a few times as an amateur and although he acknowledges that, "people say the atmosphere was special there, the atmosphere inside the marquee for the Neary fight was something else. That will take some beating." As for the Stadium itself and Andy's abiding memory of it! "I didn't like it much – it was far too cold!"

Prescot's Steve Johnson was inspired to join firstly the BICC ABC and then the famous St Helens' Star through a combination of ex-pro Brian Tonks and his idol at the time, Muhammad Ali. Steve won the majority of his 60 amateur fights, a record that included runs to the junior ABA semi-finals on three occasions, eight international appearances and a multi-nations gold in Athens. Turning pro with Frank Warren aged 23 Steve developed into a capable middleweight, winning 11 of 16 pro contests, and he met the likes of Winston Burnett, Brian Anderson and future world champion – Germany's Graciano Rocchigiani. Still living and working in Prescot, this article was compiled through interviews with Steve in 2007.

STEVE JOHNSON

Talented middleweight forced to wait for the 'House' call!

Although there was no history of boxing in his family, Prescot middleweight Steve Johnson admits that, "my Grandad and Uncle Sonny were good street fighters!" Inspired by Muhammad Ali, "he was my idol at the time," Steve was invited to the BICC Boxing Club by ex-pro Brian Tonks. "I was interested in boxing through Ali and he inspired me to first get involved. I went to the gym to have a look, liked it and started training properly when I was around 13."

After a short stay with the BICC, Steve joined the famous St Helens's Star ABC – then run by Tony Smart. "In total I had around 60 amateur fights, winning around 50. I was a junior ABA finalist once and got as far as the semi-finals on two further occasions." Steve was good enough to make eight international appearances – losing only one – including a fine win over the American Randy Smith in Gloucester in November 1981 *[ABA lost 8-4 eds.]* At the time Smith was ranked the world no. 2. I read in the programme that if you put him in a telephone booth with a gorilla – he would fend off the gorilla and make a call at the same time! Although nervous at facing him and what he could do to me I managed to win."

Five months earlier Steve had won a gold medal at the Acropolis Cup multi-nations tournament in Athens, Greece, a feat emulated by John Lyon, Keith Wallace, John Farrell, Jimmy Duncan and Tony Willis. "What a team that was!" As an amateur Steve remembers travelling to Germany, "with a North West Counties team captained by the great George Gilbody. I got drunk on Applesaf – I was only 17 at the time!"

Another time a similar select team went to Ireland. "I climbed into the ring ready to box and the fight was delayed as they had to play a game of bingo! We had to wait in the ring until someone called 'House' before we could fight. It was surreal standing there, all gloved up, listening to the numbers being read out!"

Steve turned professional when he was 23 with Frank Warren soon after his international victory against the USA, making his paid debut in January 1982 at Hornsey Town Hall stopping 'Prince' Irving Wilmot in the fourth round. Steve had four wins in the first four months of 1982, including a fifth round stoppage against the experienced Winston Burnett at the Bloomsbury Hotel, London, in March. Cardiff-based Jamaican Burnett would go on to have over 120 contests, meeting the likes of Mark Kaylor, Jimmy Price, Lou Gent, Noel Magee, Nigel Benn, Chris Eubank, Brian Schumacher and Errol Christie, in his 14-year career, so Steve was in good company with this victory.

After a five month pause Steve outpointed the useful Bethnal Green light-heavyweight George Danahar, who had lost only three of 14 at the time, including a points loss to Herol Graham. This was in September 1982 and meant that Steve had won five from five in a perfect start to his pro career. An eight round points loss to the highly rated and former ABA light-middleweight champion Darwin Brewster followed just three months later however, forcing Steve to take a break from the pro game of nearly 11 months. Undeterred, the Prescot man returned in late 1983 with two wins, both early, in the space of just two weeks. He stopped Wolverhampton's Ron (Deano) Wallace at Kirkby Sports Centre inside nine minutes on 24 November, then on 5 December Steve forced the referee to save Manchester's Chris Coady from further punishment inside five in Manchester.

Steve had just two contests in 1984, a points victory over experienced Brummie Willie Wright in Manchester in February and a return against the only man to have beaten him to date – Cardiff's Darwin Brewster. Unfortunately for Steve however, he didn't get his revenge, the Welshman again running out a points winner over eight rounds. Finchley's unbeaten prospect Danny Sullivan was next for Steve, at Warrington's Spectrum Arena in February 1985, but the Londoner's perfect 6–0 record was blotted when he was counted out in the sixth round. Two months later Steve travelled to Frankfurt, Germany to meet up-and-coming middleweight, Graciano Rocchigiani.

Steve lost on points over six rounds to give the talented German his 12th straight win as a pro. This was no disgrace however, as southpaw Rocchigiani would add his country's middleweight and light-heavyweight titles before going-on to lift the IBF Super-middleweight crown, European and WBC light-heavyweight titles, beating the likes of Nicky Walker, Chris Reid, Thulani Malinga, Crawford Ashley and Michael Nunn in the process. "I boxed well for the first two rounds against Rocchigiani," recalls Steve, "but he battered me for the next four! I just wasn't fit enough to go with the pace he set after that. Even then though you could tell he was going to be good."

Just a month before outpointing Steve, Rochigiani had stopped Brentford's Tony Jenkins in six rounds in Dusseldorf and it was Jenkins who was lined up for Steve when he returned to the ring in November 1985, on the Jim McDonnell v Jose Luis Vicho European featherweight title undercard at Wembley Arena. Although both had gained valuable experience from meeting a future world champion it was Steve who had perhaps learned the most, winning unanimously over eight rounds.

Steve had been a pro for just over three and a half years and had a commendable record of 10 wins from 13 contests, the only losses being to Darwin Brewster and Rocchigiani, both talented operators. In this time Steve had steadily risen in the domestic rankings, so much so that by the end of 1985 he was named as official challenger to Sheffield's Brian Anderson for the Central Area middleweight title the Yorkshireman had held since May 1983. To Steve's delight the contest was also named as an eliminator for the British title – then held by Huddersfield-based Londoner (Noel) Prince Rodney. Steve lost courtesy of a fifth round TKO but admits he should have done better. "I let myself down in the Anderson fight. It was my own fault. I just didn't train or prepare properly and paid the price."

Following his loss to Anderson, who would go onto win the British title himself, Steve retired from boxing but four years later however, he returned to outpoint Merthyr's Simon Collins in the Welshman's hometown. This was in April 1990 and the following month a swollen eye forced the referee to stop Steve's contest against Roberto Gigli in Avezzano, Italy, in the seventh round of a scheduled eight in the Italian's favour. Steve retired for good soon after. "I came back after such a long time because I thought I could still do a job," says Steve. "I was still in the gym, still fit and thought, 'Why not?' Once you've stopped boxing you do miss it and even now I'd come back if I could!" On his last contests, Steve remembers. "I was winning at the time of the stoppage but the Italian caught me in the eye with a thumb or something and the next thing it had really swelled up. I wore my old boots for this fight and could barely stand up, let alone box. I asked Franny if I could box bare feet but obviously he said no!"

Looking back on his career today, Steve rates his second ever fight as one of his hardest. "Although still a novice I was put in with a national schoolboy champion named Smith and he proved to have far too much experience than me. Right from the first bell he was too good and this was my first defeat."

Steve has few regrets at choosing boxing as a career and is philosophical about the standard of today's fighters. "I enjoyed the travel boxing afforded me at the time and the fact that I was extremely fit. I have no regrets at all but I think that at times I just didn't train hard enough for certain contests. There is now more money around for today's boxers – even those less talented – although I still believe that to be British champion you have to be really good."

Steve recalls the Liverpool Stadium with affection, whilst he remembers an embarrassing encounter from his pro days with a smile. "I fought at the old Stadium eight times as an amateur, once receiving the Bessie Braddock Trophy for best fighter in the Championships. The atmosphere really did compare to Wembley Arena. It was electric at times. The crowd were very knowledgeable and despite resenting me initially because I was a St. Helens' fighter, once they had seen my skill and style their opinion changed and they soon warmed to me. As a pro I remember my trainer leaving an ice-pack down my shorts. The fight was televised and 30 seconds into the third round I had to tell the ref to stop the fight to let me take it out!"

Today Steve is, "married to Gaynor and we have two children – Lewis and Olivia. I still love to train in the gym and my sporting background has influenced my children. Both are involved in lots of activities, Kung Fu, swimming, football and so on."

Little known in the UK now, Liverpool-born Jimmy Johnston emigrated to the USA with his family when he was 13 to become one of the most important, influential and well-known boxing personalities in America. He not only ran Madison Suare Garden successfully for a number of years in the 1920s, but he was also involved with a host of famous boxers and fights of the day, most notably managing Jack Sharkey for a time and promoting the Benny Leonard v Lew Tendler 1923 world lightweight title bout at Yankee Stadium, New York.

JIMMY JOHNSTON

Liverpool-born but found fame in USA

Liverpool has not only produced a great number of top class domestic fighters and fight personalities over the years, it has also spawned a number who came to prominence on the other side of the Atlantic, the majority coming to the fore in the late nineteenth and early part of the twentieth centuries, when migration to the USA from Liverpool was a regular occurrence. One of these was Jimmy Johnston, who was born in the Athol Street area of Liverpool on 28 November 1875.

Jimmy's father was an iron-moulder, making moulds for casting iron, an occupation that the advance of technology has long since made obsolete. The situation was barely any better in the harsh economic climate of the 1880s however, and Jimmy's family were forced to emigrate to America, where they settled in New York's Upper East Side, when he was only 13 years old. Jimmy attended a local public school but quit in the eighth grade so he could find employment and help his family financially. Perhaps influenced by his father's occupation before him, and no doubt aided by his tough life-story to date, Jimmy found work in a Jersey City foundry.

As well as working in the foundry by day however, Jimmy earned extra money by boxing at night. Although his boxing career was a modest one, Jimmy was considered good enough to meet Danny 'Kid' Dougherty, albeit a tenth round stoppage defeat – a man who had met future world champion 'Terrible' Terry McGovern. Jimmy, who never weighed more than ten and a half stone as a professional, received $150 for this contest, the largest of his career.

Jimmy combined both careers until he was 28 years old. He had boxed off and on for six years, but despite rising to the rank of foreman at the foundry, with up to 150 men under his supervision, he realised that there were better ways to make a living. He had seen from the inside how the fight game worked and he wanted a piece of the action himself. Billy Newman, the owner of a number of private members clubs where boxing matches where staged gave Jimmy a job as a handyman - the Liverpool-born lad was on his way.

Soon Jimmy was travelling the country with English fighters keen to try their luck in the States. He began to promote boxing shows in his own name and worked closely with Charlie Harvey, a manager who specialised in running the affairs of English boxers in America. Two of these fighters were fellow 'scousers' Billy and Paddy Gannon. They had stowed away on a US bound ship in the early 1920s. Upon their arrival in America they soon teamed up with Jimmy and boxed on a number of shows under his promotion. After returning to England, Billy would later sign for Manchester's famous fight manager Harry Fleming.

Despite his success Jimmy had bigger ideas. In 1912 he leased the old Madison Square Garden and ran it successfully for four years. He loved to tell the story of the time he sub-leased 'the Garden' to the famous boxing promoter Tex Rickard for the Jess Willard v Frank Moran heavyweight battle in 1916. Rickard paid the Liverpool man $15,400 for the privilege, little knowing that Jimmy however, had originally leased the arena for only $1,000! Before taking over at 'the Garden', Jimmy had already staged some of the biggest fights in boxing history. His Benny Leonard v Lew Tendler contest at the Yankee Stadium in 1923 (Leonard won on points over 15 rounds) hit the half-million dollar mark. He also promoted the Mickey Walker v Jack Sharkey contest (a 15 round draw) in Brooklyn in 1931. In addition, Jimmy managed numerous fighters over the years and, as a former fighter himself, he ensured he made money for all of them.

Jimmy was made ringmaster of 'the Garden' in October 1931. Perhaps his greatest achievement however, was making Jack Sharkey heavyweight champion of the world. Sharkey beat Max Schmeling for the title in June 1932 at Long Island Bowl. Jimmy then manoeuvred the 'Ambling Alp', Primo Carnera, into a match with Sharkey. They had met previously in October 1931 at Ebbet's Field with Sharkey winning a 15 rounds points decision. The return at the Bowl was in June 1933 only this time the world title was at stake. Carnera sensationally KO'd the champion from Boston in the sixth and it was

Jimmy who had first call on the new champion's services. Jimmy went on to bring huge profits into the Garden through his unrivaled business acumen and shrewd match-making.

Tea-total and a non-smoker, Jimmy fathered no fewer than ten children, one of whom, Jimmy Johnston jnr. later went on to stage fights at New York's St. Nicks' Arena. For a lad from the working-class streets of Liverpool, Jimmy Johnston certainly left his mark on the American fight scene.

Turning professional at the early age of 15 years, to help provide for his family following the death of his father in the First World War, just four years later 'Young Ash' found himself in the opposite corner to the great Peter Kane. He eventually left the boxing ring and joined Sam Barton's Booth, travelling all over the country facing all-comers in all shapes and sizes, but mostly the tough Welsh mountain towns and villages. On the outbreak of war in 1939 he joined the Army and saw action in France, Belgium and Germany before being demobbed in 1946. This chapter is based on an article written by Frank Johnson that was first published in 1973.

ASHTON JONES - YOUNG ASH

One of the great boxing booth attractions

Born in Elgin Street, Birkenhead off Argyle Street in 1916, Ashton Jones attended St. John's School in Oliver Street, but was forced to leave at the first opportunity when his father was killed in the First World War in order to contribute to the family income. Christened Ashton James Moss Jones, 'Young Ash' adopted his boxing name by taking the first three letters of his Christian name and, like many boxers of the time and as he was only 15 when he boxed professionally for the first time, the 'Young' prefix was only natural.

Although his first job was at a garage, such employment was more a means to an end rather than an occupation and soon he was making his ring debut - a third round KO win over 'Bisto' Ashworth at the Vittoria Street Stadium. His career as a flyweight was born. Although his main interest was boxing Ashton's entry into the fight game came about by accident. His friends, Robbie Griffiths and Pat Kehoe, who attended Bob Foster's gym, asked a reluctant Ash to accompany them one night after school. It took a lot of persuasion but once at the gym, the boxing bug hit him and Ashton soon became a regular.

Bob Foster became his manager and for his debut fight he earned the princely sum of 2/5d. Dick Staden trained him for his fights but they found fights hard to come by in Birkenhead and Ash only had eight contests in his first three years. He recalled stopping Mick Ollerhead in seven rounds at the old Bebington Stadium in what was a scheduled ten-rounder. A feature of that fight was the fact that the referee was the former bare-knuckle fighter of repute, Tom Spring. Ash returned to the same venue not long after to box a thrilling punch-for-punch draw with Eddie Platt of Stockton.

113

In 1935 flyweights were in plentiful supply with the likes of Tiny Bostock, Tut Whalley, Jim Warnock, Joe Curran, Jackie Brown and the great Benny Lynch, all top-liners. Also stealing the boxing headlines on his way to the top of a great career was the Goldborne blacksmith, Peter Kane, who drew huge crowds every week to the Liverpool Stadium. Kane met 'Young Ash' at Warrington in late 1935 and he stopped the Birkenhead man on a cut-eye decision in the eighth round. The fight was refereed by Fred Snell, himself a former local fighter of some repute and later, Mayor of Birkenhead. Ash did well to evade Kane's haymaking right hand which had spelt doom to a succession of opponents.

After the tragic death of Bob Foster, Ray Duncan took over Ash's management. The Birkenhead flyweight was stepping up in class and he gained a highly creditable ten-round win over the Irish craftsman, Paddy McStravick. To prepare for this fight, Ash had sparred with the great Liverpool flyweight, Joe Curran. Ash can boast to never having been knocked out in a fight but he knew what it was like to have been put out stone cold as, in a sparring session with Boy McCann, he ran onto a terrific right hand and went out like a light - and this was with 15 ounce gloves!

Around this time, a Liverpool boxer by the name of Chris Kelly was causing quite a stir and Kelly and Ash met in a great ten-rounder with the Birkenhead boxer registering one of his finest ever wins. Kelly was a clever box-fighter, and Ash had to turn it on that night in order to get the nod. A ten-round draw against Young Owens of Chester was full of drama as Ash received the makings of a cauliflower ear when a blistering right swing landed firmly on his right ear. The swelling was painful in the extreme but, fortunately for Ash, the referee was again old Tom Spring and he intervened with the doctor and told him to bathe it with warm milk. The treatment worked and his ear remained unimpaired for the rest of his life but the right-hander lingered in Ash's memory. He always maintained that Owens hit even harder than Peter Kane.

When Ash was 18 he left the boxing circuit and joined Sam Barton's boxing booth at Pontypool with Birkenhead welterweight, Larry Hamill. The booth travelled far and wide taking in Blanavon, Cardiff, Bath, Bargoed, Mountain Ash and many more of the Welsh Valley towns. They bred them tough in those parts with boxing going hand in glove with mining for so many youngsters so to take the stand as a booth fighter in that quarter of Britain was to face some of the toughest characters around. Whilst on the booths Ash recalled boxing the former Welsh title holder, Tich Smith, in a special ten-rounder.

There were five boxers in the booth and the Birkenhead man boxed six-rounders every night of the week, with three shows on Saturdays. He received £2.10s per week, out of which he had to keep himself and find suitable digs in whatever town the booth happened to be. When in Bargoed, he once went down a mine only to emerge convinced that booth fighting was a much more preferable occupation. It was at Bargoed that Ash went in with a miner, aged around the 50 mark, but magnificently proportioned, with shoulders, "like a barn door and fists like bin lids." He took Ash the distance and with a one stone advantage, he hit harder than any other booth opponent had done.

Ash returned to Birkenhead and resumed his boxing career with a fight over eight rounds at the Villa Marina in the Isle of Man against Young Andrews of Liverpool. Ash lost on points although he said that Andrews was the cleverest fighter that he ever fought. He held the Welsh champion, Pat Warburton, to a thrilling ten-round draw in Mountain Ash and he also drew with Pat Ryan who had given Peter Kane a difficult time at the Liverpool Stadium. Ash dropped a six-round verdict to the highly rated Kid Bonser at Liverpool Stadium on a bill topped by Ernie Roderick whilst he also dropped a ten-round decision to Herbie Clark but held Southport's Teddy Snowball to a draw at Ashton-in-Makerfield.

Ash had a cousin who boxed under the name of 'Newsboy' Casey who was once beaten by that fine Runcorn battler, Jimmy Stubbs. Keen to avenge the family honour, Ash met Stubbs at the Birkenhead Drill Hall and he recorded a great ten-round decision. This was a fine performance and he followed-up with a ten-round win over Billy Ashton at Bebington Stadium. In 1939 at Birkenhead Drill Hall, Ash beat Young Atherton but, with the war looming, he joined the Loyal North Lancs, who's unofficial motto was, 'Leave Nothing Loose.' On his way to the barracks at Preston he met up with the Liverpool scrapper, Peter Banasko.

Ash boxed a little in the army and he made friends with a bugle boy, Billy Holden. Apparently, Holden had been subjected to a doing over during a boxing session by an over zealous bully, a Sgt. Major Instructor. This so incensed Ash that he began to plot retaliation. He didn't disclose his former career but, on the quiet, he sent home for his full gear of boxing boots, trunks, gum shield and socks. He didn't wear these however, instead going to the gym dressed in an old pair of pumps and a baggy pair of shorts. He wanted it to look like he would be fair pickings for the bully NCO. Once he had been selected as the next victim for the slaughter however, Ash disappeared into the toilets where he swiftly changed into his boxing gear and, as he climbed through the ropes, the colour drained from the face of his opponent. The colour wasn't the only thing to drain away as life almost did when he received the mother and father of a hiding which put the Sgt. Major in hospital for a month!

Ash formed an army boxing team with Les Carter, Paddy Dunne and Gerry McLean, all Liverpool fighters. They boxed and won against the RAF down South but sterner battles faced Ash when he landed in Normandy on D-Day, +2. He fought as an infantryman at Arrowmanches and was engaged in the tough fighting around Caen. He fought his way through to Belgium and Germany and saw his fare share of action. Boxing was out in that arena but Ash recalled seeing a German submariner giving one of the hated SS men a terrible hiding as they waited to be taken away as prisoners. The British soldiers had ringside seats for that one and no-one intervened.

Demobbed in 1946 when he was 30, Ash had two more contests, both in North Wales, with both ending in KO defeats. The old snap was gone and he retired. He had no further connections with boxing and passed away some years ago.

The Mersey Fighters 2

A top amateur with Kirkby ABC in the early 1980s, local lad Dave Kenny won a European under-19 silver medal in East Germany in 1982 and made the senior ABA featherweight final the same year before turning pro with London promoter Frank Warren in 1984. Plagued by cuts and inactivity however, Dave retired from the pro game barely two years later having won three out of just six contests in the paid ranks. Still living and working in Kirkby, Dave remains active in amateur boxing and currently coaches at his former club. This article was compiled through interviews with Dave in 2006/07.

DAVE KENNY

Loved the amateurs – not so keen on the pros though!

With a father and grandfather who had both boxed for the Army during their service days, it was not surprising that Kirkby's Dave Kenny was drawn to the sport, joining his local club when he was ten years old. "I went down one night out of interest," recalls Dave, "got the bug, stayed, and enjoyed every minute of it."

Dave enjoyed it so much that he amassed around 120 bouts in the famous tuscan red and cream vest eventually, "winning about 90." He won North West Counties Schoolboy and Junior titles; was the West Lancs. and Cheshire featherweight champion three years running (1982-84); and not only represented England on a number of occasions, but also managed to win a fantastic silver medal at the 1982 European (U19) championships.

Dave won a total of five Young England vests whilst his two full England vests came in a match between the ABA and Finland in 1982. Dave won his first contest against K Hurri in Helsinki on 15 November, but lost his second, just two days later, to V Koota in Yiorjarven. Dave was one of the most promising young boxers in the country and it was this, together with his experience of representative matches abroad, that ensured his selection for the European under-19 championships in Schwerin, East Germany in September 1982.

Since its inception the tournament had been dominated by boxers from the Eastern bloc and 1982 was no exception with 10 of the 12 gold medals going to East Europeans. It was an outstanding tournament for England however, as Errol Christie won a gold at

117

middleweight, with Orrie Jones collecting a bronze at welter. In the featherweight division Dave won four bouts in ten days, including a fine win over the Pole, Dariusz Koscdowski in the semi-final, to set up a meeting with the outstanding Bulgarian, and eventual gold medallist, Borislav Blagoev. "Blagoev had KO'd everyone in getting to the final," recalls Dave, "a West German, East German and a Romanian, so I knew it would be tough. He was really strong, but going into the third round, I thought I was ahead. I got caught with a big right-hand however, and I dropped to my knees only to get back up again and see the ref count me out on my feet."

Dave Kenny (left) v Lazslo Almady (Hungary) in the European U19 championships, Schwerin, East Germany, September 1982. Source: Dave Kenny.

Later in the year Dave made the senior ABA featherweight final where he lost to St Pancreas' Herman Henry. Henry was 12 years older than the young Kirkby man however, and it was this that told in the end. "Henry was 31 at the time whereas I was only 19, and although he never actually hurt me it was the difference in experience that beat me in the final. If I had known then what I know now I should have beaten him but he was a clever boxer! He was very hard to catch up with, very slick – a bit like John Hyland from the Golden Gloves who I also met a few times."

Dave reveals that he was rarely nervous before a bout and that this was mainly due to his old trainer, Richie Lloyd. "Richie, or 'ginge' as he was known, had a clever way of making you relax before contests. You would be getting warmed up, tying your laces or putting your bandages on, and he'd start telling you funny little stories. You would be so concentrated listening to him that you wouldn't think about the bout at all. Quite often after he had finished you would end up in stitches because you'd be laughing so much! He was a real character and a real gentleman."

Looking back on his career Dave has only two regrets; "At one stage I left Kirkby for 12 months and joined Holy Name, which I shouldn't really have done, and I shouldn't have turned pro with Frank Warren either." Dave had just six professional bouts, winning three and losing three.

His paid debut was a winning one – a second round stoppage victory over Bethnal Green's Ronnie Mayer at London's Bloomsbury Crest Hotel in July 1984. A fourth round stoppage win over Welshman Tony Borg followed three months later. In November 1984 Dave gave 5lbs to Southend's Steve Cooke eventually losing, virtue of a cut eye, in the third. Two more losses followed, in March 1985 and May 1986. The combination of cuts, weight disparity and the long gaps between fights however, eventually forced Dave to retire.

"I joined Frank Warren's stable hoping to make something out of the sport but despite moving to London I was stitched up – literally! I was a proper featherweight, rarely over 9st by more than a few pounds, but bad matchmaking, against lightweights and even light-welters, cost me what should have been a decent pro career. I received bad cuts in three bouts and slowly fell out of love with the pro game. I'd had enough and just decided to pack it in."

After retiring Dave married Tina and this year they celebrate their 20th wedding anniversary, whilst they have a daughter Toni, now 16 years old. Still living and working in Kirkby where he has his own black cab, Dave still loves the amateur side of the sport and together with John Lloyd, "the best coach around," he coaches at his old club Kirkby ABC. "I had a great time as an amateur, visiting places I would probably never have gone to if it wasn't for boxing. I would do it all over again with Kirkby and hope to coach a few more champions to join the many Richie and John Lloyd have produced over the years."

Notwithstanding his desire to unearth yet more local champions, Dave feels that compared to the 1980s it is less of a challenge for today's amateurs to win titles than it was for him and his contemporaries. "To win an ABA title in our day you had to really fight for it. At every stage you were boxing another area champion, maybe even a national champion as in those days Scotland, Wales and Northern Ireland also competed. These countries no longer compete of course and this means that there are fewer fighters boxing today so it's easier to succeed simply because there is a lack of competition at certain weights."

Echoing what many top amateurs from the pre-headguard days think, "I couldn't fight now with headguards, I'm glad I boxed when I did," Dave reckons that, "a lot of today's champions wouldn't have even got out of the West Lancs. preliminaries 15 or 20 years ago!"

Dave boxed at the Liverpool Stadium many times and ranks it the best venue for atmosphere he ever appeared at. "I boxed at the Stadium in the ABA championships in 1982, 83 and 84. The atmosphere generated there was second to none. As they always have been, the Liverpool fight fans were brilliant, they always applauded a good boxer even if you were from out of town. Even boxing at Wembley Arena in the ABA final couldn't compare. It's a shame they pulled it down."

A popular and hard-hitting light-middleweight of the late-1970s and early-1980s, Joe Lally boxed for a variety of amateur clubs in the South of the city, most notably the old Lockheeds ABC in Speke, winning a number of England vests and a multi-nations bronze in the process. He turned pro with former British, British Empire and European bantamweight champion Alan Rudkin in 1974, and in a six-year career he won 12 of 29 bouts, meeting the likes of Carl Speare, Prince Rodney, Andoni Amana and Robbie Davies. Still living and working in Liverpool this article was obtained through interviews with Joe in 2007.

JOE LALLY

Light-middle Joe never shirked anyone

"I first started boxing training when I was around seven or eight years old at St Malachy's in the Dingle. I took up boxing mainly to please my Dad. He loved the sport and when I started to win a few I kept it up for him as he always enjoyed watching me box."

Joe's family soon moved to Speke, but this didn't stop him from boxing. "I boxed for All Hallows School and then Lockheeds where John Maddocks and Dinny Procter were the trainers. I also sometimes trained at the Gemini with Jimmy Burns as well because it was a bit closer to my home than Lockheeds."

Although he made a few finals, Joe didn't win any titles, but he was good enough to box at the Prince of Wales Investiture tournament in Cardiff in June 1969, where he won the welterweight title. He was also selected for England on a number of occasions, and in September 1969 he won a bronze medal at a multi-nations event in Ostrava, Czechoslovakia, the first such tournament to be held in an Eastern-bloc country.

"My style was more of a fighter than a boxer," says Joe, and for that reason he turned pro in 1974 just before he turned 23. "The pro game seemed to suit me. Alan Rudkin was my first manager before I moved to Pat Dwyer. The amateur and pro codes were a lot different to each other, even then, and I found that I was a lot more dedicated as a pro and learned a lot more."

Joe's pro debut was a six-two minute rounds points win over Halifax's George Salmon at the Anglo-American Sporting Club in Manchester in April 1974. A return at the Liverpool Stadium three weeks later saw the Yorkshire man gain a revenge eight rounds points win, although Joe disputes this. "I thought I won the return with George really. I was surprised when they gave it to him." Four stoppage wins in his next four bouts marked Joe out as an exciting, hard-hitting banger, but two defeats in two weeks in July 1975 followed.

Joe didn't box at all the following year, returning to the ring in January 1977 where he lost on points to fellow 'scouser' Carl Speare at the Stadium. Six further contests in the year yielded just two wins and a draw, although dropping a decision to Manchester-based Jamaican Eddie Smith in September was no disgrace, nor was his stoppage loss to Cardiff's Errol McKenzie in June. Smith would later KO Roy Gumbs, win and lose to Tony Sibson and would also meet the likes of Tom Collins, Mark Kaylor, Jimmy Price and Nigel Benn. McKenzie was also a top class operator meeting such men as Larry Paul, Tony Sibson and Herol Graham.

Joe recalls his early pro days with affection, especially when remembering his spars with fellow scouser Harry Scott. "As a novice pro I sparred a lot with Harry Scott in Franny Hands gym. He was a gentleman. A great man. He never took any liberties with us young lads, in fact he would rather teach you something in the ring than hurt you."

1978 was Joe's busiest year as a pro. Despite an early loss to Birmingham's Owen Robinson Joe KO'd Doncaster's Brian Gregory in Doncaster and then travelled to Copenhagen in May where he scored a great points win over local welterweight Per Mullertz. "I boxed really well here," recalls Joe. "It was a good trip in that they looked after me really well over there, but I missed my home and my wife and returned to England after just a few days." Joe made such a good impression on the promoters that three months later he was asked to travel to Scandinavia again, this time to Glyngoere in Denmark, to face exciting middleweight prospect Torben Andersen. This time however, Joe lost on points over four rounds. Andersen would go on to win 24 out of 26 pro fights.

A great KO win over Edinburgh southpaw Billy Lauder in Liverpool in October not only showed Joe hadn't lost any of his punching power, it also set him up for a Central Area title challenge against Huddersfield's Prince Rodney. Joe tried his best against the future British champion but lost in controversial circumstances. "I was disqualified in the fifth for a headbutt," explains Joe, "but it certainly wasn't intentional." A month later Joe dropped a points decision to Welshman Dave Davies at the Stadium. "I felt I was robbed in this fight," says Joe. "I dropped Davies for an eight count early on and was all over him, but I still lost. I couldn't believe it at the time." Less than a week later Joe was in action again, only this time in Spain, where he faced unbeaten Spaniard Andoni Armana in Bilbao. A fifth round KO defeat to a man who would lose a European title shot against Tony Sibson was certainly no disgrace, but made Joe think about retiring. He returned in March 1979 however, to face another exciting local scrapper in Birkenhead's Robbie Davies.

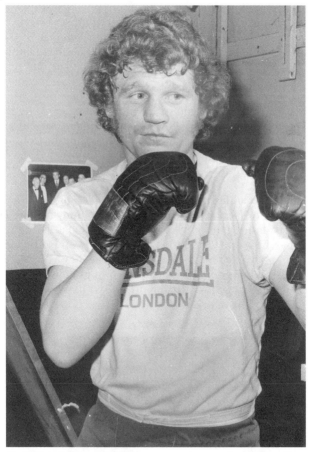

Joe Lally in training c. 1977   Source: *Gary Shaw*

Promoted as a mouth-watering local derby between two big hitters, the fight didn't fail to live up to expectations, with both boxers looking to connect with one big shot. Ultimately it was Joe who was caught first, being stopped by a powerful shot in the fourth round. "Robbie Davies was my hardest fight," says Joe. "He was always strong, tough and never knew when to give up. He caught me good in that fight."

It was to be another full year before Joe boxed again, and although he won two and drew one of his five fights in 1980, he feels that he shouldn't have returned at all. He outpointed Blackpool's Billy Hill and experienced light-heavyweight Joe Jackson in March then lost and drew one apiece in April – an amazing four fights in just six weeks. In June he travelled to Cambridge to meet light-heavyweight Jimmy Harrington but was stopped in the third. "I'd had enough by then and decided to quit. I went on too long really. I should have finished my career a lot earlier as I took too much punishment late on."

Always popular whenever he appeared in his hometown, Joe recalls the famous Liverpool Stadium with a smile. "Boxing at the Stadium was always a pleasure. It had a brilliant atmosphere, second to none, the best place I ever boxed. You can't beat boxing in front of your home crowd at a place like that, with all its history and the famous boxers who'd fought there."

On the sport and his life today, Joe remains philosophical. "You've still got to be good to succeed in boxing today. The fundamentals are the same as they always were but I wish they'd have had headguards 30 years ago as I wouldn't have took the same amount of punishment. I've been happily married to Sheila for 30 years now. We've got three kids; two girls, Lindsey and Joanne; and a boy, Joseph. Joseph wanted to have a go at boxing a while ago but I talked him out of it. I didn't want him to take the same stick I got."

A three-weight champion in his native Ghana, Elias Thomas Lartey was one of a number of African fighters who emigrated to England in the late 1940s and early 1950s and made their home in Liverpool. A box-fighting feather/lightweight, Elias served with distinction in the Far East during the Second World War before coming to England in 1948. His record reads much better than first suggested and, in his three-year career in England he won around 18 contests from at least 33 bouts, meeting the likes of Stan Gossip, Peter Gaskell, Ronnie Gladwell, Jackie Molloy and Bernie Pugh. Elias famously had two fights in one night at Northampton in November 1948 and, despite going blind after a training accident, he lived in Liverpool until his death in 1994.

ELIAS 'ZULU KID' LARTEY

Left Ghana for fight career in Liverpool

Born Elias Thomas Lartey in Accra, Ghana in April 1923, Zulu Kid Lartey was one of the best of the many African boxers who settled in England after the Second World War. An active and sporty child in his hometown, young Elias first took up boxing as a teenager and his talent did not go unnoticed by the mainly British boxing officials based in Ghana at the time and it wasn't long before he joined a local amateur club.

In 1937, then aged 14, Elias spotted the address of Tommy Craggs, a well-known Bournemouth referee, in an old copy of Boxing News and as his gym was sparse in terms of boxing equipment he wrote to the referee asking if he could donate any items. As a sign of his goodwill and keenness to be successful in the sport, Elias enclosed a photograph of himself in boxing pose – barefoot!

As in Nigeria and other British protectorates in Africa, boxing shows in Ghana in the 1930s were normally organised by British Army officials. This was a good match for Elias, for as soon as he was old enough he joined the Royal West African Rifles and it was here that he enjoyed most of his early success. Although no Zulus come from the Gold Coast, Elias bared such a striking resemblance to Young Zulu Kid, the African flyweight who had challenged Jimmy Wilde for the world title way back in 1911, that he gladly took on the moniker. Due to his success the name stuck and 'Zulu Kid' Lartey became one of the most respected and feared boxers in late-1930s and early 1940s West Africa.

The outbreak of the Second World War saw Elias, who was soon promoted to Corporal, posted to various countries abroad, including India and Burma. Not that these postings prevented him from boxing however. Already well-known in West Africa, Elias soon began to make a name for himself in the towns and cities where he found himself stationed. It was reported that after one fine performance in Madras, where he outpointed a Private Crackwell of the Royal Warwickshire Regiment on a show where Freddie Mills and Al Robinson boxed an exhibition, that none other than Henry Armstrong, the American boxing legend, wanted to sign him up for a career in the States.

Although records on many pre- and Second World War boxers are hard to verify, it is doubly difficult with boxers like Elias, who boxed at a number of venues in Africa and Asia. What is known however, is that Elias was a well-respected amateur in Ghana and that he turned pro there in 1942, some years before his arrival in England. He was good enough to win the featherweight title of Ghana and was often referred to as 'the Maharajah of Boxing' in his local press. It was reported that whilst stationed abroad he beat not only Crackwell but also, "Tiger Williams of Leicester, John Hornby of Wrexham, Jimmy Camberwell of Dagenham and so many Indian and Burmese tough fighters."

Elias was a contemporary and friend of cruiserweight Richard Armah, another popular African boxer who moved to Britain in the late 1940s, and the pair often appeared together on the same bill. Elias was also once a second at an Army boxing tournament with Seargent Roy Ankrah, another well-known African fighter who moved to Britain in 1950. Dubbed the 'Black Flash' Ankrah won most of his bouts in the UK and won the Empire featherweight title in 1952.

Soon after the war ended Elias left the port of Tokaradi aboard the Empire Bure and set sail for England. Due to the good reports he had received from European and US boxing observers the initial plan was for him to have a number of fights in Europe before touring the USA, but as it turned out he settled in Liverpool and fought only in Britain. Before he left Ghana, Elias told a waiting reporter, "I am confident that I shall not disappoint my many friends." He was waved off by his boxing friend Richard Armah.

Although internet records of Elias' British contests list 17 contests, with just seven victories, and his UK debut as an eight rounds points loss to Hull's Stan Gossip at Sheffield in December 1948, the MFBA has found at least another 16 contests (10 wins) for Elias. His first contest in Britain can be confirmed as a points loss to Nottingham's Mias Johnson at Morecambe on 8 September 1948, his performance being described as, "promising," by the *Boxing News*. A week later the Zulu Kid had his first win on British soil, when he outpointed Stoke's Jacky Ryan over six rounds at Liverpool Stadium.

Elias was certainly busy, and he had at least another eleven fights in Britain before the year was out. These included wins over; Tommy Clark of Leeds; Wigan's Peter Gaskell, who was decked three times by Elias before the referee intervened in their sixth round of their clash in Douglas, the Isle of Man; Teddy Gaynor; Bradford's capable Tommy Madden; a revenge win over Mias Johnson where, "the exchanges were fast and furious throughout," and Elias, "was perpetual motion, showering punches from every angle"; and, in a situation that would not be allowed today, two remarkable wins on the one night on 29 November.

On a show at Northampton that also featured the Nigerian heavyweight Sammy Wilde, another African boxer who regularly appeared with him, Elias beat local man Ronnie Gladwell after the latter was forced to retire in the second round with an injured right hand. Later on in the evening Elias was asked to go in with Al Binney. Elias obliged and decked the famous black Sheffield boxer three times before the referee stopped the contest in his favour, also in the second round. It was reported at the time that this was Elias' eleventh win since coming to England and both he and Wilde collected 'nobbins' that, "an excited crowd showered into the ring to show their appreciation of the Zulu Kid's prowess."

An attempt to make it three wins in just four days at Sheffield on December 3 failed as the highly rated Stan Gossip, who would later lose a British title eliminator to Bert Jackson, outpointed Elias over eight rounds. Elias finished the year off by meeting Liverpool's Bernie Pugh, then rated in the British top 10, at Liverpool Stadium, but Bernie proved too clever and won on points over eight rounds.

Tipton's Johnny (Jackie) Britton was Elias' first opponent of 1949, but the Midlander would have been better advised to stay at home as he was KO'd in the first round. A left put him down for a count of seven in the first minute but no sooner had he recovered when Elias threw a swinging right that caught him flush on the chin and decked him for the full count. A points loss to Jamaica's Black Bond at Colwyn Bay later in the month was exacerbated by news that Elias had broken his thumb in this contest and would be out of the ring for some time. He returned at West Bromwich Town Hall in a top of the bill contest on 4 March that was broadcast on the radio, boxing superbly to outpoint Chesterfield's Billy Hill.

Eddie 'Zulu Kid' Lartey c. 1948   *Source: Gary Shaw*

Just four days later Elias met Birmingham's Billy Davies who had lost only seven out of 32 contests. Perhaps unsurprisingly given Davies' record and his contest just a few days previous, Elias lost on points. Just three weeks later however, he was in action again, this time at

Bournemouth, where he was outpointed over six rounds by Brighton's Tony Brazil. The referee for this contest was none other than Tommy Craggs, the official Elias had written to for boxing equipment over a decade before!

A return with Billy Hill in May 1949 ended with Elias, despite giving away 5lbs, stopping the Yorkshireman in the fifth round. This was followed by a top of the bill points loss to Owen Johnson in Morecambe. Elias was to have at least ten more contests before retiring, beating the likes of Jackie Molloy (twice), ex-Scottish featherweight champion Jimmy Dunn in Glasgow, Jack Collins and Jim Dwyer, as well as holding Bootle's Johnny Molloy and Scotsman Jim Campbell to creditable draws. His win against Jackie Molloy in August came on the undercard of the British Empire lightweight title between Ivor (Kid) Germain and South Africa's Jimmy Toweel at Liverpool Stadium. Elias also lost to the talented Scottish featherweight George Stewart in Glasgow and, in his final contest, Ireland's Pat McCoy in Edinburgh.

It can be seen that Elias record reads much better than first suggested and that most of his losses came against local boxers fighting in front of their home crowd. With a frequency that would astonish boxers today, he also fought as often as he could. In just 16 days, between 18 August 1949 and 3 September for instance, he had at least four contests, winning three in Liverpool and losing one in Glasgow. That equates to a fight every four days! Indeed, if it wasn't for injury Elias would have almost certainly have had far more contests and developed into an even more formidable opponent. It was reported that whilst in Switzerland Elias was having his usual early morning run when a mist developed quickly and he ran into a lamp-post. The injuries were so severe that they caused him to become blind. He survived to lead a full and rewarding life however, eventually passing away in his adopted home-town in July 1994.

With a style that was reported as being built more on the quantity of shots thrown, Elias would often simply overwhelm opponents through the sheer number of punches he could put together. However, although he could certainly take a punch, as many of the fight reports testify, he could also box behind a solid jab if the occasion warranted. Whatever the style Elias adopted however, Zulu 'Kid' Lartey proved to be a tough opponent for many British feather/lightweights in the late 1940s.

Joining Caryl Gardens ABC in the hope that it would improve his weakened legs, Liverpool's Jim Lloyd enjoyed it so much he won a National Schoolboy title and an NABC championship before winning a fantastic bronze medal at the 1960 Rome Olympics and a senior ABA title in 1962 when he was in the Army. He turned pro with Len Cotteril soon after and, in four years, managed ten wins from 20 pro bouts, despite admitting he didn't enjoy his time in the paid ranks. He returned to Merseyside to set-up Skelmersdale ABC in the late-1960s and still lives in the town. This article was compiled through interviews with Jim in 2006.

JIM LLOYD

Olympic bronze medallist loved the amateurs more than the pros

Although his father and two older brothers, Alan and Leonard, all boxed, there was another reason why Jim Lloyd became interested in the sport when he was seven years old. "As a child, I had suffered from advanced influenza in my legs," recalls Jim. "My father asked my brothers to take me to Caryl Gardens ABC to help strengthen my legs. I suppose that from that first day, I became hooked on boxing."

Jim's first experience of boxing however, was a frightening one. "They told me to go into the changing room and change into some training gear. I opened the door and was confronted by a naked man. I was out of there in a minute, looking for somewhere to hide. My brother Alan discovered me hiding behind a door and when I told him what had happened, he couldn't stop laughing. This was around 1946, the war had not long finished and we were all very naïve then." The man Jim spotted was none other than Liverpool favourite, Gus Foran, who had just finished his training schedule in a gym that in those days, hosted both pro and amateur fighters. From that potentially embarrassing moment, Jim became involved in boxing for the next 20 years. "It enabled me to travel to places that I would never have been able to go to had I not been involved in the sport. It certainly broadened my outlook on life. It's a great sport for building up a kid's confidence and self respect. I've had some disappointments over those twenty years but these have been greatly outweighed by the more pleasant experiences that I've had."

Jim's trainer at Caryl Gardens was Joe Clark. "What he didn't know about the sport wasn't worth knowing," recalls Jim. "I also had my Dad and my brothers offering me help and advice whenever it was needed." Jim stayed at Caryl Gardens for the next seven years before joining the Liverpool Star ABC when he was 14. Despite trainers Billy Davies and Billy Gamble having, "a great influence on my career. I soon returned to Joe Clark at Caryl Gardens. I suppose it's like leaving home - you can't wait to get back again."

In 1954 Jim won a National Schoolboy championship. "It was my first title and I felt as though I'd won a world title. I was so proud and so was my Dad who, by this time, was unable to teach me as much as he wanted to because he was suffering from arthritis in his legs. Despite this he was always present whenever I went into the ring." Two years after winning the schools title Jim made the Junior ABA finals. A year later he won the NABC welterweight title. "As far as I was concerned, I was going to the top!" Jim was brought back down to earth in 1959 when he was ruled out of the Senior ABA championships with an eye injury. Two years later the same thing happened in the West Lancs and South Cheshire Championships. "I couldn't believe my bad luck as 1960 was also Olympic Games year and I had built up my hopes of going. It's the zenith of an amateur fighters career and I didn't want to miss it."

As things turned out however, Jim was called up for his National Service that same year. "I joined the Royal Army Ordinance Corps and this allowed me to keep up with my boxing. I won the Army welterweight title and this enabled me to progress into the ISBA Championships. My enjoyment didn't last long though because I got myself disqualified in the first round for an allegedly low blow against a guy called Parkinson who was representing the Royal Navy. It wasn't a low blow at all and it completely shattered me. Even today, if I met that referee, I would have to let him know how I felt and still feel about the decision."

Following Jim's disappointment at what he thought was the end of his Olympic hopes however, fate intervened to give him another chance at qualification. An 'Olympic Trial' had been arranged between him and the ABA Champion, Colin Humphries. "I told myself that I would make certain this time but it never came to that because Colin had to pull out when he sustained an injury. I had to feel for him because I knew full well just how he felt." Jim was in the Olympics after much uncertainty however, and, "was determined that I would do both myself, the Army and, of course, the country proud. Jim certainly didn't let anyone down as he boxed superbly to gain a bronze in Rome. "I was hoping that I could have gone higher, maybe silver, even gold, but I came up against the great Italian, Nino Benvenutti in the semifinal. Nino would go on to win the gold medal so I suppose I can say that I was beaten by the best man in the world." Benvenutti would go on to win a world title in the paid ranks whilst, "my old mate, Harry Scott, would also cross gloves with Nino as a pro."

Jim maintains that Olympic selection was the pinnacle of his amateur career. "I loved the whole experience of being there. It was a great fight against Benvenutti - I really enjoyed it. He was a very good boxer, tall for the weight and he knew what he was doing." 1960 of course was the same Olympics that introduced the world to the talent that was Cassius Clay, although Jim admits the England team hadn't heard of the American at the time, although they certainly knew some of the visitors who came to see him there. "We were billeted next to the Americans and Grace Kelly and Bing Crosby came to see Clay. We'd never heard of him but we knew Pietrzykowski from the Europeans. He was a great boxer but Clay made him look like a novice. He showed his medal off to anyone he could find, but I was equally proud of my bronze"

In 1961 Jim was still a serving soldier and he again entered the Army Championships. "This time, I entered into the middleweight division, but I lost on points to Ernie Longhurst. It was another of those disputed decisions, with many among the audience feeling that another gross injustice had been done. I must admit that I was gutted. I even reached the stage where I thought that I had had enough of the sport altogether and thought about packing it all in. I think that probably every fighter goes through this stage at least once in his career. It's a horrible feeling and you just feel as though everything is against you but I suppose that this is where the discipline kicks in and you pull yourself together and fight your way back again."

There were also rumours that Jim would turn professional. It became so unsettling that Jim was forced to speak out in his defence, going as far as to give an interview to the *Boxing News* denying the stories. In 1962 Jim, "finally achieved my ambition to win an ABA title when I outpointed Johnny Kingston Elliot in the light-middleweight final." Jim's medal collection was growing. He had won Schoolboy titles, an NABC title, an Army Championship, an ISBA championship, an Olympic bronze medal and a senior ABA crown.

Although an amateur winning so many titles and medals will invariably be approached to 'turn-over', Jim says that, "it never occurred to me to turn pro but, after winning the ABA title, I was approached by a number of managers suggesting that I became a professional. I was offered the sum of £500 by a certain manager, a tidy sum in the 1960s, but the Fisher ABC had been more of a second home to me, and I made the decision to go with Len Cottrell and trainers, Jim and Bernie Cottrell. My Dad was supportive of me turning professional. He said that I could 'make a few bob', and as I was now a married man with a young son to think of, I was thinking that I could maybe put a few shillings in the bank for my wife Pat and my family."

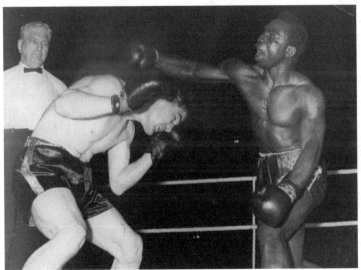

Jim Lloyd (left) v Sugar Gibiliru, Wembley Pool, September 1962. Source: Gary Shaw

Jim's pro debut came at Wembley Arena in September 1962. In the opposite corner was a man Jim knew well from his hometown, West Africa's three weight champion, Sugar Gibiliru. "We boxed a draw over six rounds. Sadly Sugar passed away in December 2005. I attended a tribute night to him not long afterwards. It was sad to think that so many things had happened to us both since that first professional fight and now he was gone. In his memory, money was raised for equipment at the Royal Liverpool Hospital, so he will never be forgotten."

Jim had a total of 20 contests as a pro, winning ten, losing seven and drawing three. "I beat Harry Wheeler on a first round KO. I also had two great contests against Billy Tarrant who, at the time, was rated the number six middleweight in the country. Both fights were complete 'sell-outs', and both were really hard. He was a tough opponent. We boxed a draw in the first contest and this made a second fight a must and I won the return on points. I also lost to Wally Swift. I was a substitute for this fight, and came in at short notice. Wally was the British champion at the time and he was a very cagey fighter who knew all the moves. Although he wasn't a devastating puncher he was very good technically and in the end he just wore you down."

Jim had no complaints about his ninth round stoppage loss to Swift but he was rapidly losing his affection for the pro game. "I was having second thoughts about having turned pro. As an amateur I loved everything about the game but the pro side was completely different - all anyone was interested in was money. I got £75 for my first fight but had to give my manager 25% and my trainer 10%. But I was the one doing the training and fighting! I managed myself for my last year as a pro and I earned more during that time than the rest of my career."

Jim continued for a while however, beating Louis Onwuna on points in his next fight before losing on an eye injury to West Ham's Johnny Kramer. In May 1966 he had his last fight against Liam Mullen, being stopped in five rounds. "I was in my twentieth year in boxing and it just wasn't there anymore and I decided to leave the game. As a pro I had boxed out of London. This meant that the family had to live there but a few years after I retired we came back to Merseyside. My family increased over the years. I now have two sons, Kevin and Martin, and two lovely daughters, Julie and Jane."

Jim didn't leave the sport altogether though. "I returned to the amateur game with my brother Alan and we started Skelmersdale ABC. In 1971 I became a qualified ABA coach. I had a few jobs; betting shop assistant, docker and then a driver of heavy goods vehicles, a job which took me all over the country and which I loved. I am also a fully committed supporter of Liverpool FC!" Jim admits that he has had a few problems over the years. "I had heart surgery a few years ago but I'm happy to say that I feel fine now. I have been attending Skelmersdale College for the past three years, studying Sports Therapy and I intend to go on attending college. I have also joined up with some of my old amateur and professional colleagues through the MFBA. It's great to meet up every month and talk over old times."

Jim states that as far as injuries go, "I was lucky throughout my boxing career. I was never seriously hurt or injured. I do have a broken nose, which I suppose is indicative of a fighting man, but the reality is that I didn't get it through boxing - I got it playing cricket. I was 14 years old and I was playing wicket keeper. I misjudged a fast ball and let it slip through my gloves, smashing onto my nose. Stuff like that never happened inside the ring did it!"

Jim thoroughly enjoyed his career in amateur boxing. The professional side is a different matter however. "Although I have no regrets at trying the professional side of the sport, give me the amateurs any time. I enjoyed my amateur boxing and the people I met there. Scotland's Bobby Keddie and I would beat the hell out of each other but were the best of mates - often going for a drink together afterwards. To me, Dick McTaggart was the greatest amateur fighter I have ever seen, and probably ever will see. He had everything, and it was an education just to watch him."

The son of former British and Empire heavyweight champion, Jack London of West Hartlepool, Brian London, or Brian Harper as he was known when he boxed as an amateur, won an Empire Games gold medal in 1954 as well as an ABA title, before turning pro in 1955 with himself as manager. In 1958 he won the same titles, British and British Empire, that his father had won in the 1940s. In a 15-year pro career, Brian had 58 fights, two for the world title, winning 37 and met the likes of Henry Cooper, Floyd Patterson, Joe Erskine, Zora Folley, Willie Pastrano and Muhammad Ali. Always popular whenever he appeared at the Liverpool Stadium - which was often - Brian still lives near Blackpool and this chapter was obtained via interviews with him in 2007.

BRIAN LONDON

Blackpool heavyweight always a big favourite at the Stadium

Having a famous boxing father, a British champion in his own right - Jack London, it may be assumed that it was perhaps inevitable for Brian London to follow in his father's footsteps. However, nothing could be further from the truth. "The truth is that I hated boxing," says Brian. "My brother Jack and I used to run with my father when he was doing his roadwork but I never had any intention whosoever of following him into the ring. It was only when I went into the RAF in 1952 that I took up boxing and it was because of who I was that they obviously thought that I should take up the sport. Both Jack and I were members of the RAF boxing team along with Dick McTaggart, a truly great boxer, and of course, we also had little Percy Lewis as well. It was quite a team."

Despite his relatively late introduction to the sport, Brian's size, power and fitness held him good stead. "My method of fighting was to leave my corner and go, 'Bang! Bang! Bang!' If the other fellow fell over, then I was happy. Sometimes of course, it was me who fell over - and then I wasn't so happy. I had some good times in the RAF. We travelled all over the place and, of course, we got the best treatment. I was called up for National Service which meant two years but if you signed up for three, you became what was known as a 'regular', and you got regular pay. This made quite a difference. You could therefore say that I always fought for the money. You got around 28s. a week if you were National Service but if you were a 'regular', then you got £3. 2s. 6d - or thereabouts, so it was well worth it."

Brian admits that, "although I said I hated boxing when I was young, I have to say that I thoroughly enjoyed it in the Air Force." He enjoyed it so much that, representing the RAF, Brian won the Imperial Services heavyweight title in 1954, then the ABA title, and made the Empire Games team in the same year - winning a fantastic gold medal in Vancouver. He also represented the ABA on seven occasions, winning five and losing two. Such success ensured that, "When I came out of the RAF, I thought that maybe I could make some money out of the ring so I turned professional.

"My Dad had been a pro for around 18 years. He had 141 contests, winning 95, and he fought men like Buddy Baer, Freddie Mills, Bruce Woodcock, Jack Pettifer, Manuel Abrew, Larry Gains, who he fought five times, Gipsey Daniels, Ben Foord, Len Johnson and so on. You name them, my Dad fought them. I had no intention of fighting as many contests as my Dad of course, but I saw it as a way of making a decent living. I never had a manager. I always looked after myself. I would never ask who I was fighting. If the phone went and someone said, 'Do you want a fight on such and such a date?', I never asked who against - only how much! I was always fit. I never neglected my roadwork or my gym work. Whether I had a fight or not, I always kept in condition. I never had to work hard to get rid of excess weight."

Brian's real name was Brian Harper, and this was the name he fought under in the RAF, but when he turned professional he took the same name as his father. Most of his early professional fights took place in the old family home town of West Hartlepool but his first pro contest was in London in March 1955. He stopped Manchester's Dennis Lockton in the first round. "It was 'Bang! Bang!, Bang!' as soon as I left my corner. It was them or me from that point on." Brian's approach certainly paid off as he won his first 12 contests, 11 of them by KO.

It was a case of unlucky 13 as far as Brian was concerned however, as he was stopped in the first round in May 1956, in London, by another 'banger' - Henry Cooper. First round KO defeats are hard to take for any boxer, and Brian was no exception. "This is where your character comes in, for you either put it out of your mind and concentrate on getting the job done in your next contest, or you let it worry you and, if you do that, then you're in trouble." Brian jokingly sees the reason for his first pro defeat however, "I think Henry had it in for me as I'd stopped his brother Jim in four rounds a couple of fights before!"

Brian certainly seemed to put the loss to Cooper out of his mind as he won his next three - again all inside the distance. "I was on a roll again but you'll always get some spoilsport coming along won't you? I was asked to go to Dortmund in Germany to fight Heinz Neuhaus and he beat me on points over 10 rounds."

Brian London (right) v Henry Clark, 6 February 1969, Liverpool Stadium
Source: Gary Shaw

Brian remained a popular attraction wherever he fought and he puts this down to his whole-hearted approach to boxing. "I seemed to be popular with the fight crowds wherever I fought, maybe because I never pretended to be anything that I wasn't. By that I mean that I always fought the best fight I could, and if it wasn't good enough, then at least I knew that I'd done my best and that was all that mattered as far as I was concerned. The fight crowds seemed to know this."

After the Neuhaus defeat Brian went on another run of quick wins, including a fine KO win over Peter Bates and a points win over dangerous Tongan Kitione Lave. Soon his record showed 20 wins (17 KOs) from 22 contests. "I must have been doing something right!" Others thought so too, and the class of Brian's opponents steadily improved. Up next was the highly rated American, Willie Pastrano. "Willie was a class fighter and he gave me a boxing lesson, beating me on points."

Four months later however, Brian was offered the fight he wanted most - the opportunity to fight for the title that his father had held in the late-1940s. On 23 June 1958 Brian met Cardiff's Joe Erskine for the British and British Empire heavyweight titles. "I stopped Joe in eight rounds to become champion. I was the proudest man in the world, but I have to say that Joe Erskine was a great fighter. Britain was well off for heavyweights around that time. As well as Cooper and myself, there was Erskine, Dick Richardson and later, Johnny Prescot and, of course, Billy Walker. I fought them all and I can honestly say that if Joe Erskine had had a decent punch, he would have been world champion, he was that good."

A British title holder at last, Brian admits that, "It felt great being the champion with all the adulation that came with it." Basking in this glory a return with Willie Pastrano in September 1958 saw him gain revenge for his previous loss with a fifth round stoppage victory. 'I counted this as a great achievement for I rated Willie highly," says Brian, "He was a great fighter." Brian's reign as champion didn't last long however, as once again, "a spoilsport came along to put the kybosh on things. This time my old friend Henry Cooper." Brian and Cooper met in January 1959 - with Cooper winning on points over 15 tough rounds.

Despite this loss, Brian was then offered a fight for the world heavyweight title against reigning champion Floyd Patterson, in Indianapolis, USA. "The Board of Control refused to sanction it because I wasn't the British champion but I didn't care because it was worth a lot of money to me. I wasn't bothered what the board thought anyway so I went over there and Patterson stopped me in the eleventh round but I'd lasted longer than Archie Moore and Ingemar Johansson so I hadn't exactly disgraced British boxing had I? Maybe Patterson's people thought I was a soft touch. If so I proved them wrong as well."

Following the Patterson contest Brian took another fight against a man who many heavyweights at that time avoided like the plague, Nino Valdes the Cuban. "He was a good fighter," recalls Brian, "as big as a house! Even Rocky Marciano's people didn't want to know him!" The tough Cuban stopped Brian in seven rounds, the same round the Blackpool man stopped Pete Rademacher in in his next contest. "He was the guy who won the Olympic Gold Medal and then fought for the world heavyweight title against Patterson in his first professional contest. I'll bet he got a few bob for that!" Next up was Welshman Dick Richardson in Porthcawl with the European heavyweight title at stake "I was stopped in eight rounds and there was a bit of trouble at the end of the fight. It was all good fun though."

Brian then stopped tough Texan Howard King in the open-air at Blackpool's Stanley Park, one of four fights he had in is hometown. He was of course ever popular here, but he also fought at the Liverpool Stadium nine times and the Merseyside venue holds a special place in his memories. "Without doubt one of my favourite fight venues was the Liverpool Stadium. I fought there a few times and I always enjoyed the experience. The crowd there were great and they always treated me well, like an adopted 'scouser' really. What made it better was the fact that I could come straight home afterwards.

"I was always top of the bill and there was always a full house when I appeared there. The atmosphere was great. I remember the first time I fought there - it was against Johnny Prescott and at the end of 10 rounds, the referee gave the fight to Prescott. There was no way that he'd beaten me and the crowd made their feelings known immediately. There was tremendous booing, and one thing led to another and to say that things got out of hand would be an understatement. There was an even bigger fight than the one we'd just had so I suppose the Liverpool fight crowd got two fights for the price of one!"

Film of the Prescott fight shows the Liverpool crowd singing Brian's name - perhaps the only time 'scousers' have sung the name of another city at a sporting event. Brian also beat California pair Roger Rischer and Amos Johnson at the Stadium, as well as New York's James J. Woody and the talented Zora Folley of Dallas. "I had some great fights against some top Americans at the Liverpool Stadium," says Brian, although one of the best 'yanks' he met was Eddie Machen. "I fought him in London in 1961 and he stopped me in five rounds. He gave me a working over." Machen later met Ernie Terrell for the world title.

Brain also met another famous American - Muhammad Ali. Their August 1966 meeting at Earls Court was for the world title. "Ali stopped me in three rounds and I had no complaints. He was amazing, he was so fast for a big man, and he certainly was big. It was incredible how fast he was. The only man I think could have beaten him was Marciano."

Of boxing today, Brian takes some interest still. "I still watch boxing if it's on the television. I don't go to shows anymore but I still keep in trim. I run every day except Sunday and I punch the bags I have hanging in my garage for about 15 rounds every day. I'm as fit as any other 72-year old former fighter! Would I do it all again? Yes, definitely, but I would probably do it differently. Get myself a good manager and go to London, but saying that boxing's been good to me. I made a good living and that's all a man can ask."

Undoubtedly one of the finest British amateurs ever to have boxed, St. Helens' John Lyon won a record eight senior ABA titles, the first in 1981 and the last in 1989. As well as representing England/Great Britain on numerous occasions throughout the decade, including two Olympic appearances, both as team captain, John also won Commonwealth Games' gold and silver medals and multi-nations tournaments galore. Still living and working in the North West, where he is a coach at Wigan ABC, this article was compiled through interviews with John in 2007.

JOHN LYON MBE

Record Breaker John – king of the amateurs

With a record eight ABA senior titles, a host of multi-nations gold medals, a Commonwealth Games gold and silver medal, Olympic appearances and a fantastic ten-year England career (1980-1990) it would be understandable if St. Helens' amateur boxing legend John Lyon found it difficult to pick a defining career highlight. For John however, such a dilemma is easily answered, as a year after retiring he was awarded the MBE for Services to Boxing. "Receiving the MBE from the Queen herself at Buckingham Palace was definitely my greatest achievement," says John, "even accounting for the honours I won."

Gaining the long list of honours he accumulated over a fantastic ten year international amateur career, and the reward and recognition that went with them, must have seemed a world away for a 13-year old John who, despite some family background in the sport, was only persuaded to attend his local club because a friend asked him to accompany him. "My four older brothers had all boxed, with Gerard having over 100 contests, so I knew a bit about boxing before I joined a club. One of my mates fancied going one night and asked me to go with him. I said yes, went along and caught the bug from day one."

In a record breaking amateur career, John boxed for Lowe House ABC, then Greenalls St. Helens/St. Helens Star. It was whilst with Lowe House that John first came to national recognition. In 1980 he made the ABA light-flyweight final but found himself the only Merseyside finalist from six, the others being Keith Wallace, Ray and George Gilbody, Tony Willis and Jimmy Price, to lose, going down on points to Repton's Terry Barker. Only 18 at the time however, John would gain revenge over a number of Repton boxers in the years to come.

Although disappointed at losing his first national senior final, the defeat isn't what John remembers most from that night. "I was only 18 at my first ABA final at Wembley in 1980 and I was very nervous. When I walked out into the arena and I saw the BBC cameras and the size of the crowd - there were thousands there - my bottle went. My old trainer Albert Freeman got me in a corner and asked me if I wanted a quick swill of my mouth. I said yes and he got out an old whiskey bottle that he had earlier filled with water. The problem was he must have left a bit of whiskey in the bottom of it. I was tea-total at the time but I knew straight away it was whiskey. As it hit the back of my throat I near choked! I coughed and spluttered and quickly had to spit it out, and could still taste it a bit when the bell went for the first round."

Later in 1980 John gained the first of many England vests when, together with John Hyland and Joey Joynson, he represented the ABA U19 in a match against East Germany. A first round stoppage loss in Senftenberg in October was followed a month later by a points win over Hungary in Milton Keynes; his long and illustrious international career was on its way.

In 1981 John made the ABA light-flyweight final again, where he met another Repton boxer in the shape of Alan Masterton. In what was to be the first of four straight ABA final victories, the disappointment of the previous year was forgotten as John ran out a clever points winner. In 1982 John beat another Reptonian, John McBride on points, whilst in 1983, boxing for St Helens Star, he beat Danny Porter (Hitchin Youth) to win a hat-trick of titles. A change of name for the St Helens club to Greenalls St Helens couldn't stop John from winning ABA title number four a year later when Trelewis' Wayne Williams was also beaten on points.

By now of course John had become a virtual ever-present in the England senior squad. A gold in the 1981 Acropolis Cup in Athens, Greece was a welcome addition to his ABA title of the same year. Likewise, John's 1982 ABA title was soon being kept company by the silver medal he won at the 1982 Commonwealth Games in Brisbane, Australia. John had a great tournament here, eventually losing to Kenya's A Wachire in the light-flyweight final.

Not wanting to keep his 1983 ABA title alone too long without a Greek companion either, John's burgeoning trophy cabinet was swelled further with the addition of another gold at that year's Acropolis Cup.

Later in the same year, he headed to Belfast and added a Commonwealth Federation championship gold. John's increasingly frequent international appearances included matches against East Germany and a combined ABA/Canada match against the USA in Reno, Nevada in November 1983. The 1984 Olympics had been allocated to Los Angeles and, with many suspecting Eastern-bloc countries would boycott the event in retaliation for the USA's boycott of the 1980 Moscow Olympics, this appearance was perfect practice for Britain's aspiring Olympic boxers.

John's 1984 ABA title ensured he was selected for the Olympics. Indeed, all 12 ABA winners that year made the squad. Despite a team that also included John Hyland, Pat Clinton and Brian Schumacher however, and the Eastern-bloc boycott, only super-heavyweight Bobby Wells returned with a medal. As many talented British boxers have found to their cost, the draw at major tournaments often conspires against their progression. A Sudanese boxer and then an Israeli in the first and second rounds were dispatched easily enough by John, the St. Helens man winning both bouts 5:0 on the judges cards, but the draw had also matched him with pre-tournament favourite and local hero Paul Gonzales in the quarter-finals. Like John, Gonzales had enjoyed a clean sweep on all five judge's scorecards in his early rounds.

Despite trying his best however, the American proved too strong for John and he lost 4:1. With Gonzales winning his semi-final 5:0 and then gaining a walk-over in the final however, John found solace not only in the fact that he lost to the eventual winner, but also that he was the only one of Gonzales' opponents to get the nod of any of the judges who saw the talented American box that summer. Gonzales was also adjudged the outstanding boxer of that year's tournament, winning the coveted Val Barker Trophy in the process, so John's defeat was certainly no disgrace. With an Olympic gold medal behind him, Gonzales turned pro the following year and enjoyed a highly successful pro career, challenging Orlando Canizales for the IBF bantamweight title in 1990.

John's progress in Los Angeles did have its downside however. "At the 1984 Olympics Kevin Hickey, our trainer, wouldn't let any of the squad sunbathe until after they had finished boxing. We all knew sunbathing sapped your energy. I got through to the quarter-finals so it only left me three days to enjoy the city. We duly headed off to Venice Beach to relax and would you believe it I got sunstroke and was ill for the rest of my time there. I guess being from St. Helens I just wasn't used to it. Just my luck!"

Although John lost in a preliminary round to eventual winner Mark Epton in the 1985 ABA championship, the year proved to be another successful one. A seasoned international performer, he won another seven ABA vests this year, visiting Rostock in East Germany, Dublin, Belfast and Prague in the process. He also lost to the outstanding Hungarian amateur and 1980 U19 European champion J Varadi in Milton Keynes in November. As far as multi-nations tournaments were concerned, John won a gold at Canada's Quebec Cup and was unlucky in the draw for that year's European Championships, where he was captain, in Budapest, losing to the eventual champion Dieter Berg of East Germany in the first round.

John Lyon (right) v Leonard Makhanya (Swaziland), flyweight final, Commonwealth Games, Edinburgh 1986.   *Source: John Lyon*

Domestically John returned to winning ways in 1986, this time at flyweight, to win ABA title number five by outpointing Croy Miner's Drew Docherty. Selected for that year's Commonwealth Games in Edinburgh he was also given the honour of captaining the England boxing team that won medals in every division bar light-welter and light-middle. John himself beat Swaziland's Leonard Makhanya in the flyweight final to add a gold to the silver he had won four years previously. Canada's Dan Sherry and Lennox Lewis were the rising stars of this tournament, both going on to enjoy great success in the paid ranks, but it was another boxer in the weight category won by Lewis that John was forced to remember recently. "I was shocked to hear of the death of our super-heavyweight at the Edinburgh Commonwealth games, James Oyebola," recalls John. "He had a great tournament to win a bronze medal, only losing to Lewis in the semis."

In 1987 John added another ABA title, beating the Army's John McLean on points. This, his sixth senior ABA title, equalled the long-time record held by Middleton ABC's Joe Steers way back in the early days of the ABA in the 1890s, when the flyweight division wasn't even recognised. Steers won the heavyweight then middleweight titles in 1890 and 1891 (the year Val Barker won his title) respectively, before adding, in a scenario that would not be allowed today, both the middleweight and heavyweight titles in 1892 and 1893.

John represented the ABA twice in 1987, winning on each occasion in Prague and Slupsk, Poland. 1988 was another Olympic year, this time in Seoul, South Korea. Many thought it would be the first for some time that would not be boycotted by the world's leading boxing nations. Nevertheless Cuba, then as now, the leading boxing nation in the world, refused to take part due to North Korea not being involved in the organisation of the Games. With both the USA and most Eastern-bloc countries participating however, medals for British boxers were just as difficult to come by. Indeed, only Richie Woodhall won a boxing medal for Britain at these Games, with John losing in the first round to Turkey's Ramzan Gul.

His disappointment at not going further was tempered to a certain extent by the fact that, for the second major championships in a row, John was named team captain. He would also of course, win yet another ABA title this year; his seventh and therefore a record. By again outpointing Drew Docherty in the final John was now officially the most successful senior amateur boxer in British history.

Not one to rest on his laurels however, John added an amazing eighth ABA title in 1989, the last finals to be held at Wembley, by repeating his 1987 victory over Scotland's John McLean. He also captained the small ABA team that took part in that year's world Championships in Moscow, where he came up against a Korean in the quarter-finals.

"This was the hardest fight I ever had," recalls John. He was strong and skillful." The scoring system, whereby judges awarded a boxer the round if they thought he had won it, had been changed after Seoul to one where points were awarded for scoring shots, much like today, and John recalls that, "there were just two points in the fight going into the last round, but every time I threw two shots he managed to come back with three. Time and again he just seemed to step up a gear just when it mattered most. I don't know where he got the strength from. It was the first time in over a hundred bouts that I had come up against such a tough, hard, strong challenger."

Nearing the end of his career, John boxed in a few more international tournaments, including the 1990 Commonwealth Games, where he again captained the team, but lost to his old adversary John McLean in one of the tournament's major shocks. He then moved up a weight and proved there was life in him yet by winning a bronze at bantamweight in one of his favourite tournaments, the Acropolis Cup. This was in June and a few weeks later he retired.

Never one to regret the choices he made in his career, John looks back on what he achieved and says simply, "I had a very happy and fulfiling boxing career and wouldn't change a thing. I am still involved with the sport as a coach at Wigan ABC and I still train the England squads too." One of the main beneficiaries of the unsurpassed knowledge John accrued in his career was his son, Craig, one of John's three children - Joshua and Daniel being the others. In yet another show of modesty, John notes that, "Craig boxed as a schoolboy and later became a double ABA champion himself." Like his father, Craig also boxed for England and would probably have won another two titles had injury and illness not affected him.

Talking of his family life, John is keen to show his gratitude for the help and assistance they gave him throughout his career. "After leaving school I started working for Pilkington Glass, where I still am to this day, fitting the boxing around my shift work and family life. I was married at 17 and had three children while I was boxing and I would like to take this opportunity to thank them all for their love and support throughout my career. I couldn't have achieved all I did without them."

On a parting note, John is also keen to mention the Liverpool Stadium and his local boxing fans. "My first appearance at the Stadium was as a 17-year old in my first ABA Championships. I remember I beat Paul Fletcher on points. It was probably the most memorable night of my boxing career really. The Stadium was one of the only places I have ever boxed where I could really feel the crowd pushing me and urging me on to win. I have boxed all over the world and never felt the buzz that I got from the Liverpool Stadium and the crowds there."

Birkenhead's Martin McCarthy was a popular and hard-hitting bantamweight from the post World War One era. He turned pro with local manager and ex-pro Bob Foster aged just 15 – his father was a cripple and he immediately became the main breadwinner in his household. More tragedy struck barely a year after his pro debut when his mother died but Bob went on to have around 65 professional contests plus numerous encounters on the travelling boxing booths. This chapter is based on an article by Frank Johnson, that was first published in 1972.

MARTIN McCARTHY (YOUNG MACK)

10 fights a night - on ham and eggs!

Martin McCarthy (Young Mack) earned his fame as a hard-hitting Birkenhead bantamweight in the days following the First World War. The interest he had shown in the sport while attending St. Paul's School was given plenty of opportunity to blossom when he left at the age of 14 and came under the expert wing of the late Bob Foster. Boxing in those days was almost a way of life for many local youngsters, and Martin rapidly absorbed some hard-won lessons at the Conway Athletic Club. Training was rugged with some of the sparring often the prelude to mini-wars, the boys giving everything as they endeavoured to attain peak fitness.

There were so many good boxers about that anybody who entered the ring half fit was on a hiding to nothing. Martin, who soon assumed the ring name of 'Young Mack', was a dedicated trainer and never shirked a job no matter what the strength of the opposition. Refusal would only have opened the door to another budding fighter and when 'Young Mack' was offered his first pro fight at the age of 15, he jumped at the chance. His opponent was George Davies, a boxer of some repute as he had had at least 20 previous bouts, many against quality opposition. From the opening bell Martin was given a hard lesson on what boxing was all about. Davies hit hard and often with both gloves but the packed crowd at the Central Hall, Hoylake gave 'Young Mack' a great ovation as he kept going back for more, even when his knees buckled from the power of some of Davies's haymaking rights to the head and body. 'Mack' stayed the course and through bloodied lips, watched enviously as the referee held the gloved fist of Davies aloft to signal a convincing win. 'Mack' went home sore and grimly clutching his 7/- 6d purse money.

Out of defeat emerged a fighting spirit which never left him however, and in his second fight at Chester 'Mack' took on local hero George Boswell and dispatched him to the canvas for the full count midway through the third round. The first lesson had been well and truly learned and with Bob Foster as his manager, they forged a formidable team. Training at Bob Foster's Club were local boys Charlie Tonner, Ray Duncan, 'Kid' Foggo, Billy Fletcher, Billy Quinn, Nat Stewart, Billy Earle, Charlie Smith and Arthur Holsgrove. There was hardly a night when one or more of the boys were not in action at a wide variety of Merseyside venues and, as success followed success, the name of Birkenhead was well to the forefront of boxing.

'Mack' fought another local boxer, 'Red' Tim Kenny at the Victoria Stadium on the corner of Conway Street, and he won in the fourth round after referee Jack Hanlon had called both boys to order for more action. In an open-air tournament at Ashton-in-Makerfield, 'Mack' boxed a ten-round draw with the Manchester pocket 'Hercules', Pat Flynn, the crowd showering the ring with 'nobbins' which came to £4. This was a handsome sum in those days and made a nice addition to his purse of £3.10s. As his earlier manager Bob Foster, had been tragically killed in a motor cycle accident, his manager at the time was Ray Duncan and it was Ray who was in his corner for the Flynn fight. It was toe-to-toe with both fighters hammering away incessantly, with fortunes swaying in thrilling style. The pace was incredible and the Birkenhead man came back twice from the brink of defeat to crack fierce left hooks to Flynn's midriff, to fully earn a share of the spoils.

Mack was an orthodox fighter, possessing a sleep-producing left hook and endless courage when up against it, all the ingredients for a man who was definitely hungry, not only for money, but for success - and how 'Mack' worked to attain his success. He boxed at Seaforth in Sam Barton's boxing booth, with his local hero Charlie Smith also in the camp. 'Mack' remembered that across a field from the booth was a ham and eggs stall where an ample plate full could be bought for a shilling. After as many as ten bouts in a night, a plateful of ham and eggs was just the job to revive lost energy! Another boxer on the staff was cruiserweight 'Battling' Sullivan whose son, Johnny Sullivan, would win the British middleweight title after the Second World War. Billed as 'The Bruising Cruiser', Sullivan was a fearsome fighter - they had to be as some of the challengers were not climbing through the ropes simply for laughs.

Martin's mother died when he was just 16 years old and, with his father crippled owing to injuries sustained in the First World War, the role of bread-winner fell upon the stocky shoulders of 'Young Mack'. With six brothers and sisters to bring up, boxing therefore became a necessity. With a total of 63 contests in his professional career, not counting numerous booth fights, 'Mack' averaged a fight a fortnight and his maximum purse was £5. He always reckoned that his first opponent, George Davies, was the toughest man he ever met.

Martin had a wealth of stories from his ring career and once recalled boxing first on the bill at Ellesmere Port. After he left the ring he got into a meat van and hurried off to Wrexham to box last on the bill there, with his total nights purse money coming to £4. He also recalled being in Charlie Tonner's dressing room the night he fought Alf Howard and was stopped in the eighth round. Tonner went to hospital with a split lip after that fight but local pride was saved when his future manager Bob Foster, beat another Birkenhead man, Frank Price on the same bill. In later years, Mack worked at Cammell Lairds as a compressor driver before retiring as a clerk in 1971. He passed away some years ago.

An injury prone right hand affected Scotland Road's Gerry McNally throughout his career, yet this didn't stop the middle/light-heavyweight from boxing for several Merseyside clubs during his amateur days; winning a junior ABA title in 1949; nor from becoming one of the country's top light-heavyweights during the late-1950s and early 1960s. Indeed, at one time Gerry was ranked No. 1 contender for Chic Calderwood's British title but was overlooked for a title shot. After his ten-year professional career (1953-63) he became a successful businessman in Camberley, Surrey, where he had been based since the early-1950s. He passed away in 2006 after a short illness.

GERRY McNALLY

Injuries to right-hand affected title chance

It is highly probable that Gerry McNally held a record that no other British boxer let alone Merseyside boxer can match. His achievement? In his first contest as an amateur, for the now defunct Lee Jones ABC, and under the tutelage of Harry Ives, Gerry won a Liverpool Boy's Championship at the Liverpool Stadium. Gerry moved on from the Lee Jones to join Luke Gregson at the famous Star ABC and it was with the famous old south-Liverpool club that he won a junior ABA title at Wembley in 1949. Soon after this Gerry was on the move again, this time 'over the water' to another famous old Merseyside club, Birkenhead ABC. Training with Gerry here, under the guidance of Jack Peel and Tom Murray, were the likes of Mickey Flanagan, Wally Thom, Vic Harrison and Jim Allsopp. With this kind of quality available in the gym, it was no wonder that Gerry went on to enjoy further success as an amateur.

Growing up in the 1950s meant that Gerry, together with most of his contemporaries, had to complete a period of National Service. He duly joined the 4th Batt. RAOC but this didn't mean his boxing was curtailed. Indeed, Gerry boxed for the Army often and was considered good enough to represent the ABA against Italy in his first year in uniform where he dropped a points decision to S. Burcchi in November 1951, the ABA eventually losing 3-7.

It wasn't long however, before Gerry's fledgling boxing career began to have an effect on his brittle hand. Gerry injured his hand on countless occasions. It seemed that it could not stand up to the stress and punishment of the ring. So much did his father believe this, that he tried to get Gerry to give up the sport altogether in case his son was injured so severely that not only would he have to stop boxing, but also stop him from earning a living at another occupation. In an attempt to correct the problem, Gerry had a number of operations over the next few years. These had little effect however, and prevented him from competing for what Gerry wanted most - a senior ABA title. Undeterred however, he decided that the best way to overcome the problem was simply to develop his left hand even more – and this he did to great effect.

Upon completion of his National Service, Gerry decided to turn professional and he signed with John Simpson. Gerry said that becoming a full-time boxer was a natural progression for him as not only had he been training with professionals throughout his amateur career, but he had also fought on fairground booths since he was 14-years old. His first bout as a professional however, took place not in Liverpool but in Watford – a third round stoppage of Leicester's Harry Harvey in January 1953. Unable to find employment in the North West, Gerry had returned to Camberley in Surrey, where he had spent part of his National Service. This turned out to be a smart move on Gerry's behalf as not only did he manage to find work in the building trade, but he also married Gretta, whom he had met whilst he was in the Army, and they raised three daughters.

After his debut win, Gerry drew, won and lost his next three fights respectively, and was then matched with his toughest opponent to date; the former 1953 ABA middleweight champion, West Ham's Ron Barton. Barton, himself a novice professional, stopped Gerry in the second round at Leyton baths in March 1954 and would later go on to become British light-heavyweight champion. Many years later Gerry recalled that following this defeat his manager appeared to lose interest in him. With hindsight this may appear to have been understandable, after all Gerry had lost two out of five contests as a pro. However, Gerry also thought that, "it was a mistake...to have joined a stable with two British champions...". The inference being that most of his manager's time and efforts were taken up in looking after them. Gerry did concede however, that he gained excellent experience sparring with one of the champions in question, future British light-heavy and heavyweight champ, Don Cockell.

Despite this however, Gerry did become disillusioned with the sport. This wasn't helped when his manager handed him his license back. Although Gerry continued to train, in an old Army gymnasium with no trainer, supervision or the quality sparring he was accustomed to, he began to drift away from the sport. However, boxing manager Frank Lambert from Farnborough convinced him that he still had plenty to offer. With renewed interest and vigour, Gerry began to train properly once again and although out of the ring for nearly a year, he returned in December with a six rounds points win over Gambia's Fred Balio at Wembley Town Hall.

Gerry remained unbeaten throughout 1955, gaining wins over Jimmy Edwards, Ron King, George Roe, Charlie Lake and Ralph Scott. He also drew with Jimmy Lynas. He had managed to get his boxing career back on track and he was convinced that he would at last, begin to make an impression on the British ratings. His plans suffered a dramatic setback, however, when Frank Lambert died suddenly of a heart attack. His death affected Gerry tremendously.

Determined to keep up his good work in the ring, and to honour the memory of the man who had convinced Gerry to return to boxing, Gerry vowed to continue and he signed with the brothers Billy and Terry O'Doherty. Gerry's first contest under their control would take him to Blackpool's Tower Circus and a win over a man who would later win not one, but two world titles; Nigeria's Dick Tiger. Fighting out of Liverpool, Tiger was having only his second contest in England but, as described in the first volume of *The Mersey Fighters*, his early boxing career was anything but memorable. The points win over eight rounds in January 1956 was well deserved by Gerry, but was just one of four straight defeats Tiger suffered in his first six contests in England. He would later win world titles at middleweight and light-heavyweight, and was named *Ring* fighter of the year on two separate occasions.

Despite this victory Gerry suffered four losses from six contests in 1956. In March 1957 he lost on points over eight rounds to Cardiff's Phil Edwards (Cilia) in Manchester. Edwards, "one of the best fighters I ever met," would later contest the British middleweight title, losing twice to Terry Downes. The loss to Edwards was one of only two contests Gerry had in 1957. The following year he managed only one as worries resurfaced about his troublesome right hand.

Despite this however, Gerry managed to break into the domestic top 10 for the first time. He was ranked the No. 10 light-heavyweight in Britain in 1958, and with four wins and a draw from five contests, he rose to No. 9 the following year. Wins over Stan Cullis, Tommy

Gibbons, Don Sainsbury and Redvers Sangoe pushed Gerry even higher – No. 2 in 1960. He was now competing against the best men in the division. In 1961 he beat Yolande Pompey and then outpointed a former British champion, the still highly regarded Alex Buxton. These wins meant that Gerry was now ranked the No. 1 contender for Chic Calderwood's British title. His dream of fighting for the title appeared to be within his grasp.

While he was waiting to be named as the official challenger for the British title, Gerry took contests in Germany and South Africa. Although losing on points to Gert Van Heerden in South Africa, Gerry made such a good impression that he was offered four further contests there. Following his close points loss to Van Heerden Gerry remarked humbly that he had, "never believed in disputing a decision – you have to accept these things as all part of the game." Respected journalist Piet Lourens meanwhile said of Gerry's performance, "I consider Gerry to be among the best of British boxers to come to South Africa" whilst even Van Heerden himself paid tribute to Gerry when he confessed, "I have never been hit so hard." Gerry later revealed to *Boxing News* that he had injured his hand again when he landed a right to Van Heerden's head in the fifth round. It was later examined in a local hospital.

Further disappointment was in store for Gerry however, when it was announced that Bristol's Stan Cullis, whom Gerry had already beaten the previous year, had been chosen to fight Calderwood for the title. Calderwood KO'd Cullis in the fourth round at the National Sporting Club in February 1962. In an attempt to get back on the title trail Gerry went to Bristol the following November but was beaten by Cullis on points over ten rounds. Gerry had fought so well – he had broken the Bristol man's' nose as early as the second round – that even the local fight fans showed their displeasure when the decision was announced. Gerry immediately issued a challenge for a return with a £500 side-stake but it was never accepted.

Just three days after Christmas 1962 Gerry lost on points over ten rounds to Stockholm's Lennart Risberg - in Orebro, Sweden, and although still ranked highly, he had only one more fight after this. In February 1963 he accepted, "a substitute job against Ron Redrup *[Gerry was ranked No. 2, Redrup No. 3 at the time eds.]* and I got my eye cut in the seventh round. I lost interest after this defeat and I never boxed again."

Upon retiring Gerry carved out a career as a successful businessman in Camberley, but he also retained an interest in the sport by training heavyweight Les Stevens. Stevens would later win the Southern Area heavyweight title. Although he remained in Southern England, Gerry kept up his membership of the MFBA and paid periodic visits to his friends here.

He became Chairman of the Slough Ex-Boxers' Association (EBA) and Vice-President of the Reading EBA. Remembered affectionately by his friends and colleagues at the MFBA, as well as being one of the top light-heavyweights in Britain for many years, he also acted as a sparring partner to Chic Calderwood, Terry Downes and Alex Buxton amongst others. It makes you think what he could have achieved with two good hands!

Born in 1915, Danny (Mack) McGowan had no amateur experience when he turned professional in 1934, but this didn't stop him from amassing almost 100 pro contests over the next ten years and developing into one of the toughest fighters of his generation. Danny, who also boxed under the name 'Danny Boy Smith' feared no-one, meeting featherweights, welterweights and even middleweights during his career. He rarely turned down a contest and his never-say-die attitude ensured he became a firm favourite wherever he appeared. He passed away in 1984 aged 69 years.

DANNY (MACK) McGOWAN

Rushed to Leeds by US Military Police for one fight - but still lost!

Danny Mack had his first professional contest in February 1934 when he was 19 years of age. He had been spotted in a street fight with a much bigger boy by local manager Wally Evans OBE. Wally saw instantly that young Danny was giving his opponent all the trouble he could handle and after the scrap he immediately suggested that Danny come along to the gym he ran in a cellar in Penrhyn Street off Scotland Road. Out of curiosity Danny went along and was immediately hooked on the sport. He reckoned it was a good way of keeping fit and of course of earning some extra money in the hard economic climate of the 1930s.

Danny's first contest was a losing one however, as he was stopped in two rounds by 'Jocker' Johnson at Bebington in February 1934. Danny wasn't deterred however, and he returned to the town in October to challenge Teddy Jones. The game youngster was beaten again however, although this time he managed to go the full six rounds. Another six round points defeat followed two weeks later in Liverpool, but this was an improvement of sorts as Danny's opponent was 'Jocker' Johnson, the man who had stopped him inside six minutes on his pro debut.

Next Danny travelled to Wigan where he gained a creditable draw against Widnes' capable Bert Chambers. Three losses and two draws from his next five contests meant that by September 1936 Danny had yet to win in two years as a professional, albeit he had had only nine contests due to work commitments. This changed soon after however, when he was matched with Mick Howard at the Liverpool Stadium.

Although it was an obvious step up in class, Danny wasn't overawed and he was declared a points winner after six rounds. Howard demanded a rematch and a fortnight later the two met again with Danny forcing Howard to retire in the fourth.

Danny was beginning to get himself a regular following at the Stadium. The crowd knew that he would probably never become a champion but they also knew that whenever he appeared the Liverpool man would give his best, never take a backward step and, more often than not, would still be there at the final bell, no matter who the opponent. This spirit was exemplified in December 1936 when, after travelling to London for a few contests, Danny was matched with an up-and-coming lightweight by the name of Boy Boone – believed to be none other than Eric Boon. Danny lost on points over four rounds but had impressed many by his tremendous courage and application and it was no surprise that he soon found himself in demand as a sparring partner for the more accomplished fighters of his generation.

He was engaged by world Champion Freddie Miller in the early 1930s, when Miller had a string of contests in Britain, most notably his two victories over Nel Tarleton for the world featherweight title. He was also employed by Ernie Roderick when the talented Liverpool welterweight was preparing to meet Henry Armstrong in 1939. No doubt Roderick's backers saw Danny's non-stop style as perfect preparation for 'Homicide Hank'.

When Danny travelled to London to meet Boon he did so alone, and on arrival he had to pay one of the local seconds 10 shillings to bandage his hands for the contest. Sharing a dressing room that evening was legendary Welsh heavyweight Tommy Farr, and when Danny returned Farr is alleged to have told Danny that he had won the contest and that he should demand a return. A second contest never came off however.

When not fighting Danny earned his living working as a docker. In June 1939 Danny was working on an American ship when he was told he had been engaged to meet the vastly experienced Nottingham featherweight George Marsden that same night. Marsden had had over 280 contests in his career to date. The only problem however, was that the contest was scheduled for Leeds. Danny had no means of getting there in time but he managed to make it thanks to some US Military Policemen who were keen boxing fans. They drove Danny all the way to Leeds in a jeep – but their kind gesture was in vain however, as they saw their new friend lose on points over ten rounds.

One particular fight Danny was always keen to discuss was his August 1942 bout against the more than capable Warren Kendall at the Liverpool Stadium. Danny decked Kendall nine times over the course of their ten round contest but somehow still managed to lose on points! He would later state that the referee in that fight had officiated in three previous contests and that the decision had always gone against him. This reverse however, was a rare set-back for Danny, especially over the longer fight distances. His first 12-rounder was against Perry Skitts in Morecambe in September 1938, a contest Danny won easily enough. A week later he lost over eight rounds at Liverpool Stadium, but a fortnight after this he beat Johnny Chadwick also over eight at the Stadium.

Danny was having his best winning sequence and three wins followed, all of which showed his willingness to fight anywhere at anytime;- a ten round points win over Jimmy Dempsey in Morecambe on November 17; an eight rounds points win over Bill Robins at Blackpool a week later; and just three days after this Danny travelled to Newcastle to beat local man Norman Demmy over 12.

Although difficult to compile it is believed Danny had around 66 contests during his 11-year career, with more losses (34) than victories (25). Magnanimous in defeat however, Danny always said that the results of his contests often meant little to him. He simply turned up, gave his best, took his money and went home again. He just loved to fight and as long as he felt that he had given the audience value for their money then he was happy. He was more than just a journeyman however, and he was good enough to beat the likes of Warren Kendall, Johnny Fox, Billy Barton and he managed to take both Eric Boon and Ronnie James the distance.

On one occasion Danny was working at Aintree racecourse replacing the fences when a loose horse jumped the fence and landed on him. Danny suffered a broken arm and leg, and was unconscious for eight hours in intensive care. The horse in question was Pearlish Gold and after leaving hospital Danny went to see the trainer to discuss claims for compensation. He was given short thrift by the trainer however, who exclaimed that Danny should be giving him compensation as the horse never raced again! How times have changed.

Despite never really being interested in boxing for titles as an amateur, Stockbridge Village's Joey Moffat enjoyed a successful unpaid career with Cantril Farm ABC, then Tuebrook, and finally Kirkby, before turning pro with the former Welsh world title challenger Colin Jones in 1990. A popular, aggressive box-fighter wherever he appeared, Joey lost his pro debut but won his next nine, before retiring in 1993, when he was on the verge of an eliminating contest for the Commonwealth title, to concentrate on his trade as a publican. This article was compiled through interviews with Joey in 2007.

JOEY MOFFAT

Debut 'loss' robbed Joey of unbeaten record

Joey Moffat first became interested in boxing when he was 10 years of age. Although like many former fighters, there was a family connection behind his reason to take up the sport, "my brother John had boxed a bit, as had my Dad, Billy, when he was in the Army," Joey acknowledges that the main reason he took up boxing was because, "it was something to do. There was nothing going on for kids in the area at the time and I just went out of interest."

A fire at the gym used by Cantril Farm ABC forced Joey to move to firstly Tuebrook, and then Kirkby ABC, where he sparred regularly with Gary Ryder and Paul Hodkinson. "My cousin Freddie Joyce boxed for Kirkby at the time and he said that if I went he would pick me up and drop me off and so on, as it was a far way from my home." Despite Freddie's assurances however, Joey soon had to sort out his own transport. "I think I saw him once at the gym and after that I never saw him there again!"

Altogether Joey had around 28 amateur fights, losing only a handful. He remembers training with a North West Counties team prior to a match against Canada. "After training we would have something to eat and then play a game of 5-a side football to burn our meal off. The team was mainly made up of Liverpool and Manchester lads and that was how the teams were usually split – Liverpool v Manchester. You can imagine what happened next. Even though we had the likes of Andy Holligan, Gary Thornhill and Nigel Wenton, both sets of lads would be kicking lumps out of one another. Then we would all calm down and go and spar! Both Gary Thornhill and I boxed at similar weights at the time and after our fights against the Canadians I couldn't believe how lucky he had been in his match-up. The lad he boxed was pretty poor and Gary won easily, but the lad I boxed was like Sugar Ray Leonard! He kept talking to me as we were fighting, saying things like, 'That's not the way to do it man! Is that all you've got man? Come on, give me more!' and so on. He really wound me up!"

Despite this fine amateur record Joey admits that at the time he, "wasn't really in the amateurs for the titles," and he turned pro with former world title challenger Colin Jones in 1990. "I thought I may as well get paid for fighting. It was only after Colin had asked Billy Aird what I was like, and Billy replied that he thought I could have won the ABA title that year, that I thought I maybe should have stayed amateur a bit longer."

Joey's pro debut was a six rounds points loss to Swansea's David Jenkins, in Bristol in March 1990. "This was a terrible decision," says Joey, "I was well robbed." It was to be a full 18 months before he boxed again, this time forcing Manchester's Paul Hughes to retire on his stool after four rounds. "This was probably the best I ever boxed. Everything felt right. I decked Paul a few times and each time I kept talking to him, telling him to get up and carry on. I was really fired up for it. After the fight I remember Andy Holligan coming into the dressing room afterwards and saying that my performance had reminded him of himself!

A fortnight later Sheffield's Kevin Lowe was outpointed over six rounds on the Andy Holligan – Steve Larrimore Commonwealth light-welterweight title bill at Liverpool's Central hall. A return two months later saw the same result. Two third round stoppages in the next three months were followed by an eight round stoppage over Birmingham prospect Scott Doyle in May 1992. Four months later Doncaster lightweight Carl Tilley was outpointed over six rounds. This contest, on the Andy Holligan – Tony Ekubia, British and Commonwealth light-welterweight title show at Everton Park, is a particularly memorable one for Joey.

"As an amateur I had never really struggled with my weight. In fact I probably could have made super-feather with a bit of effort. For some reason however, the pros were different and I started to have to work a bit to make the weight. A few days before the Tilley fight I was a few pounds over. It was the same the day before and I panicked a bit, taking a few laxatives instead of just one. I made the weight but was constantly having to go to the toilet, even on the night of the fight. I had to walk past the opponent's dressing room to get to the toilet at Everton Park and after the third or fourth time I could see him looking at me strangely. I thought to myself, 'this lad thinks my bottle's gone!'

"Staring at your opponent while the referee gives you instructions in the ring had never been my way of doing things and this fight was no different. I just stood there looking down at the floor, as usual, but when the referee asked us to touch gloves I held my hands out and Tilley brought his down on top of mine - hard and fast. I looked back at Colin Moorcroft in my corner and he could see I was angry. He managed to calm me down a bit but I came out all guns blazing and managed to deck Tilley in the first round. I tried to stop him early, and probably could have done if it wasn't for the problems I'd had before the fight. By the end of the third round I was completely drained although I managed to hold on to the end to take the decision. This was my hardest fight physically.

"In the dressing room afterwards a young lad came to see me to tell me that the crowd had threw 'nobbins' in after the fight and he asked what he should do with the money he'd collected. I could hardly lift my head up I was that tired. I turned to look at him and could see he only had a £1 coin! I told him he could keep it! I was still going the toilet days later!"

In a little over two years Joey had built up a fine record of seven wins from eight contests and was making steady headway up the British rankings. A nine-month lay-off followed however, before his next contest against Birmingham's Norman Dhalie at the Devonshire Hotel. "I was looking to get back into proper shape with this fight," recalls Joey, "and give the game a real good go. I was hoping for an easy work-out, nothing too difficult, but when Dhalie caught me with a big right hand in the first that cut and near decked me – it later needed five stitches – I remember going back to the corner and saying, 'Where did you get this fella from?' I thought they'd got me Naseem Hamed, throwing big shots from all angles." Joey survived his unconventional opponent however, to force a stoppage in round four.

Three months later Joey had what turned out to be his final contest in the paid ranks, a six rounds points win over Doncaster's durable and vastly experienced Dean Bramhald. "I was down to fight Tony Foster for the Central Area title. I think I would have beaten him as well. It was also going to be an eliminator for the Commonwealth title but Foster was injured two weeks before the fight was due to take place and pulled out. No substitute could be found and, having just started in the pub game - I had the Deysbrook then - I realised that I didn't really need the money anymore so I decided to pack it in.

Joey Moffat c. 1992   *Source: Joey Moffat*

"I missed it a bit at the time but time seemed to go past so fast and before I knew it, it was too late to comeback. Saying that however, I did think seriously about it a few times. Even when I was 36 I could still make lightweight easy enough."

Despite his all-action style, and his draining win over Tilley, Joey found sparring more difficult than the actual fights. "I sparred with some good lads and they were always tough. I remember sparring with Andy Holligan for his fight with Larrimore. He caught me behind the ear with a really good shot. It hurt at the time but even though sparring made it worse, especially around my jaw and face, I thought I would get over it. In the end however, it got so bad that I went to the hospital thinking that I'd somehow broke my jaw but they said there was nothing wrong with me. After I beat Kevin Lowe on the same bill however, it swelled up really bad. It looked like I'd had a stroke after the fight – my mouth was all lopsided. It turned out that I'd damaged nerves in my face and that was why it hurt and looked so bad.

"Another time I was sparring with Peter Harris for his European title fight against Paul Hodkinson He was a lovely person. A real gentleman. I had never really liked headguards and although Peter was wearing one I chose not to, even though his trainers were worried I might catch him with my head and cut him. I assured them I wouldn't however, and Peter seemed OK with it, but then what do you know, we come together and I catch him with my head and cut his nose! His trainers all screamed and jumped in to have a look. It was really embarrassing and I was so apologetic it was unreal. Peter was great though. He just said it was one of those things."

When asked about boxing today, Joey reckons that is still a tough sport in which to succeed, but that, "it isn't as hard as in my day. Head-guards give a false sense of security in my opinion, and this makes some boxers take more headshots than is probably necessary."

Still living and working in Liverpool, Joey has been married to Tracy for 24 years and they have three children. "Natalie is 24 and has recently given us a grand-daughter, Joei; Jennifer is 21; Gary, who boxes for the Rotunda, is 19 and Jordan is 17."

It was perhaps inevitable that Birkenhead-born Tommy Molloy would take up boxing as a career, for his brother was former fighter and Liverpool Stadium favourite Jimmy Molloy. Jimmy, featured in the first volume of The Mersey Fighters, boxed all over the world during his 13-year career (1939-52) mainly due to his time with the Merchant Navy, but was ever popular at Liverpool Stadium. Although highly rated, Jimmy never got the title chance his skill and efforts deserved, but his younger brother Tommy did, winning the British welterweight title in 1958 by defeating London's Jimmy Newman at the old Streatham Ice Rink. In an eight-year career (1955-63), Tommy won 34 of 43 contests, with six losses, two draws and one no-contest. Now 73, Tommy currently lives in the Wirral and is ever welcome at the MFBA monthly meetings.

TOMMY MOLLOY

32-fight unbeaten streak took Tommy straight to British title

Such was Tommy Molloy's desire and determination to make it as a boxer that his first amateur contest, for the old St. Francis ABC when he was nine years old, took place just a year after he caught pneumonia. For a while Tommy was even placed on the danger list, but he managed to pull through and he stayed with the club for ten years – right up until his call-up for National Service. For a while the club was captained by Johnny Best jnr., and amongst other members over the years were such Liverpool fighters as Bernie Pugh and Steve Walsh. Tommy always said that his time with St. Francis' was one of the happiest periods of his life and he thoroughly enjoyed his amateur career.

Although Tommy spent much of his National Service in Germany with the Queen's Bays, his boxing talents were not overlooked. Whilst in the Army he won the BAOR, Army and ISBA championships, losing only 11 out of 110 bouts. The two bouts which gave him the greatest pleasure however, were his two victories over Nicky Gargano – the 1954, 1955 and 1956 ABA welterweight champion. "One was in the Army trials and the other in the semi-final of the 1953 ABAs at light-welter,"remembers Tommy. Gargano also boxed for the Army, and was one of Britain's top amateurs at the time. The Elton Manor man represented his country on numerous occasions and won Commonwealth Gold in 1954, a Bronze in the 1956 Olympics and a European amateur title in 1955, so Tommy's victories were outstanding achievements. Despite his 1953 ABA semi-final win however, Tommy didn't win the title that year, eventually losing out to Cardiff's D. Hughes. At the same championships Liverpool's Frank Hope lost in the welterweight final.

Tommy had carried his elder brother's bag to fights when he was younger, and he continued this level of mutual respect when he turned professional in 1955 by naming Jimmy as his manager and trainer. Indeed, Tommy even wore Jimmy's old protector for some fights. Tommy's pro debut was a six rounds points win over Leeds lightweight Johnny Delmore at Liverpool Stadium in February 1955.

Tommy Molloy with Lonsdale Belt c. 1958   *Source: Jim Jenkinson*

166

Whilst Jimmy's undoubted experience and advice was an enormous help to Tommy, it did have its setbacks, for the rules of the sport at the time stated that no blood relation of the first degree could assist in a fighter's corner. Nowadays of course this rule has been relaxed, but during Tommy's early career it meant that in certain contests the one man whom he trusted more than anyone else was prevented from doing so. However, what advice Jimmy imparted to his younger brother must have been heeded, for Tommy went on a winning streak that would take him straight to the British title.

A fantastic 31-fight unbeaten start to his career saw Tommy rise from the No. 9 British welterweight in 1955 (Birkenhead's Wally Thom was the champion), to No. 3 in 1956 (Peter Waterman champion), and then No. 1 challenger to Waterman by 1957. Waterman retired undefeated as champion in 1957 and Tommy was paired with Walthamstow's Jimmy Newman – ranked No. 2 – to contest the vacant title at Streatham Ice Rink in July 1958.

Tommy had already met Newman in the ring twice before. He had stopped him at Harringay in October 1956, before drawing their second contest at Earls Court in March the following year. Contemporary accounts thought both Tommy and Newman were not at their best in their title fight, but this mattered little to Tommy who won comfortably on points over 15 rounds. Although a wide margin winner, the victory was hard earned and the capacity crowd at the old venue gave both boxers a standing ovation for the final three rounds. It was Tommy's 32nd consecutive victory. Amazingly he had yet to taste defeat as a pro.

Tommy defended the title just twice in two years, the first a sensational victory over London's Albert Carroll at the Stadium in October 1959 that is still recalled by old-timers today. The Londoner appeared to be cruising to an easy points win until Tommy finally managed to land one on target in the twelfth round. Carroll took a count of eight before getting back to his feet. Tommy caught him again for another eight count however, and in no position to defend himself the referee rightly called a halt and the home crowd, some of whom had been preparing to leave before Tommy's sensational finish, went home ecstatic. It is still regarded as one of the most exciting finishes to a contest Merseyside has ever seen as for much of the fight a Molloy victory had seemed remote.

Four months later Tommy took his title to Nottingham to defend it against the notoriously difficult to hit local favourite Wally Swift. Tommy tried in vain to get inside Swift's legendary defence but was repeatedly caught with the straight left and he duly lost on points. A further three contests followed but Tommy never challenged for a title again and he retired in 1963 with a fine record of 34 wins from 43 contests; two draws, six losses and one no-contest – a July 1957 meeting with Dundee's Jimmy Croll that saw referee Fred Hampton stop the contest after warning both boxers for persistent mauling, holding and not breaking! He also met the likes of Roy Baird, Syd Greb, Leo Molloy, Paul King, Hippolyte Anex and Johnny Melfah.

Tommy currently lives in retirement on the Wirral side of the Mersey and, health permitting, occasionally visits his friends in both the Merseyside and Wirral Former Boxers' Associations.

Born in Liverpool in November 1971, Kirkby's Alex Moon grew up watching local hero Paul Hodkinson progress from Kirkby ABC to world champion and enjoyed a successful amateur career with the club himself. He followed this with an outstanding professional career, the highlight being his reign as Commonwealth super-featherweight champion 2001 - 2002. Alex retired in 2003 after meeting the likes of Jonjo Irwin, Charles Shepherd, Affif Djelti, Dean Pithie and Phillip N'dou. Still living and working in Kirkby, this article was compiled through interviews with Alex in 2006.

ALEX MOON

Followed clubmate 'Hoko' to boxing glory

Former Kirkby ABC boxer Paul Hodkinson turned pro in 1986 and went on to win the British, European and WBC featherweight titles with Irish promoter Barney Eastwood An early defence of 'Hoko's' British title took place at Kirkby Sports Centre in December 1988. In the audience that evening was a young Alex Moon, then an up-and-coming amateur with the same club. "I went to see 'Hoko' and got hooked," recalls Alex. "The rest is history."

"My uncle Billy Moon, had boxed for the Army and I believe he was very good. He didn't continue when he came out however, so I don't think I followed anyone into the sport in that respect. If anyone attracted me to boxing it was Paul Hodkinson – he was the big thing in Kirkby at the time. "I had always been very sporty. I was good at football and was in and out of a few teams, but I remember going to Kirkby ABC for the first time mainly because of 'Hoko'. Everyone was saying he was going to be the next Barry McGuigan, and they weren't wrong!"

As an amateur with the Kirkby club Alex won a multi-nations bronze at Liverpool in 1995, boxed for Young England and made a winning appearance representing the ABA v Ulster in Portstewart in June 1993. Not everything went as smoothly as this however. "I remember winning my first three bouts but then losing my next nine - although most were majority decisions. I was only 17 at the time and I did get a bit disheartened. In fact I came close to packing it all in." To the delight of Mersey fight fans however, Alex continued and went on to win around 50 out of 70 amateur contests. A career in the pro ranks beckoned for Alex and he signed for local promoter John Hyland in 1995 when he was 23.

His debut was a solid third round stoppage of Birmingham's Marty Chestnut at Everton Park Sports Centre in September 1995. Chestnut had previously lost to other local fighters Paul Lloyd and John Sillo. Just like the start of his amateur career however, Alex's fortunes soon changed and in his next contest – a little over two months later, he was forced to retire in the second round against Alfreton's Godfrey Goddard in Chester. Undeterred however, the Kirkby man then went on a run of 12 contests undefeated (two draws, one against the ever awkward Welshman Miguel Matthews) culminating in a 12 rounds points win in October 1998 over Khayelethu Booi for the vacant WBU inter-continental featherweight title at St Georges Hall.

With just one defeat from 14 contests, Alex was climbing high in the British rankings and was soon named as challenger to the much more experienced Doncaster fighter (John) Jonjo Irwin. Irwin had already won, then lost, both the British and Commonwealth featherweight titles and in his previous contest had scored a classy points win over the talented Esham Pickering. He had also met the likes of Michael Armstrong, Colin McMillan and Paul Ingle – all top rated fighters - so it was a tough proposition for Alex and despite putting everything into their February 1999 meeting at Newcastle the Kirkby boxer was adjudged the loser after 12 hard rounds.

Three wins out of four contests followed before Alex met reigning Commonwealth champion Charles Shepherd in Glasgow in March 2001. Out of all his 27 pro fights Alex reckons this was his hardest. "I had just signed with Scottish promoter Tommy Gilmour. One day he rang my trainer John Smith, and asked him how fit I was. I was ticking over in the gym and John replied that I was reasonably fit and looking forward to my next fight. Tommy then asked if I fancied meeting Charlie Shepherd for the Commonwealth title – the following week! Chances like that don't come around often in boxing so there was no way I was going to turn it down." Just like his meeting with Jonjo Irwin however, Alex knew he was going to have to be at his very best if he wanted to wrestle the crown from the tough Burnley man.

"Charlie was built like a mini Mike Tyson and it seemed as if he was just as strong. I tried not to get into a war with him – to keep him on the outside. 'Jab! Jab!', John kept telling me, but by the eighth round I was just too tired and the fight became a bit of a brawl. I remember the bell going at the end of the 11th round and I walked back to Shepherd's corner convinced that it was mine – I even wondered why Charlie was walking back with me! How I got through the 12th I don't know! All I kept thinking was, 'Keep moving your head. Keep moving your head!' When the bell finally went I was so relieved to have got through the last round never mind the entire contest, that I forgot all about the decision for a few seconds, but then the referee came over and raised my arm. I can't describe how I felt – the years of training, everything I'd sacrificed…it all seemed worth it. It was just brilliant!"

Alex followed this victory up with two successful defenses before losing narrowly on points to Dean Pithey in Coventry in July 2002. He decided to retire not long after. Despite his achievements however, Alex does have some regrets. "I honestly think that I didn't achieve as much as I could have in the professional game. It was a great achievement and honour to be Commonwealth champion, but I should definitely have won more titles. I sparred regularly with British, European and world champions and I always held my own. Indeed, I often got the better of them in the gym.

"When I fought for the IBO world title *[October 2001 v Frenchman Affif Djelti in Manchester eds.]* I was convinced I was going to win. I'd never been put down in my career and all he had was a solid left hook. Throughout my training John Smith kept telling me to keep my right hand up, 'Protect your chin' he would say. However, I'd think to myself, 'He's not going to knock me out. No way!' Then what happens in the fight? I throw a right hand to the body and he catches me with a left hook to the head. I had never been hit so hard. I remember sitting on the canvas thinking to myself, 'How did I get here?' If there is one thing I'd love to do it's to go back to that night and have the fight over again."

This loss should be taken in context however, for Djelti was no mug himself. The Frenchman had turned pro at 30 years of age in 1996 but had been mixing it with top class super-feathers and lightweights for some time. He had lost to Colin Dunne in a world title fight in 1998 and had already beaten Charles Shepherd (TKO 6 February 2000) and Dean Pithie (KO 6 October 2000) before beating Alex. He would later go on to hold the European super-feather crown before losing it to the talented Boris Sinitsin.

With Liverpool currently the centre of excellence as far as English amateur boxing is concerned, and the sport itself now paying boxers to stay amateur and hopefully decline offers to turn professional, Alex is philosophical when comparing his generation with today's stars. "When I boxed as an amateur I got very little financial help. Even when you boxed for England and had to travel to Crystal Palace to train you weren't guaranteed expenses.

"Saying that though, I think it's great that amateurs who represent their country today are receiving the financial help they do. If I had received the same package when I was an amateur then I probably wouldn't have turned pro. That's not to say I don't think it's any easier to succeed in the sport now than it was in my day. The truth is you get what you put into it. Boxing has always been tough! The top boxers are so dedicated – it doesn't matter if they are boxing today or ten years ago.

"My training programme for a fight was eight weeks. Wake up at six in the morning and go for a five or six mile run. Then back to bed. Then the gym for 12 o'clock. Get home about 3pm and try to relax. Have your evening meal about 5pm then maybe go for a walk about 8pm, making sure you're in bed for no later than 10 o'clock. That's it. Day in day out – for eight weeks!" With a training regime that tough it's no wonder Alex isn't keen to start his career over, although he does admit, "I definitely miss the buzz of getting in the ring."

The monetary reward that professional boxing can offer is another aspect of the sport that intrigues Alex. "When you look at what today's footballers are paid, for the training they do – it just doesn't compare. Money for boxers has improved over the years with TV money and so on, but in my opinion it's still not enough. We put our lives on the line every time we enter the ring and although the elite few can earn a lot of money, sometimes millions, more could certainly be provided for the majority."

Although the buzz of entering the ring may be something Alex would like to re-live, this modest professional is keen to acknowledge the support he received from family, friends and fans over the years. "The Liverpool fight fans were unbelievable. They got right behind you. I loved boxing in Liverpool, especially at Everton Park Sports Centre. Out of 17 amateur fights there I only lost two, and I never lost a fight there as a professional. I remember my first year in the ABAs and walking out to hear the crowd shouting my name. All my friends and family had come to see me. The hairs on the back of my neck stood up - it was very emotional."

Now retired from the sport he graced with such commitment Alex has one final message for anyone who may look up to him as he once did with 'Hoko'. In order to succeed in the hardest sport in the world Alex's message is simple; "You've got to put your heart and soul into it and not switch off for a second."

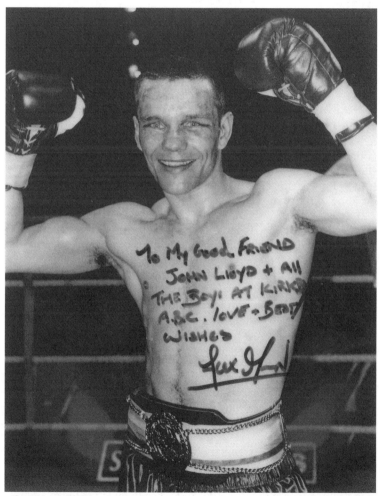

Alex Moon c. 1998   *Source: John Lloyd*

A throwback to the days when men turned pro with no amateur experience whatsoever, cruiserweight Tony Moran's dedication and perseverance overcome a debut loss, work commitments and sceptical boxing commentators to fight for Area, British, Commonwealth and world titles. In his near six-year career Tony won 14 of 20 fights, meeting the likes of Matthew Ellis, Mark Hobson, Paul Bonson and Gyorgy Hidvegi. The most recent boxer in 'The Mersey Fighters 2' to retire, Tony still lives and works in Liverpool and this article was obtained through interviews with him in 2007.

TONY MORAN

Belief took Tony to world title shot

At the age of 13 Tony Moran got involved in martial arts, namely freestyle karate and, "by the age of 14 had won my first national title. Wanting a new challenge I went along to Everton Red Triangle boxing club a year later and found that I was also pretty good in a boxing ring." Tony trained at the boxing club for a few months before deciding to return to martial arts.

Tony started work at 16 and, "doing what most teenagers do at that age, drink and partying, that was the end of my serious training for about a year." At 20 however, Tony decided to start training again. "I took up my martial arts training again and won national and international titles in freestyle karate. I then decided to get in the teaching side of things when I was about 25." It was during this second stint in martial arts though that Tony got a real bug for boxing. "A friend and boxing trainer by the name of Dave Ash (Huyton ABC) started to take me on the pads. He told me from my first pad session that I had a future in boxing if I wanted it and tried to convince me to start training as an amateur. I was working shifts at the time however, running community martial arts classes and working three nights as security on nightclubs, trying to save for a house with my now wife, Adelle and I just didn't have the time."

With such a hectic life, training of any description was put to one side and it was a full two years before Tony's frustration at his inactivity resurfaced. "I went to see Dave again, and another friend named Ray who was a trainer at the Rotunda, and asked them to get me fit enough as a boxer so I could go and put myself forward to pro-trainers and see if they would consider taking me on. After a couple of months I felt confident enough to put myself forward for spars/training sessions in pro gyms to see if I had what it took and, knowing the name of just one pro-manager in Liverpool at the time, I decided to visit his office to see if he would give me an opportunity."

After finding local promoter John Hyland's office in the Moat House Hotel, "I knocked and found a room full of people all turning to see who had just walked in, with John sitting behind his desk. Every face is looking at me as if to say what do you want? So I just asked, 'Is there any way you would consider giving me a try out as a pro.'Now I'm not saying the people in the room openly laughed at me, but I could definitely notice the mild expression of humour on many faces. To his credit, John remained businesslike, but put the obvious questions to me like who was I and what had I done as an amateur? After explaining myself, John was good enough to arrange a training session for me with Colin Moorcroft and after this session Colin advised that I go and get myself an amateur career first.

"I thought about this and although it was a good idea, I was now 27. I have a lot of respect for amateur boxing but I wanted a taste of the real thing before I was too old. The challenge excited me, and as I am the type of person who doesn't like to think of future regret, for my dreams and ability not to be put to the test, I was determined, even though I knew only the very basics, to give it a go. Several months later I got my chance when a friend was working with John Smith and told him about my desire to be given at least a chance of showing my raw talent to a prospective trainer. John invited me down to Stockbridge Village ABC for a workout and I impressed him enough with my fitness and basic boxing for him to arrange aba proper test - a sparring session with heavyweight pro Darren Chubbs at Kirkby ABC.

"I was only 13st with no amateur experience and Darren had been a decent amateur, so when he, either because it was his way or he was simply following instructions, was pummelling me on the ropes, my first thought was, 'Tony, what the hell have you got yourself into?' My next thought however, was, 'You better prove yourself or go home,' and that I did, going on to give a very good account of myself. With John having seen enough to give me a chance, I embarked on a near six-year career that would not only see me fight for an Area, British, Commonwealth and world title, but also put me on the verge of a breakdown with the stress I put myself through."

Having been thrown in at the deep end, Tony trained hard for four months before going to the BBB of C to convince them he had what it took to be a professional. John Smith then linked him up with Tommy Miller, a manager who, "unbeknown to me at the time I signed, was basically a manager of journeymen." Although Tony had great respect and admiration for these men, "it was a route I was unwilling to go down as in my mind I was going to be a champion."

A few months later, Tony's first fight was arranged in Gateshead - a six x two minute bout against local prospect Shaun Bowes. "We had a real good tear up and, although he got the decision, he came off a lot worse than me in the looks department! He even followed me into the shower room, his face covered in blood and bandages, to ask me who I thought had won. I told him he did, because that's what the referee had said!"

Miller offered Tony a fight nearly every week after that but the game Liverpool man kept turning them down. "I was fit enough because I never missed a days training, but I wasn't prepared to be a journeyman, so told him I wanted notice in order to train and prepare properly. As he was at the mercy of bigger managers however, this wasn't something Tommy was able to offer. I wrote him a letter explaining that I was never going to be a journeyman and no matter if anyone thought I had ideas above my station, I would rather walk away than be treated as cannon fodder. Good enough, Tommy gave me my contract back and I then wrote to another manager, Tommy Gilmour, and convinced him to give me a chance."

Tony had to wait almost seven months for his second pro contest however, and although never away from the gym, it was a frustrating experience. "It got even more more frustrating when I was beaten fair and square by Paul Bonson, one of the toughest journeymen around. This was my first fight for Gilmour and I had wanted to prove myself to him but was taken to school really by Bonson." Four months later Tony was matched with Southern prospect Graham Nolan. "Everything came together that night. I gave the lad such a boxing lesson and beating that he never boxed again. His manager, Jim Evans, even called me a 'ringer' as he thought I was too good for a supposed novice!"

Five more wins followed for Tony in 2002, with another four victories in 2003. In October Tony was offered his biggest fight to date. "I was on a roll when they offered me a fight with Blackpool's Matthew Ellis, a man I had seen on TV a few times. He was promoted by John Hyland and billed as the next great British heavyweight hope. To me this all seemed like destiny and, although I was going against my own rules by taking a fight on a few days notice, I knew I had to take chances like this when they came up. Ellis was a nice man but he definitely had a high opinion of himself, as did his entourage, so they were probably all shocked when I blitzed him inside four rounds, making his transition to cruiserweight a painful one. He was also managed by Jim Evans and again Jim thought he wasn't being told something about my record."

This victory earned Tony a top ten domestic ranking for the first time (No. 6) and British and Commonwealth champion Mark Hobson duly selected Tony for his next defence in Huddersfield. "I couldn't believe that after only two years of real boxing experience - the first year being somewhat wasted as well - that I was going to be fighting live on Sky Sports for two major titles. I was really buzzing and gave myself a full six weeks to prepare." The 'buzz' lasted just two weeks for Tony however, and then, "reality kicked in."

"I firmly believe that had the fight been after my first two weeks of training then my chances of winning would have improved massively. I could have run through walls with how fit and strong I felt, but then it all went horribly wrong. Come the middle of my third weeks training I was exhausted. A wreck. I didn't feel ill, it was just that I had no energy whatsoever. I was useless in the gym. With hindsight it is easy to understand why, but at the time it was soul destroying because I felt my dream was slipping away from me."

Ordered by trainer John Smith to take a week off and see how things were when he came back, Tony rested. "Although I was much better than I had been before the rest, I was still nowhere near as good as I felt in the first two weeks. I still couldn't manage more than a modest workout the first few days but by about half-way through week five I was able to start putting the work in again and had a good last week. John and I spoke about pulling out, but I knew I was going to fight no matter what. John wanted me to fight as well but we both knew that there was no way I was fit enough to go 12 rounds."

Tony needn't have worried about lasting the distance however, as the fight itself was all over inside nine minutes. What a three rounds it was though - good enough to be named the sixth best domestic fight of the year by *Boxing News*. "Jim Watt made me a happy man with his commentary that night because he knew from what he said that I was there to either win by KO or be KO'd myself out." Unfortunately for Tony it was the latter. "Near the end of round three I was totally depleted physically and even though I had just had Hobson going about 30 seconds before hand I didn't have a drop left in the tank to capitalise and he caught me. I earned his respect that night however, and I was there to support him a couple of months later when he defended his titles in the same place beating Lee Swaby.

Although Tony received many plaudits for such a brave performance, any hopes he had that it would boost his career were sadly misplaced. I was naïve to believe that my performance against Hobson would help me. In fact the opposite happened, no-one wanted to take me on and it was 14 months before I fought again." Although two wins and a defeat followed in 2005 for Tony, including a fourth round stoppage loss to Rotherham's Neil Dawson in Altrincham that saw both boxers down a total of six times, he was left kicking his heels in the gym for a further five months waiting for another fight.

"I was then offered a fight in Paris against the number one ranked contender for the WBA and WBC titles, Valery Brudov. At the time he had had something like 30 fights and 30 KOs and it was just an eight rounder, a warm-up really, as he was due to fight Virgil Hill for the title. The call came through just three days prior to the fight date and I said yes straight away. I was fit and knew I had nothing to lose. I started getting excited, telling all my mates, but I was then told they were going with someone else because, as Jim Evans told me, I seemed too keen. Because of this they knew I must have been willing to have a go when all that they really wanted was a body to work out on."

A four rounder in December, on an empty show in Liverpool, thrown together for Sky at a weeks notice, was all Tony had in the rest of the year. In February 2006 however, just as he was preparing for a six round contest in March, Tony was asked if he fancied a week's sparring with Enzo Maccarinelli in Swansea. "I jumped at the chance and spent a great week sparring with a great champion and meeting a great bunch of very hospitable people. After getting home I had about four weeks left to train for the six rounder and coming into the last week of what had been a good build up I got a call that was unbelievable. I was being asked to fill in, at late notice, to fight for the WBF world title against Hungary's Gyorgy Hidvegi."

So excited was he at the news, that Tony, "ran a 12 miler that night instead of my usual six!" John Smith began to plan Tony's workouts for the next five days to ensure he was ready to go the 12 round championship distance. By Thursday afternoon however, Tony was brought back down to earth, "because the people backing my opponent, putting the money up for the fight, didn't want me as the opponent and said they were looking elsewhere. I was back to the six rounder, as planned, until Friday came and I was told the world title fight could be back on but I'd have to wait until Monday to find out for sure."

Although Tony was meant to be off work for the next two days he remained in the gym, "testing myself in spars and on the pads with 12 round workouts. I was feeling good." A call from Matchroom organiser John Wishausen on the Monday telling Tony, "they were sorry for me being messed about but they simply did not want their boy to have to fight me," seemed to have scuppered his title chances. Eventually however, "John told them it would be me or no-one whether they were putting the money up or not."

In the days leading up to the fight Tony had a lot of thinking to do. "My wife was due to give birth to our first child and here I was taking a world title fight with just four days notice. Although I knew I was fit enough, I also knew the wife and my family would think I was mad and would only be worrying. I therefore made the only choice I could under the circumstances and told no-one other than a few trusted friends who I was sure would not tell anyone else. I was worried my wife would suffer stress at a time she really didn't need it and I didn't need to be worried about her worrying about me. So I set my plan in action, I told my wife I was going away to train for a day but because it was a couple of hours away I would not be finishing until late so may as well stay the night. I then rang the local newspaper and asked them not to print anything in case my wife or family heard about it and they agreed.

"So off I go on the Thursday morning to Scotland with John and two close friends and by the afternoon I am there weighing in for my chance to become a world champion, albeit a WBF champion but a world champion all the same. I am a great believer in fate and thought that the gods really were in my corner. I was going up to Scotland for one thing only; to win and return home the next day as a world champion to surprise everyone."

It wasn't to be however, as Tony suffered a knock-down in the seventh round. "I got up on unsteady legs and instead of holding like a pro, tried to fight back like a novice and took another eight count, the referee waving it off. It's the only fight I have regretted because up until then, win or lose I had always given my all, either to the point of excellence or the point of exhaustion. That night however, I just threw it away and I'm still not sure why. There may be any number of reasons but the fact is I just didn't perform to the best of my ability and

Tony Moran (right) and Enzo Maccarinelli, February 2006
Source: Tony Moran

the best of my ability would have been more than enough to beat my opponent. It's frustrating when you know that and don't take the action necessary to realise it."

Tony arrived home at 3am to wake his wife and, "tell her two bits of bad news, one is I'd lied to her and the other was that I'd lost out on a world title. She was great about it though, gave me a kiss and a hug and went back to sleep." Although obviously depressed at losing his world title fight, events over the next few weeks put things into perspective for Tony. "A 33-year old best friend of my wife died suddenly and my daughter, Amelie, was born. I thought shame on me for giving my feelings over what amounts to very little in the big scheme of things, so much importance.

"Being a father is truly the greatest gift in the world and puts anything else in the shade and it's with that feeling that I embarked on becoming the best dad I could be. For nearly a year I never give boxing much thought until a call came to fight for the Area title in February 2007. I shouldn't have taken it really. I had already decided boxing no longer had a place in my life, not because I still didn't want to compete but because to find a spare four hours a day to train properly for a fight would be four hours spent away from my beautiful daughter. I eventually took the fight however, gave it my all, and although it looked like it was all over in my favour in the first three rounds I then tired before I could take advantage."

Although he lost in the seventh round to Manchester's Chris P Bacon, Tony remained philosophical in defeat. "I was happy in everything but the win as again I had given it everything. That is the thing I am most proud of in my career. Those who know me best and what I'm about as a person know I always gave it everything I had in trying to achieve my goal."

Looking back on his career today, Tony says that he drew strength from all those that doubted his ability and belief. "Everyone, from my close family and friends to my own trainer, believed I was only entering into boxing for a bit of an experience. After losing my first two fights, although it was with goodwill and good intentions, I knew I was being humoured when I stuck to my belief in what I believed was still possible. Those already established in the game, trainers, managers and boxers, thought I was a dreamer and in their minds I was good for one thing and that was as a game sparring partner to assist with their rise to the top. A couple of these hard hitting heavyweights who turned pro at the same time as me and had all the perks of sponsorship and promoters appreciated my tenacity in being there whenever the need for sparring arose, but I know that in their minds and the minds of those around them, it was them headed for titles not me. For all this apparent certainty however, they never came as close as I did.

"I have no ill feeling over these words or thoughts however, because, with hindsight, how could they think any different of my chances, when I had no history to prove otherwise. For me, all that mattered was knowing that I had given it my best shot. I entered into boxing so as not to have to live with the regret of never having tried it and then, when my career became a reality, I trained, sacrificed and fought so as not to have to live with any regret in my later years of what might have been."

Tony admits however, that such belief and dedication did have its drawbacks. "Many times I questioned my common sense about what I was doing. Often, every part of me was pleading to just give up what, at times, seemed like a pathetic attempt at a dream. I pushed myself to exhaustion not because I could not handle the training of a fulltime professional boxer, but because I was committing the time and effort of such whilst also working 40/50-hour weeks as a shift worker in the homeless service. One of these jobs alone can be draining, add to it a couple of nights per week as a martial arts instructor and two or three working security on clubs and you have a recipe for burnout.

"My schedule over the years was exhausting to say the least. Nights were by far the worse in terms of how I felt - both physically and mentally, but they also afforded me the best opportunity to train for fights as I worked a 12-hour shift from 8pm till 8am. John only trained his fighters of a morning anyway, so day shifts were out. My schedule coming up to fights would therefore consist of me swapping as many shifts as possible with colleagues so I could get on nights.

"I would then work all night, sleep for nearly two hours in the staff room, wake up feeling awful and then race to the gym session which started at 10am. I would then have a punishing workout for two hours or so, go home and sleep from about 1pm till 6pm, get up and then run for a few miles before starting my shift again at 8pm. I did this in cycles of four nights per week and then my other commitments took over for the rest of the week.

"As anyone who does shift work will tell you, nights can be tough, they leave you feeling spaced and pretty low both mentally and physically. I can see now that my work schedule and my training schedule was harming me. My dream to succeed was like an addiction however, and even though I knew I wasn't doing myself any good I just couldn't stop myself."

Tony admits that the hardest times were when he was not getting fights. "I would go to the gym to spar after a night shift and would suffer the consequences of having no sleep combined with getting punched around a ring by an equally fit and determined man who had more than likely had a good nights rest and had the good fortune of being a fulltime fighter.

"Apart from the catastrophic events in life, day to day hardship cannot get much worse than a 'no sleep then a punch in the head' combination. It really is gruesome and these times had a seriously negative affect on my mental state. Not only because the overall effect could be draining, but also because there was nothing good coming out of all the pain and sacrifice. I was well aware that because of my slow reactions I was taking far too many punches to the head. At times it seemed like all I was doing was suffering for weeks or months on end - for nothing. Apart from the obvious impact on myself, my personal relationships were also suffering and I was really quite unhappy most of the time."

To emphasise the sacrifices he made in order to fulfil his dream, Tony is keen to describe the build-ups he had to some of his major fights. "The fight I took with Ellis, which gave me the opportunity for my crack at Hobson, came at just three days notice and I was working right up until the day before the fight. For my fight with Hobson I worked and trained to the regime I described earlier, working constant nights for six weeks up until the Monday of the week of the fight.

"By contrast, Hobson took nearly all of the same time off work to prepare fulltime. The six round training regime that I had been doing up until that point was, literally, doubled overnight. That was the reason my first two weeks were wonderful and the rest was so bad. My body was shocked and simply shut down until I gave it some rest.

"My fight with Dawson came after a forced layoff of 14 months followed by having three fights in as many months. This doesn't seem a lot, but training at a fight preparation level for nearly three months and working more or less constantly does have an effect, and although I knew I was not right for that fight and hinted at pulling out, I let myself be talked into it. In order to fulfil my desire to train with Maccarinelli for a week I worked a night shift on the Sunday, left work on Monday morning straight after the shift and drove for five hours to Swansea before climbing in the ring for six rounds of sparring. Being the only sparring partner willing to stay the agreed course, I then sparred everyday until the Friday.

"After our last spar on the Friday afternoon, I simply climbed back in my car and drove home for 5 hours before starting another night shift." If such a schedule doesn't seem bad enough, Tony admits he fought twice on shows in Liverpool, "before getting changed and heading straight for a night shift in the homeless hostel where I work."

With such an interesting story, it's no wonder Tony has mixed thoughts when looking back on his career. "Sometimes I think I was stupid to even think of doing what I did, but sometimes I also feel that it was the most life affirming thing I could have done. In many ways it's just too early to tell. My boxing career is not long over and although I am a stronger person because of it, I don't know if I truly loved the sport as some do, or was just flirting with my own romanticism of what I hoped I could achieve."

Tony is keen to express his thanks to all those that followed him and believed in him during his career. "Thanks to John Smith, Dave Ash who pushed me into the sport and Christopher Duff, my biggest supporter, the lads at Allerton Injury Clinic, Mark Quinn and the coaches at Stockbridge Village ABA." Tony currently lives in the Woolton area of Liverpool with wife Adelle and young daughter Amelie.

The Mersey Fighters 2

One of Britain's top flyweights in the 1920s, Birkenhead's Billy Morris made his debut at the old Liverpool Stadium in Pudsey Street, and went on to have around 200 contests, meeting most of the best fighters in the division. He had countless 10 and 15-round fights, and faced the likes of Elky Clark and Kid Socks in his near ten-year career. This chapter is based on an article written by Frank Johnson that was first published in 1973.

BILLY MORRIS

Top Birkenhead flyweight from yesteryear

Born at the turn of the century when people could still remember seeing the great bare-knuckle battlers of the 1890s, and the flyweight division had not even been formed, Birkenhead's Billy Morris made his debut in 1916 and went on to secure a place near the top of the domestic flyweight ratings, meeting the likes of Elky Clark, Young Johnny Brown and Kid Socks along the way.

As a youngster, Billy attended St. Mary's School and the Birkenhead Higher Elementary School in Conway Street. While furthering his scholastic career, he also had a before school job in a fish shop in Chester Street from 8am to 8.45am and all day Saturday, for which he received 1/- and a cod's head. The job went however, when the shop boss asked Billy to clean the windows and he refused. The boss then decided to do the job himself but fell through a window, at which point he vented his feelings on the luckless Billy and immediately fired him.

In 1916 Billy got a job at Cammell Lairds as a handling lad with the riveters and it was at this time that he first took a real interest in boxing at the Shaftesbury Boys Club in Thomas Street under the wing of George Carter. Billy had a talent for boxing which soon became apparent, and he moved on to Joe Nolan's gym at the Haymarket and after six months training he signed under Joe's management.

Billy's career was under way with a second round KO over Young Fleetwood at the famous Pudsey Street Stadium in Liverpool, a contest for which he received 30/- in purse money. With his career successfully launched Billy chalked up several more impressive six-round wins. He soon moved up to ten-rounders where one of his most impressive wins was over the rugged Billy Hampton of Dowlais, South Wales. Billy received £4 for this July 1920 win, with the great British heavyweight

185

Frank Moody also appearing on the bill at Pudsey Street. The Liverpool crowd took all-action Billy to their hearts and his fierce punching, especially his perfectly timed right hooks, sent many a tough prospect to the canvas, most notably the normally hard as nails Wattie Williams.

The Birkenhead scrapper was moving up the scale gradually and he was only narrowly outpointed over 15 cracking rounds by Cardiff's highly rated Frank Kestrel at Pudsey Street Stadium for a £12 purse. This contest sparked off a three fight series against Kestrel, and over the same distance at the NSC, London, Billy got the nod. In their third meeting at the Ulster Hall, Belfast, they drew in a real humdinger of a contest. Billy also enjoyed a three-fight series with Bethnal Green's talented bantamweight George Stockings, who boxed under the name 'Kid Socks'. Billy lost two and won one of his fights against the Londoner, who fought for the British title in 1926.

Near the top of the flyweight tree in those halcyon days of the ring was the legendary Scotsman Elky Clark from Glasgow. Billy met Clark in Glasgow in August 1923 losing by KO in the eleventh of a scheduled 15. These of course were the days of 20 round championship fights! In a return at the NSC some six months later, Billy held his own before succumbing to Clark's power in the eighth round. Two fights later Clark would win the British title vacated by none other than Jimmy Wilde, and as well as defending it successfully on numerous occasions, once against Kid Socks, he would later go on to win the European crown as well as challenge Fidel LaBarba for the world title.

Billy also dropped a hotly disputed points decision to Jimmy Wilde's chief sparring partner Johnny Jones at the NSC. Before a return fight could be made however, Jones was tragically killed in a pit disaster. He was also forced to retire against Plymouth's top flyweight Frankie Ash. Ash had a win over Bugler Harry Lake when they met in May 1921 at Plymouth and would go on to defeat Bushy Graham and Dom Volante, as well as challenge Pancho Villa for the world title in the United States in 1924, so Billy's retirement was certainly no disgrace.

One of the most exciting British fighters of the 1990s, light-welterweight Jimmy 'Shea' Neary boxed for the old Imperial ABC as a teenager before, after a spell in the Army, joining the Golden Gloves. It was at the famous Dingle club that Jimmy, who in honour of his father would box professionally under the name Shea, met George Scholfield for the first time and the two continue to enjoy a highly successful relationship. A tough, hard-hitting, two-fisted fighter straight out of the old school, Shea won 23 out of 25 pro contests (16 KOs), winning the WBU light-welterweight title of the world in the process, and in his eight-year career met the likes of Hugh Forde, Terry Southerland, Darryl Tyson, Jeremiah Malinga, Andy Holligan, Eamonn Magee and Micky Ward. Still living and working in Liverpool, where he has opened up a pro gym with George Scholfield in Old Swan, this article was obtained through interviews with Jimmy in 2006/07.

JIMMY 'SHEA' NEARY

World title for hard-hitting 'Shamrock Express'

By his own admission, James Patrick Neary, had little interest in boxing as a youngster, instead preferring to spend his time playing football. "All the way through school football was my sport. I'm a mad Evertonian and my Dad used to take me to all the games. I had a no. 10 shirt as Duncan McKenzie was my idol at the time." It was only when Jimmy reached the age of 14 that he began to take an interest in boxing. "I was playing football for fun but I began to be *told* to play it and it started to become a task rather than something I enjoyed. We moved house and I started to mix with different kids and it was then that I first started going to the gym and I quickly found that I enjoyed boxing - the training and the discipline required. I used to watch the big fights, Ali and Conteh, as a kid - my Dad used to watch them, but I was never going to be a boxer, it was always a footballer. But that all changed once I became interested in boxing."

Jimmy took up boxing at the old Imperial ABC under the guidance of Tony Silvano. He was a quick learner and a dedicated trainer but Tony Silvano detected something more. "Jimmy was always asking questions. Why do you shift your weight this way when slipping or throwing a punch, and so on. So I'd show him. He'd practice and practice. He'd make mistakes yes, but he'd keep at it until he got it right."

Despite his family's Irish ancestry, and after having only a handful of amateur contests for the Imperial, Jimmy joined the Army in 1985 when he was 18. With unemployment high in Liverpool during that time, it was more a job than a career but Jimmy is keen to stress that, "I enjoyed the time I had in the Army. The comradeship you got with the lads and the discipline involved." The Army were more than keen to maintain Jimmy's interest in the sport and given every encouragement to continue his boxing career, he did so with a vengeance, having four contests in four days, "All first round stoppages!" for the King's Regiment to win an Army Novices Competition.

On leaving the Army Jimmy joined the Golden Gloves ABC, where he teamed up with George Scholfield. George remembers Jimmy as being, "raw but very determined. He took some punches but he was very strong, very hard and had a big heart. That's what got him through because he was stopping lads bigger and heavier than himself." George sparred with Jimmy and remembers him as not only being extremely fit and strong after his military service, but also with a tendency to stand with his guard too wide - a habit George quickly corrected. "I sparred with him myself and put him on his knees with a great body shot. Right under his high guard. He didn't do it again!"

Although he had been good enough to fight his way to the local finals of the ABA Championships previously, Jimmy had never been successful in winning an ABA title. "I got beat by the same lad twice, Lee Rimmer. He was too classy for me at the time. A good boxer." After winning 10 out of 13 contests for the Gloves however, the pursuit of amateur honours was forgotten when he turned professional with local manager Brendan Devine in 1992. "My Dad had died in 1989 and when I turned pro a few years later I decided to call myself Shea. His name was Seamus but everyone, family and friends, called him Shea."

Shea trained with George Scholfield above the Claremont pub but soon moved to the famous Everton Red Triangle gym. His pro debut was as spectacular as they come - a first round stoppage win over Wolverhampton's former martial arts expert and black belt, Simon Ford at Everton Park Sports Centre in September 1992. A stiff jab put Ford on the floor near the end of the round, and two further visits to the canvas, courtesy of Shea's devastating left-hook, were enough for the referee to wave it off just as the bell sounded.

Three further victories in the year, two of which also came early, marked Shea out as an exciting prospect. His all-action style of fighting endeared him to the Liverpool fight crowds and, entering the ring Tyson style in plain black shorts and boots, Shea quickly became a TV producers favourite. His six rounds points win over Barnsley's future British welterweight champion Chris Saunders in December was his first fight shown on TV. With Saunders having previously met the likes of Billy Schwer and Ross Hale, many thought Shea was over-matched but he won unanimously on points over six rounds. The exposure this gave him made the national boxing press sit up and take notice of the latest fighting sensation to emerge from Liverpool.

George Scholfield then took Shea to work with legendary local trainer Charles Atkinson snr., the man who had guided Kirkby's John Conteh to world title glory in the 1970s. After Conteh left Liverpool to go to London, Mr Atkinson had avoided local fighters but the renowned coach responded to boxers who were dedicated trainers - and Shea was certainly one of those. Jimmy remembers that, "Mr A wouldn't take no slacking. He'd say, 'If you don't want to do it - there's the door.'" A first round KO over Newport's Vaughan Carnegie in February 1993 was followed by a fine six rounds points win over experienced fellow Liverpudlian John Smith. With six wins from six, Shea had enjoyed a fantastic start to his pro career but it would get even better however, as an explosive run of 10 stoppage victories from 10 contests propelled him to the verge of a world title shot.

Amongst these wins were a sixth round retirement victory over Birmingham's talented and former Commonwealth super-featherweight champion Hugh Forde, a stunning second round KO over Sheffield's Nigel Bradley that won Shea the Central Area title, and a heart-stopping second round KO over slick Cincinnati welterweight Terry Southerland, "the hardest fight I'd had up until that point." MC for the contest was the famous American Jimmy Lennon jnr., and Shea later admitted that it was a tremendous feeling to hear Lennon introduce 'The Shamrock Express' in his unique style. 'I thought to myself - I've made it here!"

Enjoyment soon turned to horror however. After a good right hand by Southerland in the second round of their February 1996 contest at Everton Park, Shea was on the verge of being stopped due to the resultant cut over his left eye. "The referee, Mr Green, stopped the bout and took me to the corner, telling them to clean it up. He looked at it and said, 'Because it's you Shea I'm going to give you until the end of the round.' I thought I was going to get beaten for the first time but

189

George just said, 'Go out and do him Jim.' And that's what I did. From then on I just tried to catch him with a big shot. I think my Dad was looking down on me that night." Within seconds a massive overhand right sent not only Southerland to the canvas and through the ropes but also Shea's supporters delirious. More importantly however, the watching TV executives were more than interested and, with few domestic managers willing to match their men with Shea - even for national honours - the search was on for a suitable opponent and belt for his next contest.

In October 1996, under the guidance of John Hyland, Shea's new promotional team matched him with Washington's Darryl Tyson for the vacant WBU version of the world light-welterweight title at Everton Park. With just nine losses from 57 contests, Tyson had been a decent contender at lightweight for a few years, losing on points in two previous bids for the IBF and WBC crowns. A fighter who was coming off a KO defeat to none other than Oscar de la Hoya was certainly a step-up in class for Shea but, despite hurting his hand early on, his constant pressure gradually told and he won unanimously on all the judges scorecards to claim the vacant title. "When they raised my hand at the end I thought I'd made my mark in life." With Charles Atkinson snr. terminally ill and unable to attend the contest however, an emotional Shea took his newly acquired world championship belt to his hospital bed for him to admire the very next morning. Mr Atkinson passed away soon after.

Charles' son Mike Atkinson and former fighter Judas Clottey now took over the reins. Shea beat South Africa's Jeremiah Malinga in March 1997, and then came one of the most exciting contests ever witnessed on Merseyside. In his early days as a pro Shea had often sparred with Liverpool favourite Andy Holligan - a former British and Commonwealth light-welterweight champion and a man who had challenged the great Julio Cesar Chavez for the WBC light-welterweight title in 1993.

A contest between these two local battlers was a fight that all of Liverpool wanted to see but the question was, where to hold it. Since the sad demolition of the former Liverpool Stadium, the city had been deprived of a suitable arena for staging battles such as this. Everton Park was too small for the 5,000 or so fans that the promoters expected, so they came up with the idea of erecting a huge marquee in Stanley Park. Everything pointed to an exciting and unique boxing event - the fans and watching millions on ITV weren't to be disappointed and on 12 March 1998, the 'nark in the park' was on! Shea has admitted that he used to be nervous before a fight, especially in his early career, but by the time of this contest he had managed to put such thoughts to the back of his mind. "I used to be nervous, thinking 'Why am I here?' and stuff like that, but by now it was different. It was more like, this is what it's all about, lets get out there and do it."

Shea acknowledges that this was his hardest fight as a pro, not only due to what was at stake, but also due to the pressure he inevitably experienced in the build-up. "This was my hardest fight because it was all about pressure. As soon as the fight was announced the pressure began. It seemed to be that everywhere I looked, in every paper or on the radio, the TV, people were talking about the fight. It only got worse the nearer we got. It was a big local derby and a lot of pride was at stake. It was also a lot of pressure for me because of who I was fighting. Andy was a hell of a boxer, hard and tough, and I respected him a lot as a person and a fighter. It was a tough fight."

Amidst a cauldron of noise, both men went at each other from the first bell, neither taking a backward step. Shea dropped Holligan onto one knee for a count of eight in the sixth round courtesy of a cracking left-hook, right uppercut combination. On rising, a barrage of blows pinned the former champion to the ropes and, with 2.42 of the round gone, referee Darry Ribbink stepped in to wave it over.

Four months later Shea was matched with tall, awkward South African Naas Scheepers. "He'd never been stopped," says Shea. "He was a tall, fast, awkward southpaw. I knew, despite people telling me that I'd knock him out, that it would be a tough fight." Shea's misgivings were well founded and, in one of the fights of the year, he finally wore the South African down to claim a unanimous points win. The magnificent setting of Liverpool's St. Georges Hall was the scene for Shea's next defence of his title against another man who had never been stopped, Argentina's Juan Carlos Villarreal. Another tough fight saw Shea declared the winner on points - after the ring had collapsed prior to the fight! A fourth round stoppage win over Cleveland's Mike Griffith followed in Dublin in June 1999, Shea's only fight of the year, before he was matched with America's Micky Ward on the undercard of Prince Naseem Hamed's WBO featherweight title defence in March 2000 against Vuyani Bungu at London's Olympia.

Ward had been a solid pro for 15 years and, despite losing nine out of 43 contests at the time, was ranked high with all the governing bodies. He had fought for the IBF light-welterweight title in 1997, losing to Vince Phillips, and had also met the likes of Reggie Green and Zab Judah. Ward was a tough test for Shea and the Liverpool man admits he was the toughest man he faced. "Although the Holligan fight was my hardest fight, the toughest man I met was definitely Micky Ward. I couldn't believe how hard he hit nor how much punishment he could

Shea Neary c. 1998   *Source: Terry Churchill*

take." After another classic non-stop encounter, Shea was stopped with just five seconds remaining of the eighth round. Ward of course, who later said that his greatest accomplishment in boxing was coming to the UK and beating Shea, would go on to have three legendary bouts with another light-welterweight warrior, Arturo Gatti.

Obviously disappointed at his first loss as a pro, Shea returned with a solid 10 rounds points win over Northampton's Alan Bosworth four months later. He was then matched for the Commonwealth title with Belfast's tough Eamonn Magee at Belfast's Waterfront Hall. Despite appearing to many at ringside, boxing commentators and writers, to have won however, Shea was declared the loser after 12 rounds. "I thought I'd won this well. The plan was not to go out all guns blazing, but to take my time and win on points - something I thought I'd done. I wasn't even breathing hard at the end." Despite some reports after the fight stating that the referee had come under pressure to secure a 'home' win from local underworld figures, Shea realised, "that it was as good a time as any to get out and so I did."

Although a challenge to WBU champion Ricky Hatton in 2001 never materialised, Shea kept fit and active by training at wrestling but returned to boxing by opening a pro gym in Old Swan with his long-time friend and trainer George Scholfield. If any of Shea's aspiring pros have just half the success he had in his career, "it's still a tough sport," then Liverpool fight fans can look forward to even more good times ahead, especially as Shea's son, James Metcalfe is a promising amateur with the Salisbury ABC.

Proud possessor of a cauliflower left ear and victor of over 300 of his 340 fights, Bob Nelson is firmly established as one of the greatest boxers that Birkenhead has ever known. Although born in Belfast, Bob's family moved to the Wirral town when he was young and it was here that he first became interested in boxing. Making his debut in 1929 when he was just 17, Bob was the only 'Merseysider' to have tasted victory against Ernie Roderick. This chapter is based on an article written by Frank Johnson that was first published in 1973.

BOB NELSON

First fight earned him just 7d.

Born in Belfast in 1912, Bob Nelson was only a youngster when his family moved to Birkenhead. He attended Brassey Street School while living in Myrtle Street, off Saxon Street, with his father, mother, three sisters and a brother. He first became interested in boxing when he was 14 years old when he attended Alex Powell's gym in Watson Street. Here, the local heroes were Charlie Tonner, Larry Bonner, Billy Fletcher and the trainer was Billy Bland. Keen to get into the action, Bob asked Powell if he could spar with him and, after putting his mentor on the canvas, he was quickly told that he had all that was needed to fight his way to stardom.

Always a fitness fanatic, Bob never shirked the hard grind of training and he was always willing to learn the tricks of the trade from the leading fighters of his day. He would travel all over Merseyside to train and spar with the likes of the legendary Ike Bradley, Nel Tarleton, Ginger Foran and Tommy Bailey.

At this time, Frank Davies was promoting boxing regularly at Hoylake Central Hall and one night, after watching Billy Fletcher drop a close decision to Albert Harvey, Bob asked to appear on the next bill. He made his debut in a six rounder against fellow townsman Billy McKay winning courtesy of a fourth round KO - his purse a princely 10 /-. Out of this bonanza Bob had to pay 5/- for his license, 4/- to his seconds and, from his remaining shilling, five pence for his train fare home!

Despite the low monetary gain, Bob was determined to succeed but the hard facts of the fight game were driven home in his second contest at Southport's Kew Gardens when he dropped a 12 rounds point verdict to local man Len Mott. Bob conceded just over a stone to the tough Jewish middleweight, but he remembers receiving £7.10s for his troubles - with entrance to the open-air venue costing 11/6d including the boxing and a tour of the gardens.

The start of the 1930s heralded hard times in Britain but, as unemployment in the main cities rose, boxing thrived. Bob boxed regularly for Frank Davies and bowled over Larry Bonner and KO'd Albert Harvey (Ellesmere Port) in two rounds. In 1929, at the age of 17, Bob went to work for a Hoylake butcher and was fortunate to come under the wing of keen boxing fan and shop manager, Mr. Robinson, who did all he could to foster Bob's interest in boxing.

Eager for success and plenty of work Bob, now managed by Ike Bradley, remembers a great win over British welterweight contender, Tommy Taylor of Liverpool. Bob boxed Taylor seven times in total at Hoylake and at the Birkenhead Drill Hall - winning three times and forcing four draws over the 12 and 15 rounds course. He also had a six fight series against George Boyce (Birkenhead), out-pointing him four times, stopping him in four rounds at the Vittoria Street Stadium and beating him at the Empress Ballroom, Wigan for Harry 'Kid' Furness.

Bob boxed regularly, indeed it wasn't uncommon for the Birkenhead man to have five fights a week. Most of these were over 15 rounds, giving him a potential tally of 75 rounds every seven days! Once he even boxed six times in a week with Johnny Best, Harry 'Kid' Furness and Frank Davies the promoters concerned and all achieved after a hard day's work at the butcher's shop in Hoylake.

By 1931, Ernie Roderick was emerging as a serious contender for national honours and, as he was considered a tough opponent, it was only natural that Bob's name would be linked with the Liverpool welterweight. The pair met at the Birkenhead Drill Hall with Bob gaining a merited ten rounds points win after a terrific scrap - the only 'Merseysider' to defeat Roderick. Bob said that, whilst Ernie was certainly clever, he felt that he could have beaten him anytime due to his skillful counter-punching.

The cornerstone of Bob's success was his willingness to learn and he toured all of the Merseyside gyms to seek out knowledge and experience. He sparred many rounds with the great Nel Tarleton and remains convinced that 'Nella' was the greatest boxer he had ever seen. Prior to meeting Roderick, Bob trained with Tarleton and Dom Volante, and he felt that this was the launching pad for his ultimate success. After beating Roderick, telegrams poured in with Continental agent Nick Cavalli offering Bob a three-fight European trip but Bob's father stepped in to put the blocks on the proposal as he thought the money insufficient.

At Billy Metcalfe's gym in Liverpool at this time were Tommy Bailey, Harold Higginson, Tommy Rose and a host of others. All helped to perfect Bob's natural left-hand ability and in particular, his lethal left hooking. Bob's association with Tarleton blossomed and as the great featherweight soared to world title standard, Bob appeared on many of the same bills including the world title fight at Anfield against Freddie Miller and also when Tarleton boxed Al Brown. For these fights, Bob was paid a pound a round but he didn't complain as he was displaying his ability before huge crowds, who liked his style and speedy punching.

Regular fights kept Bob in top class trim and he beat Frank Davey twice and KO'd Albert Johnson in two rounds at Manchester. Johnson was the brother of the famous black fighter Len Johnson who later ran a successful boxing booth. Bob also KO'd Pat Murphy in three rounds at Hoylake, beat Jack Daley in London and put the skids under the rated Jimmy Walker.

One of the highlights of Bob's career was his 12 round fight against the Liverpool 'Iron Man' Jimmy Stewart who had a third round stoppage victory over world title contender Jack 'Kid' Berg. Bob met Stewart at Hoylake and lost narrowly on points, although he had the rare distinction of putting Stewart down for a count of seven early on. After the fight, Stewart told Bob that he would never have knocked him out, even if he had had a hammer in each glove. Stewart refused to box Bob again but they later trained together at Ted Denvir's gym in Aigburth with Ginger Foran. Reflecting on his scrap with Stewart, Bob remembered being hit harder than at any other time of his career. Although he refused to go down after taking a terrific right to the jaw, he remembers he, "saw stars and about seven Jimmy Stewarts!" Upon reaching his corner, trainer Charlie Whiteman poured champagne over Bob to revive him.

Bob boxed and defeated Paddy Bennett seven times. After six points wins, their last fight was stopped in the last round with Bennett in bad shape. Bennett had the reputation of being one of the hardest men in the game. Bob also dropped a points decision to his friend Eric

Harkness from West Kirby *[featured in the first Mersey Fighters eds.]* and also lost to Northern Area welterweight champion Tommy Marren, who had in his corner at Liverpool Stadium, Nel and George Tarleton. Another of Bob's rare defeats was a 10 round points loss to Cock Moffitt, the all-action Liverpool puncher. This verdict had the crowd in uproar with the referee, Dave Richards, being suspended for six months after the outcry. Such was the power and accuracy of Bob's counter-punching that after the fight the Liverpool man, who had been down twice for long counts, was rushed to hospital for immediate facial repairs.

In 1936 Bob won the Jem Mace Belt Tournament at Morecambe with the five-fight series spanning three months. He won the belt, some glory but little money for this feat, and then had to return the belt to the organisers. One of the most avoided fighters of the day was the Rotherham tearaway 'Butcher' Gascoyne. Never one to refuse a challenge however, Bob met Gascoyne at the Winter Gardens, Morecambe and, after a terrific scrap, dropped a close points decision. In a return at the same venue not long after, their fight was declared a draw although Bob recalled that Gascoyne was the only man to ever really hurt him with his body shots.

On a Dom Volante bill, Bob defeated Tommy Niblett (Birkenhead), and he also boxed in Belfast for Jim Rice in 1937, when he out pointed the local hero, Billy O'Connelly. He also boxed the late Bob Foster in the all-Wirral ten stone competition at Hoylake Central Hall. Both of them boxed Congleton men in the semi-finals, with Foster scoring a second round KO and Bob gaining an eight rounds points verdict. In the final later that same evening, Foster beat Bob over ten rounds. With the purse money being £10 to the winner and £5 to the loser, Bob had been forced to box 18 rounds in the one night for his earnings. Bob also beat Charlie Smith twice, his skillful countering upsetting Charlie's big-hitting. They had been schoolmates at Brassey Street.

As the memories flooded back, Bob remembered many of his opponents, declaring that Ernie Roderick was the cleverest man he ever fought. He gave the toughest accolade equally to 'Butcher' Gascoyne and Paddy Bennett, and had no hesitation in awarding Jimmy Stewart the 'hardest hitter' medal. Bob reckoned that Jimmy hit with the power of many a heavyweight - with either glove.

Bob sported just the one sign of his chosen profession - a cauliflower ear from one of his greatest ever fights; a 15 rounder at the Kelvin Hall, Glasgow, against tough Scottish welterweight champion, Jack McCall. Later, while under treatment for the injury however, Bob tore his bandages off and travelled to Bolton to hand out an eight round hiding to the rugged miner, Tommy Foster.

Bob admits that his ring earnings were never great, with £75 his top reward when he dropped a fifteen rounds points verdict to the polished Canadian champion, Paul Schaffer in London. He received a similar amount when being narrowly out pointed by British welterweight champion, Dave McCleave over 15 rounds. A brilliant left hand paved the way for most of Bob's successes but he could also bang a bit, and when Eddie Shuck came to St. Laurence's School, Birkenhead, with a tremendous run of 21 consecutive KOs, the crowds flocked to see if Bob would be number 22. The reverse happened however, with Bob decking Shuck for the full count in the second round with a powerful left hook.

A credit to boxing Bob had no regrets over his chosen career. Although never one to decry the modern boxer, he always insisted that his era, "was the golden age for boxing." Bob was a member of both the Wirral Ex-Boxers Association and the MFBA right up until his death some years ago.

The son of an Olympic Gold medal winner, Con O'Kelly followed his father into the boxing ring with great success. From humble beginnings in the rings of Hull, Con graduated to the bigger boxing halls of Liverpool Stadium, Newcastle's St James Hall and then to London's National Sporting Club and even New York's Madison Square Garden! His last contest took place at Anfield in 1938 on the undercard of the Peter Kane v Benny Lynch drawn contest and he retired with a very creditable 51 wins from 74 professional contests. He then famously joined the priesthood and became a popular figure around the streets of Birkenhead where he was parish priest of Our Lady's Church (Immaculate Conception). Father Con died in September 1968 aged 61 at Nantwich Hospital and was buried near to his mother, father and sister in St Joseph's Cemetery in Cork, Ireland.

CORNELIUS (CON) O'KELLY

'Father Con' boxed at Anfield and Madison Square Garden

When you are the son of a 6' 5" wrestler who won gold at the 1908 Olympic Games in London, it perhaps comes as no surprise that you would be encouraged by your father to follow in his sporting footsteps. Con O'Kelly was born in Hull in March 1908. His father, George Cornelius O'Kelly, was a Cork man who moved to England and joined the Hull Police Force when in his twenties. A promising wrestler, he was selected for the 1908 Olympic Games in London where he duly won a Gold medal by beating Norway's Jacob Gundersen.

Upon his return to his adopted home town, George was given a grand civil reception. He continued his wrestling activities with the Hull Amateur Wrestling Club and as a result of his success he received offers to appear all over the country. After an application to his Watch Committee for leave of absence to meet the Spanish champion was turned down, George resigned from the force and became a professional wrestler. His first contest as a professional came against John Lemm, for the world heavyweight title but unfortunately he lost. He also met the legendary Russian wrestler Hackensmidt but, like many before him, he tasted defeat in this contest also.

In addition to his wrestling skills George was also a more than capable boxer and for a time he combined both sports. Indeed, he was actively participating in both when he decided to test his skills in America - taking the then two-year old Cornelius with him. This was in 1910 and, after settling in Boston, George had his first boxing contest in the USA in July the same year - beating Con Comiskey inside two rounds. He decided to concentrate on his boxing after a chance meeting with the great Bob Fitzimmons, who felt that the giant Irishman would make more money and be more successful in the USA if he retired from wrestling and became a boxer.

George was managed by former world light-heavyweight champion Tommy Ryan, who had taken Jim Jeffries to the world heavyweight title. Ryan felt that he could take the Irishman all the way to the top, and further inside the distance wins followed. After a dozen or so contests in the US George felt he had earned enough from his sojourn and, as he was also feeling homesick, he returned to England. His boxing career continued however, and he was confident enough in his own ability to challenge Bombardier Billy Wells for the British title but the contest never materialised and he retired for good in 1914.

Only 26 and the landlord of a public house in Hull, George still maintained his healthy lifestyle and duly opened a gymnasium at the rear of his house. It wasn't long before he had a number of local fighters training at his gym - the young Con amongst them. Con made his first appearance in a boxing ring in 1919 when he was 11 - in the 7st weight class at the city's Sailors' Children's home. The following year he won the 7st 12lb schoolboy title and the year after that, the 10st 8lbs schoolboy title.

Although his parents desired a professional career for their son, hopefully in the medical profession, young Con was not as academic as they would have liked and he became devoted to sport, especially boxing. He joined St Mary's ABC and learnt his boxing both here and at home under the guidance of his father. In winning the North of England amateur light-heavyweight title in 1924 when he was only 16, it was clear Con was, like his father, not only growing into a giant of a man but also developing into a more than capable boxer.

Con's achievements soon came to the notice of ABA officials and, like his father before him, he was selected for the GB boxing team for the 1924 Olympics in Paris. Unfortunately, Con was defeated in the first round of contests. Not long after this he turned professional, with his father as manager and trainer, and he stopped Ike Clarke in four rounds in his first pro contest in November 1924. He then went on a great unbeaten run - defeating Sonny Webster, Ellis Powell, Harry Moody, Gunner Bennett, Stoker Stubbs, Trevor Llewellyn, Stanley

Glen Brooks (Con's first contest at Pudsey Street Stadium) and George Hetherington. All were inside the distance stoppage victories. The first opponent to take him the distance was none other than Kid Moose of Southport - who was outpointed over 15 rounds at Hull Artillery Barracks in October 1925. The referee for this contest was none other than former world heavyweight champion Tommy Burns! That year Con had a total of 16 contests but suffered his first reverse - a 15 round points loss to Charlie Chetwynd at Hull's Madeley Street baths.

Con was becoming a popular attraction wherever he appeared and in 1925 he also fought at Newcastle's Free Trade Hall, St James Hall and the NSC in London. His all-action style, coupled with his size, appealed to the boxing public, ensuring sell-out crowds whenever his name appeared on the bill. Seven wins from 10 contests followed in 1926 with a further dozen more contests the following year - including a 10 round draw and a 15 rounds points loss to Ted Sandwina - the famous Native American heavyweight of the day, at the Royal Albert Hall.

1928 saw Con follow in his fathers footsteps once more and he set sail to try his luck in American boxing rings. A wise move considering he had 36 wins (30 by KO) in 45 contests in just over three years as a professional and if his career was to progress then America was surely the right place to improve.

Father and son travelled from Liverpool to Boston in July 1928 before moving to New York. Con's first contest in America was 5 November 1928 at the famous Madison Square Garden with Al Friedman the opponent. Billed incorrectly as the heavyweight champion of Ireland - though this unsurprisingly did not dissuade people from attending his fights - Con won on points. Two weeks later he met Jack Gagnon at the Mechanics' Building in Philadelphia and earned a ten rounds points win.

Young Con's American trip was proving both successful and profitable, with the Irish-American crowds showing their appreciation of the new heavyweight sensation. His next contest, against Boston's Jim Maloney, topped the bill at Madison Square Garden but he didn't have things all his own way. In a tremendous scrap Con suffered a cut above his right eye early in the contest but hung on to earn a creditable draw against a tough opponent. A third round stoppage victory over George Gemas in Syracuse followed before Con and Maloney were matched again -

this time at the Boston Garden, Maloney's hometown. At the end of another hard fought ten rounds Maloney was adjudged the winner - Con's first reverse for 18 months and his first since arriving in America.

An up and coming young German boxer was also active in America at this time but, despite offers, a fight between Con and future heavyweight legend Max Schmeling never materialised. In February 1929 however Con was matched with another rising star, New Jersey's Ernie Schaaf who would tragically die following a contest against Primo Carnera three years later. Con beat Schaaf on a sixth round disqualification. Two defeats followed, both ten round points reversals before Con was matched again with his old rival Jim Maloney, this time at the New York Coliseum in the Bronx. Referee Danny Sheridan stopped the contest in Maloney's favour in the third round of their April 1929 contest following a severe cut above Con's left eye.

Three losses in a row forced the 'Fighting O'Kellys' to regroup and they decided that, even though Con had lost only nine of 54 contests to date, his interests would best be served with a break from the rigours and demands of training and fighting, and they duly returned to Hull. By February the following year father and son decided to once more venture to the States and they set sail again from Liverpool bound for Boston, this time taking the rest of their family with them. On 17 June the same year Con returned to the ring with a seventh round KO of Jack Dudley in Portland, Maine. Two months later at the same venue Tiger Tom Dixon lasted just a round longer.

Con had a further 12 contests (three wins, seven losses) in the US in the next 12 months, including a points victory over Al Friedman, and a ten round points loss to King Levinsky - who would later meet Joe Louis - although this loss was disputed by fans at the Boston Arena, many of whom felt Con's persistent jab had won him the decision. Tragedy forced the O'Kellys to return home however, when Con's sister Mona died suddenly of appendicitis aged just 20. Instead of Hull however, the family moved to Ireland but soon after returned to England this time settling in Sale, Cheshire and it was here that Con decided to return to the ring in 1937 - a full five years after his last contest in the USA.

Although many ex-boxers return to the ring in search of glory and perhaps extra money, Con's motives were altogether more spiritual as he needed the money to finance religious studies he was required to complete before entering the Roman Catholic Clergy. Con proved he hadn't lost any of his power however, and he posted three wins from three contests in 1937 - two in Hull and one at the new Liverpool Stadium. Another three victories from three contests in 1938, one over Lynemouth's Harry Lister for the vacant Northern Area heavyweight title, saw Con finally hang up his gloves for good, his last contest taking place at Anfield on the undercard of the Peter Kane v Benny Lynch world flyweight title bill. This meant that Con had the unique distinction of having boxed at the old and new Liverpool Stadiums, Anfield and Madison Square Garden. Quite a feat!

Con became a popular and well respected Catholic priest at Our Lady's Church, Birkenhead. He never forgot his boxing background and was was always willing to help and advise young boxers in Birkenhead in the 1940s and 50s.

One of the best known amateur fight trainers in the business, Alex Powell received offers from all over the world to train boxers – including one from Adolf Hitler! The Birkenhead lightweight earned the title of 'Merseyside's Iron Man' and although he took part in over 350 bouts he boasted that he was never counted out. Alex still led boys through his strict training and weight-lifting regime as an amateur coach in Birkenhead when he was in his late-60s, and he passed away some years ago.

ALEX POWELL

'Iron Man' asked to train boxers - by Hitler!

Birkenhead's Alex Powell came up the hard way. When he was 12 years of age he ran his blind father's coal business, delivering fuel from 7.30am until 8.30pm. The night he sneaked away from the coal yard to see a one-man circus show at a local picture house however, changed his life completely. There, for the hard-earned 2d he had paid to get in, Alex saw a man lift a 56lb weight - with his teeth. The man claimed to be the only person in the world to perform this feat but young Alex decided to learn how to do it himself.

The first time he tried it, with a 56lb weight at his father's coal yard, he nearly broke his jaw. Alex was determined to do it however, and by practicing every day he was soon able to not only lift the weight off the ground with his teeth, but also to swing it round and throw it the full length of the yard. His father's friends often used to go and watch Alex perform the trick, and the lad then decided to take a bodybuilding course.

At 14 Alex started work in the foundry at a shipyard for four shillings a week. It was there that he caught the attention of the work bully, who used to wait for Alex and trip him up or clip his ear. The day came when he could take no more and Alex challenged the bully to a fight. The scrap started outside the works gates and continued all over the yard as policemen and works overseers broke up the crowds who had gathered to watch. They fought nine times – lasting nearly half the day – and the fight eventually ended outside the gates after they had clocked off when young Alex, both eyes puffed, and bleeding from numerous cuts, smashed his bigger opponent to the ground so that he couldn't get up without assistance. That was the last time Alex was bullied at work.

The next day Alex was introduced to a man whose brother was an amateur boxing champion, and he advised Alex to take up boxing. He went along to a local club and he immediately became fascinated with the game. He had his first fight at the age of 14, won it and received a medal for his efforts. When Alex later discovered that his prize was worth only 3d however, that was the end of his amateur career.

Club boss Joe Nolan decided that Alex was too good for the amateurs, so he turned professional. His first paid fight was at the age of 15 was against 'Kid' Levene on a bill topped by Freddie Welsh at the old Adelphi Theatre in Christian Street, Liverpool. Then a bantamweight, Alex licked Levene on points over 10 rounds to collect the winner's purse of five shillings. His dynamic punching and perfect fitness made him tough for anyone to handle, and he soon became a firm favourite at the old Pudsey Street Stadium in Liverpool. Purses in those days Alex recalled, were between 30s and £2, but he often agreed to fight for, "a purse of silver," which sometimes turned out to be no more than a couple of shillings. He was so tough that it took a good man to put Alex on the boards, and even then he was usually back on his feet in seconds ready for more.

A period of travelling with a booth, taking on all-comers, honed Alex into one of the roughest and toughest scrappers in his profession. Then came the First World War and, already in the Royal Navy Volunteer Reserve, Alex was one of the first to be called up. At a camp in Deal, near Dover, Alex teamed up with a heavyweight from his own town – Arthur Townley. The big fellow had ambitions to make a name for himself as a fighter, and he asked Alex to teach him the business. As soon as he saw Townley shape up, Alex knew the big man would make the grade.

At the battle of Gallipoli, Alex and Townley took part in some fierce hand-to-hand fighting with the enemy. Alex was shot through the head at close quarters, his right eye being cut in two by the bullet. His first thoughts were for his fight career and it was only when doctors told him that he would certainly go blind if it wasn't removed that he consented to have the eye out. On returning home, Alex found that he was a 'dead man'. He went into a local barbers shop to have his beard shaved when the barber asked, "Aren't you Alex Powell the fighter?" "That's me," replied Alex. "But you're supposed to be dead!" came the reply. Apparently Alex had been reported as having been killed in action.

With only one eye everyone in the fight game assumed that Alex had had his last fight and an announcement was even made to this effect when he was introduced from the Liverpool Stadium ring a few weeks later. One eye or not however, Alex was determined to box again. He resumed training, running halfway round Birkenhead every day for a fortnight, returning home each day, "for a hot salt bath and a glass of milk with a raw egg." The boys at the club thought he was joking but soon learnt not to disbelieve him when he floored some of them to show he wasn't messing around. Alex went to Liverpool promoter 'Pa' Taylor, who managed to get him a fight, and Alex climbed into the ring once again. He was given a 10-rounder but managed to knock his opponent out in the first round. "I didn't get a chance to see you in action properly," said Taylor, "You were too quick!" In his next fight Alex took a little longer – winning by *second* round KO!

By now Arthur Townley had also returned home and, although a heavyweight, he could often be found sparring with Alex. This of course didn't do either one of them any good, so Alex took Arthur to Nolan's gym. Townley impressed Nolan so much that he was signed up immediately. Alex concentrated on training fighters now and, as well as Wally Thom and Pat McAteer, another local star he worked with was Cock Moffat. Alex remembers that Moffat had a habit of turning to look at spectators while he was fighting so one night in training Alex had someone deliberately draw Moffat's attention from the ring. Once he turned to look however, Alex jumped into the ring and caught Moffat flush on the chin to send him to the deck! "That cured Moffat of his habit," said Alex

Despite his fighting days supposedly long behind him, Alex's last fight was at the age of 52, when he stepped in to fill a vacancy at a Birkenhead club bill. He won the 12 round points decision and then decided to call it a day. He then concentrated on running a club for amateurs, although over the years he turned down numerous offers to become a professional fight trainer. One of his strangest possessions was a signed letter from Adolf Hitler received just prior to the Second World War in which Hitler asked Alex if he was interested in going to Germany to help train, 'German Youth.' Wisely, Alex didn't even bother to reply.

Toxteth's Jimmy Price first boxed with the old York House ABC when he was 16. Despite his late start, Jimmy quickly developed into one of the country's top amateurs, winning two ABA titles, a Commonwealth Games gold medal, a top multi-nations tournament in Kenya and a host of international appearances before turning pro with Frank Warren in 1983. Despite boxing at a weight which didn't suit him, Jimmy won 17 of 19 pro bouts in a little over two years, meeting Herol Graham for the British middleweight title in the process. Forced to retire on medical advice in 1986 when a contender at light-heavyweight, Jimmy still lives and works in Liverpool. As elusive to find outside the ring as he was in it, this article was obtained following interviews with Jimmy in 2007.

JIMMY PRICE

Middleweight pro contender preferred the amateurs – where he was top class

By his own admission, Jimmy Price had a tough childhood. "With a father whose family came from Sierra Leone and a mother of Italian extraction, you can imagine the problems I had as a child. Add in the fact that they were never married and split up when I was still young, these problems only increased as I grew into a young man. I always believed that I had a purpose in life though, and that choosing boxing was something that was meant to happen to me."

"I was a late starter as far as boxing was concerned," says Jimmy, "although I'd always taken some interest in the sport as my idol at the time was Muhammad Ali. My Dad, Michael Leonard Cole, was also a good amateur in his day and had been Army champion when he was based in Germany so when a friend, Danny Duffy, asked if I wanted to go with him to the York House Boxing Club, near the Anglican Cathedral, I agreed straight away. I lived with my mother, Maureen, at the time and I boxed under her family name, Priceppi, although this had been shortened by then to Price. My grandad had had to change his name when he enrolled in the Army. As anyone who knows the history of Liverpool's Italian community will know, this was advisable for many Italian immigrants at the time.

"I was 16 when I went to 'the Yorkie' as we called it, and although Danny didn't last long I was hooked immediately and I stayed. The coach then was Eddie Stevenson. I then joined the Golden Gloves in the Dingle. George Treble, Billy Harding and a cracking fellow named Barney were the coaches there and Billy's two sons, Paul and Franny, also boxed for them, as did top heavyweight Andy Palmer, who won the ABA title in 1979. After a while I left the Gloves to join Wavertree ABC with Tony Darby. All went well until I was down to fight in a miner's village in Yorkshire.

"After travelling all the way there it turned out that Tony had forgotten my medical card. He said it was OK to use another lad's card, which I did, and I duly won. About three months later however, the ABA discovered that I had boxed under another name and they banned me. I appealed against the decision but even though I was successful, saying that I didn't know anything about the change until I was in the ring and by then I thought it was too late to do anything about it, the process dragged on for nearly a year. During this time of course I couldn't box. Because of this I never boxed for Wavertree again and I left to join the Holy Name ABC in Fazackerley with my great coach and mentor, Martin Ventre. Under Martin and the Holy Name I won two ABA titles, a multi-nations in Kenya and a Commonwealth Games gold medal."

Jimmy's first taste of the ABAs was not a happy one however, as he was a losing finalist in the West Lancs light-middleweight division in 1978, going out to future Commonwealth champion Kenny Salisbury. The following year he made the semi-finals in Belle Vue, Manchester, beating future British champion Mark Kaylor in the quarters on the way. Determined not to taste defeat so close to the finals again however, the following year saw a significant improvement. Jimmy was crowned Northern Counties light-middleweight champion before adding the ABA title by outpointing one of the rising stars of British amateur boxing at the time, Bristol's Nick Wilshire, in the final.

The victory over Wilshire was a great one for Jimmy. The Bristol boxer had won a silver medal at the world U19 championships in Yokohama in 1979; added the ABA middleweight title the same year; and just a few months before his 1980 ABA final loss to Jimmy he had come back from the European U19 championships in Rimini, Italy with a gold medal.

Despite this victory, Jimmy didn't make the 1980 Moscow Olympic boxing squad for Great Britain – the ABA opting to go with experience and send Wilshire instead. It's a decision that still rankles with Jimmy. "I beat Wilshire easily enough in the final. I boxed his head off. I expected to get picked to go to Moscow but he had been to major tournaments before and I hadn't. That was probably why he was picked ahead of me."

Perhaps to make up for this disappointment Jimmy, together with featherweight Mo Hanif, was sent to Nairobi for the American sponsored 'Alternative Olympics' later in the year. He duly justified his selection by winning a gold medal. "It was a great experience. The Yanks sent a really strong squad – Don Curry boxed there - but they were a bit arrogant and flash. Maybe that's why the Kenyans supported me against them. I felt like Ali in Zaire! They kept shouting 'Pricey, Pricey, Pricey!' I won five bouts in ten days in Kenya, including a win over the American no.2 Dan Bowers. By contrast Nick Wilshire, who I'd beaten in the ABA final and despite having the benefit of Olympic squad training at Crystal Palace for weeks on end, lost in the first round in Moscow. All I'd had was a bit of training in the Holy Name with Martin taking me on the pads!"

In November the same year Jimmy made his first international appearance, "the phone wouldn't stop ringing once I back from Kenya!" albeit a first round stoppage loss to the then powerful Hungarian team in Budapest. The ABA losing the match 7-2. A surprise loss early in the 1981 ABA's to Steve Johnston, "a very under-rated boxer, he was very awkward. Nothing felt right during that contest. I just had an off night," didn't prevent Jimmy from being selected for that year's European championships in Tampere, Finland. As in previous and subsequent tournaments however, East Europeans dominated and no home boxer won a medal. "I got to the quarters but lost to the Dutch boxer Pedro Van Rammsdonk, who did well in the pros later on," recalls Jimmy. Indeed, a winning appearance for the ABA over Scotland was arguably Jimmy's only highlight of the season.

A victory over Ireland in January the following year however, was the precursor to not only Jimmy's best year as an amateur but also his last before turning professional. He added another ABA title, this time at middleweight. Fellow Liverpudlian Brian Schumacher had won the title in 1981 whilst representing the Navy and would go on to make numerous international appearances over the next two years, including the Olympics, before turning pro and twice fighting for the British light-heavyweight title. Jimmy and Brian met in the semi-final of the ABAs in Gloucester, with the Holy Name boxer emerging victorious and going on to KO Cosmos ABC's C Harrison in the final.

Jimmy's ABA title saw him selected for the 1982 Commonwealth Games in Brisbane. He produced some fierce shots to halt the dangerous and big hitting home favourite Doug Sam in the final, Harry Carpenter famously saying that, "Price threw a boomerang Sam didn't want back!" This was a highly successful tournament for England with all nine members of the squad winning medals including John Lyon and Ray Gilbody, and Jimmy has especially strong and thoughtful memories of it.

"The thing I remember most about the Commonwealths in 82 wasn't winning the medal. It was more a thought about what might have been, and to this day it still gets me thinking. We were picked up from the airport by coach and driven to our accommodation at Brisbane University. During the ride it became obvious that there was a huge Aborigine Land Rights march taking place at the same time.

"As fate would have it, the only Aborigine member of the Australian squad was Sam, a boxer in my weight division. I made the final, beating a Kenyan and a Nigerian - who gave me a perforated eardrum - and then came Sam. I won the gold, and was glad I'd won it. The sacrifices I'd made all seemed worth it and I was pleased for Martin and all the people who'd believed in me and helped me to get there, but there was something missing.

"I'd always been a deep thinker. I'd had enough time on my own as a kid to get used to my own company, and I often thought about more profound issues than merely boxing. My thoughts following this tournament were a case in point. I often wondered what would have happened had I let Sam win. Would he have become a role model for the Aborigine people, who lets face it needed all the help they could get at the time? Although he went on to turn pro and got high in the world rankings he never won anything and the thought that somehow by beating him I may have prevented him from perhaps fulfiling a greater destiny, a bit like Kathy Freeman later on say, haunted me for a long time."

Any boxer returning from a major amateur tournament with a medal inevitably has thoughts about turning professional, and Jimmy was no exception. "Even on the plane coming back from Brisbane we were talking about it. Chris Pyatt had won a gold too, and he, Jim McDonnell, who won a silver, and myself were all sitting together talking and asking each other if we would be turning pro. Kevin

Hickey asked me not to, saying that he would make me team captain for the 1984 Los Angeles Olympics if I did, but I didn't heed his advice and I turned pro soon after."

Hindsight is always a wonderful thing, especially in sport, and Jimmy doesn't buck this trend. "If I'd known then what I know now, I certainly wouldn't have turned pro. In many ways it's the worst thing I could have done. Amateur boxing is a sport, a tough one yes, but it's still a sport. Pro boxing isn't – at all. It's a business, and a ruthless one at that."

To illustrate this last point, Jimmy mentions just one factor – his weight. "At the Commonwealths I boxed at 11st 10 lbs, but I was only 21 and I was still growing. Instead of going up a weight as a pro however, I was forced to come down and box at 11st 6lbs. It was too much. I was never a middleweight. You could see the reasoning behind it from a promoters view though. The middleweight division then was the glamour division in world boxing, both around the world and in England. All the big names boxed at or around the weight; Tony Sibson, Ayub Kalule, Colin Jones, Sylvester Mittee, Marvin Hagler, Thomas Hearns, Mike McCallum and so on, so I suppose they thought if I did well they would make good money."

Saying this however, there were aspects of the amateur game that Jimmy also found disturbing. "I remember training for the Commonwealths with the England team in Crystal Palace. One night we were given blazers to wear and taken to the Thomas A'Beckett gym for a function. It was to raise cash for our spending money whilst we were in Brisbane! There was no lottery funding in those days. In fact it wasn't uncommon for some lads to get their benefits stopped if they boxed for England abroad, even in the Olympics and the Commonwealths, because they were deemed to be unavailable for work!"

Jimmy's amateur career had marked him out as a boxer to watch. He was tall for his weight, could hit with both hands and had superb defensive skills. Coupled with these attributes were other important factors; he was a southpaw and supremely fit to boot, spending long periods of time in the gym. It seemed only a matter of time before he turned pro. Sure enough none other than Frank Warren came calling for Jimmy's signature. At the time Warren was relatively new to boxing management and promotion but had already created huge excitement and interest in the sport by virtue of his challenge to established monopolies like the BBC and the Duff/Barrett promotional banner. Jimmy signed for Warren, with the latter promising his new star that he would deliver a British title fight within two years, although this came with a caveat that the young 'scouser' would have to move to the capital. "London was seen by many as the place to go if you wanted to make it as a pro, but I didn't enjoy it really and should have stayed in Liverpool. I still talk about this to my loyal friend and confidant Franny Hands."

Jimmy made his pro debut at the Bloomsbury Crest Hotel in London in February 1983, running out a points winner over six rounds against Peckham's Jamaican born James Cook. Cook, a rising star himself, had won his three pro bouts to date, so it seemed a stern test for Jimmy's first fight since turning over. "I told Frank that I wanted to get to the top quickly, and that he shouldn't be getting me any easy fights." Just two weeks later Jimmy emphasised his point by stopping the experienced and durable Martin McEwan in the second round at Alexandra Palace and was on his way.

Three further wins on the spin and Jimmy was already being talked of as a future British champion. This was no idle boxing talk however, as he ended the year ranked no. 4 in the British ratings. A July trip to Atlantic City was next up for Jimmy, another contest he has particularly strong memories of. "I stopped the Canadian Bobby Bland inside three rounds. It was a strange trip. I didn't get paid anything for this contest, being told that my flight, hotels, meals and everything were being paid for and that the fight was more for 'experience'. Although I'd had a few pro fights by then I was still only 22 and was certainly naïve as far as the business side of boxing was concerned."

Jimmy did have some interesting times whilst in America however. "I had the honour of meeting former middleweight champion Rocky Graziano - in a lift. He had heard of my fight the night before and once we got talking - he still looked great for a man in his late-60s - he wished me luck and gave me a good old Italian kiss, cheek to cheek. I didn't even have a camera with me!" Jimmy also remembers visiting an Italian Restaurant in the middle of the day. "It was very dark and gloomy inside, and what with the characters in there it was like something from the Sopranos. With my mother's background I was introduced as being part-Italian, there was even a chance I would revert to boxing as Jimmy Priceppi while I was over there, and soon everyone was very friendly with me. Frank Warren's trainer at the time, Vic Andreeti, had a house in Miami and he wanted me to stay, to try and make a name for myself in America. Again though, I was just a 22 year old lad from Toxteth and it was too big a step to take at that time."

Jimmy Price in training c. 1984   *Source: Gary Shaw*

Jimmy ended the year with another four victories, including a fine win over Houston's Raymond Gonzales at Kirkby Sports Centre, his first and only pro outing in his home city. Early 1984 wins over Manuel

Jimenez and Ken Whetstone, "I remember Telly Savalas was ringside at that one," then saw Jimmy matched with his toughest test to date, an April 25 contest against the top 10 rated and former world light-middleweight champion Ayub Kalule.

Born in Kampala, Uganda but raised in Denmark where he boxed for the famous Team Palle promoters, Kalule had been a pro for eight years and had lost just three times in his 43-fight career to date. It was certainly a tough contest for Jimmy, made even tougher by his problems making the weight and his condition before the fight. "With two losses in his last two fights they obviously thought the time was right to meet Kalule, but it didn't turn out that way." These losses however, had been to top operators Davey Moore and Mike McCallum, whilst Kalule's only other previous loss was to none other than Sugar Ray Leonard. "I was living in a tenth floor flat in a tower block in Kensington at the time and I really struggled to make the weight. Remember I was over six foot and had come down in weight from my amateur days. I was literally sucking on lemons for days before hand."

The battle to make the weight - it was the least he had weighed as a pro so far - obviously weakened Jimmy and he picked up all sorts of infections. "Jim McDonnell and his fiance Kim, now his wife, came to see me the night before the fight. I was taking all kinds of cold remedies and inhalers and when Jim saw the state of me he told me not to take the fight. I didn't listen though and was stopped with more or less the first right hand Kalule threw. I was that weak from the weight loss and the cold I had that anyone, even one of my sons, could have decked me that night!"

Five months later however, Jimmy returned to meet James Cook, the very man he had outpointed in his pro debut just over 18 months previously. Cook had come on since that defeat and had risen rapidly through the British rankings, so much so that the contest was sanctioned as an official eliminator for the vacant British middleweight title. Cook hadn't improved as much as Jimmy however, and the Londoner was stopped in the second round courtesy of a stunning left cross – thrown, such was Jimmy's style, while he was going backwards!

A seventh round stoppage win over Spanish middleweight champion Adoni Amana in Southend in November 1984 followed. Jimmy was then matched with Sheffield's undefeated Herol 'Bomber' Graham, a former British, Commonwealth and European champion at light-middle. It was one of the most eagerly anticipated British middleweight title fights for years. To say it was explosive would be an understatement – but for Jimmy it turned out to be yet another struggle. "If you see a tape of the fight now you wouldn't believe it was me in the opposite corner to Graham. I look so drawn and tired. Like the Kalule fight it had been really tough to make the weight. I remember at the weigh-in Graham's training team staring at me really hard. They couldn't believe how drawn I looked. They must have been thinking, 'Look at him. He's there for the taking. Get after him and take him out quick.'" Their views were soon proved true, and Jimmy suffered another first round stoppage loss, being decked three times in the first 100 seconds. "I was so weak again, that all Graham had to do really was wave his fist at me and I went down," says Jimmy, "I was just so tired. I should have leaned from the Kalule fight really."

Jimmy's battle with the scales was drawing to a close however. "Six months later I had my last fight for Warren, an early stoppage win over Eddie Smith, who had wins over Tony Sibson and Roy Gumbs. I then signed for the Lynch brothers, Paddy and Tommy, from Birmingham, and it was like a whole new world. The first thing they said to me was that I was definitely not a middleweight. I could hardly believe it. One of the first things they did was to buy me a steak dinner! They were real gentlemen too. They said they wouldn't take any money from me until I was earning good money myself, from title fights and eliminators.

"In my first fight for them I beat Nottingham's Roy Smith, later to be British cruiserweight champion, and then beat London-based Jamaican Hugh Johnson. I weighed 175lbs for this fight, the heaviest I'd weighed in my pro career. I was then matched with Tom Collins in an eliminator for the British light-heavyweight title *[no super-middleweight division existed in England at that time. eds]* but even though I think I would have had a great chance of winning at my proper weight, the fight never came off."

Unbeknown to Jimmy, his ring career was also coming to an end. Faced with a number of fatalities in the previous two years, the Board of Control had started to give all British boxers yearly CAT scans to ensure they were fit enough to box. Despite the fact that Jimmy had boxed as a pro at the top level for three years, notwithstanding his long and successful amateur career, he failed the scan; the top of his skull being found to be much thinner than the rest. An appeal and a second opinion failed to provide an alternative answer and that was it - Jimmy was forced to retire. "I was devastated obviously. I just didn't know what to do with myself. I remember sitting in a car outside my hotel with Paddy Lynch. Again he proved to be a total gentlemen. He gave me a train ticket to Liverpool, £400, said he was really sorry for me, shook hands and told me to look after myself. They'd still never taken a penny from me. I'll never forget that. Thanks lads."

Jimmy returned to Liverpool with no idea what to do with the rest of his life. "I didn't really have anything. I was skint. About a year later however, my old Golden Gloves colleague Andy Palmer (God bless him) got in touch, offering me a job on the doors at The Grafton. He died not so long ago Andy. With nothing else to do I took it, worked a lot of doors and went on from there."

Whilst working in Liverpool Jimmy met Patsy, "and she blessed me with two beautiful daughters, Nikita and Naomi. Unfortunately," says Jimmy, "it didn't work out - through no fault of Patsy's. I look at life through its ups and downs and believe it all to be part of a journey in life - either for good or bad. I firmly believe that God will judge us all though." Now married to Nikki, "who has blessed me with two beautiful sons, Evander and Sonny - not named after two former heavyweight champs honest! I really am lucky, God willing, because the mothers of my children get on really well, as do my daughters with Nikki and my sons with Patsy."

Looking back on his career and life today, Jimmy is adamant that boxing provided him with an escape route to better things. "Without boxing I wouldn't have been able to go to the places I went to or meet the people I did. It's been a long journey and like all journeys it has had its positives and negatives, although I like to think I've had more of the former!" Although one can spend many an hour reminiscing with Jimmy, a firm believer in a higher power and purpose, he can sum up his career and life in just a few words. "The first two verses of Peter Gabriel and Kate Bush's 1986 hit *Don't Give Up* certainly ring true for me. I grew up in Liverpool - a proud land and was taught to fight, taught to win. I really didn't think I could lose. But then of course you do - few boxers remain unbeaten - and it's true, no-one wants to know you when you lose. The important thing to remember in any area of your life though, is not to give up. Just like the song says!"

Although Jimmy has few regrets about choosing boxing as a career, there were some aspects of it he would change, the switch from amateur to pro being the most significant. "I really loved the amateur side of the sport, even though it too had its problems at the time. Not being picked for the 1980 Olympics was one of the hardest things I had to deal with, but this was more than compensated for by winning the gold in Brisbane. When the flag was raised and the anthem played I didn't think I'd won it for England, but rather for all those who had provided support for me such as Ken Birch and Martin Ventre. The proudest I ever felt was seeing a photo of Ken, a proud Jamaican man who was a father figure to me when I was younger, and myself with the gold medal in the *Echo* when I got back from Australia. That was the best feeling I got from winning it."

When asked who his hardest opponent was, Jimmy rates his spars with tough former British and Commonwealth middleweight champion, Roy Gumbs, as being physically more demanding than any of his pro fights. "Yes I met Kalule and Graham but they weren't really hard fights because they just didn't last that long! Roy was a really good boxer. He was also a powerful puncher and very, very strong. I was his sparring partner and we had some tough sessions. I really felt I'd been through the mill physically after a session with Roy, even including Joe Bugner who I was also asked to spar with on occasion. I'd also have to rate Mark Kaylor as one of my toughest opponents, whilst Terry Culshaw was definitely the hardest puncher I met - every shot hurt."

Jimmy's fights against Kaylor and Terry were in the amateurs and it is to here that we return when he picks his toughest opponent. "This was Martin Hughes, who used to box for Highfield ABC. He's an actor now," explains Jimmy, "known as James McMartin and he's appeared in a few good films, *Going Off Big Time* and *House of Cards*."

Arguably one of the least well-known Liverpool boxers to win a British title, and certainly one of the most under-rated, Kirkby super-featherweight Kevin Pritchard enjoyed a modest career with his local amateur club before turning pro in 1981. Originally a lightweight Kevin was unlucky to turn pro at a time when there was no domestic super-featherweight division. He could make featherweight easily enough but sometimes fought as high as 140lb and this versatility at the weights together with his fight anyone, anywhere, anytime attitude meant that he fought all the leading feather and lightweights of the day – and sometimes even full welterweights! His nine-year 23 wins from 48 contests record (22 losses) is much better than first suggested and he met the likes of Pat Cowdell, Steve 'Sammy' Sims, Najib Daho, John Feeney, Vincenzo Limatola, Pat Doherty, John Docherty, Jean Baptiste Mendy, Jean-Marc Renard, Hugh Forde, Robert Dickie, Jimmi Bredahl (who would later meet Oscar de la Hoya) and Colin McMillan. Currently living and working in Preston this article was obtained through interviews with Kevin during 2006/07.

KEVIN PRITCHARD

Fought the best at six different weights – but eventually won British title!

Although there was no real history of the sport in his family, "I preferred athletics and football before boxing," Kirkby's Kevin Pritchard joined the old English Electric ABC in 1971 when he was 10 years old and never looked back, enjoying spells at Kirkby ABC, then the Rotunda before rejoining Kirkby and meeting the likes of George Gilbody. Like many local boxers of his generation, Kevin's childhood hero was Kirkby's very own John Conteh. "Conteh was a hero to me," says Kevin. "His old club, Kirkby ABC, was just down the road from me and it was an honour to join the club where my idol used to train."

Hoping to emulate Conteh's achievements Kevin turned pro at lightweight in 1981 when he was 21 with the Manchester promoter Nat Basso, and he made his debut just four days before Christmas that year with a solid six rounds points win over JJ Barrett in Bradford. Less than three weeks later Kevin had his second successive victory, scoring a first round KO over Widnes' Vince Griffin at Liverpool's Holiday Inn. Despite having height and reach advantages Griffin was unable to halt the barrage of punches that came his way and, bleeding from nose and mouth and in no position to defend himself, the referee stepped in with just one minute 50 seconds of the contest gone. Although turning pro at lightweight, Kevin was really a super-feather, and for the first few years of his pro career he was forced to box at a variety of weight divisions; feather, lightweight, light-welter and even welterweight, until the super-feather division was re-introduced in the UK in 1986 *[a junior lightweight division had existed 1968-69 eds.].*

Two six round wins followed within seven days in February 1982 but, in his third fight in as many weeks, Kevin tasted defeat for the first time when local southpaw Tommy Cook took the decision in Glasgow. This was the first of many contests Kevin had in his opponents back-yard and, as many boxing fans know, you have to box extremely well to take the judges decisions in those type of fights. Undaunted by his first reverse Kevin was back just a fortnight later to gain a six round decision over Greenock's Billy Laidman, yet another Scottish southpaw. This was the start of a fine run, and he won five of his next six contests (one draw), including three victories over Bradford based Ghanaian Rocky Mensah.

With just one defeat in his first dozen pro contests Kevin stepped up a gear in his next fight meeting Sheffield's durable and awkward lightweight Glyn Rhodes for the Central Area title in November 1982 at the Liverpool Stadium. It proved unlucky thirteen for Kevin however, as he was stopped in the fifth due to a badly split lip. "Glyn was a real tough cookie. He was very tall for his weight, and very flash. He was a bit like Sugar Ray Leonard in that his shots would come from all angles, with his long arms and reach. I just wasn't experienced enough at the time and That's what cost me in the end."

Five wins from Kevin's next eight contests followed, including a fine second round KO of Cardiff welterweight Mervyn Bennett and commendable points reverses against the unbeaten Mark Davey and Gary Knight, again both full welterweights, before Kevin had his first contest abroad. Danish based Ugandan Mohammed Kawoya would lose a European light-welterweight title challenge in October 1987 so great things were expected of him when he faced Kevin in Copenhagen in October 1986. Kawoya proved his backers right by forcing a stoppage in the second round. Kawoya was very tough too but it was a non-fight for me really. I was offered good money to go and took it. I didn't have major promoters or managers behind me like other fighters did and I had to take fights like this."

The following month saw Kevin meet the man he considers his toughest opponent, Liverpool featherweight Jimmy Duncan. Duncan had been a talented amateur with the St Helens Star ABC, had won a host of local titles and made the 1981 ABA final before signing with Frank Warren in 1982. With two losses from his nine pro fights to date, one of which was against Barry McGuigan, Duncan was certainly a tough proposition. "The fight against Jimmy Duncan at Kirkby Sports Centre was probably my hardest fight," remembers Kevin. "He was a handful for anyone – very tough, very determined and he never gave you a seconds respite. It was a non-stop punching local derby and the crowd loved it, especially the large support that Jimmy always had wherever he boxed. In the end I lost on points over eight rounds but it was close."

A trip to Belfast in January 1984 saw Kevin upset the city's fight fans by forcing a sixth round stoppage against local hope Gary Muir. This was the first of six contests Kevin had in 1984, his quietest full year to date as a pro. Although he won only three of these however, the calibre of opponent he met this year show why he ended it ranked in the top ten British featherweights for the first time. To add to the victory over Muir was a fine points win over Queensferry's Ray Hood, the reigning Welsh lightweight champion, and a second round stoppage over former British champion and European title challenger, Steve 'Sammy' Sims. Losses to Swansea's Michael Harris and Scotsman Ian McLeod were no disgraces, especially as the Welshman would later challenge not only for British lightweight title, but also the British and Commonwealth light-middleweight crowns, and the talented McLeod would later lose a British lightweight title challenge to Tony Willis. The McLeod fight was also, like many of Kevin's contests, in his opponent's hometown.

The third reverse Kevin suffered in 1984 was in the return, after 18 months away from the ring, of one of Britain's greatest ever boxers the former four-time ABA champion, Commonwealth Games gold medallist and British and European champion Pat Cowdell. Throw in the fact that Cowdell had also lost world title challenges to Salvador Sanchez and Azumah Nelson and you can see what a daunting task this was for the Kirkby man and it was no disgrace for Kevin to be stopped in the fifth round. "I had a good 10 weeks or so to train for the Cowdell fight but his class and experience told in the end. He was just too good for me at that stage of my career."

Although suffering a number of reverses so far in his career, Kevin was undaunted as he knew he was improving all the time. "I was one of Barry McGuigan's main sparring partners for a long time and I learned a lot from him. I went all over with Barry, Ireland, England, Europe. Together with my own experience as a pro I knew I was improving all the time."

Kevin had just three contests in 1985, however this was also the year the BIB of C re-introduced the super-feather division and with fine wins over some of the leading featherweights of the day, as well as many lightweights, Kevin had high hopes of forcing a title shot. His credentials were underlined when he was adjudged a points winner over Manchester's Muhammad Lovelock at Liverpool Stadium in March 1985 and he was then matched with the talented Manchester–based Moroccan Najib Daho to contest the new Central Area super-featherweight title at Manchester's Free Trade Hall.

A year before Kevin had weighed in at 141lbs in his contest against Michael Harris and although he often made 130lbs with no problem he seemed to overdo the weight here and he scaled in at 126 3/4lbs as opposed to Daho's 129lbs, The 2lbs may have been the difference however, as Daho scored 98 points to Kevin's 97 but Kevin is philosophical when thinking about this fight. "It could have gone either way really. It was a fight to remember and certainly one of my hardest contests. It went the distance and I gave it my best but Daho got the decision on his home ground."

A month after the loss to Daho, who would later win not only the British super-featherweight title but also challenge unsuccessfully for both a European and IBF title, Kevin was matched with Hartlepool's former British bantamweight champion – and four-time European title challenger, John Feeney. Again however, Kevin was adjudged a narrow points loser over eight rounds, 79-78. It was a further four months before Kevin stepped into the ring again, an eight round draw against Manchester's Mike Whalley. Although he was as game as ever, it seemed that decisions just weren't going Kevin's way. This would appear to have been the case as Kevin would win only two of his next eleven contests. However, four of these reverses came against top quality foreign opponents in their own country and, to highlight the calibre of opponent Kevin was forced to meet in this period, they are worth looking at in greater detail.

Italian Vincenzo Limatola stopped Kevin in the seventh round of their March 1986 contest in Falconara, Italy but Limatola would later challenge for the European title on two occasions. In November 1987

French-based Senegalese, Jean Baptise Mendy, KO'd Kevin inside four rounds in Antibes, France. Mendy later won and successfully defended the European title six times before winning the WBA world lightweight title in 1998. In a fight against another highly rated Gallic star Kevin was stopped in three rounds by Belgium's reigning European super-featherweight champion Jean-Marc Renard in Grivegnee, Belgium in April 1988. The following year Renard challenged for the WBA world featherweight title. Unbeaten Italian Gianni Di Napoli KO'd Kevin in the fourth round of their October 1988 contest in Rome. Less than two years later the Italian challenged for the European title.

Kevin Pritchard c. 1990   *Source: Kevin Pritchard*

If Kevin's European opponents in this period weren't enough to fill even the most capable domestic super-featherweight with dread, his British opponents during the same time frame were almost as highly rated. Losses against Pat Doherty, John Doherty, Mark Reefer and Nigel Haddock were certainly no disgraces, whilst his two victories over Rocky Lawlor and Harry Escott, "he kept trying to tickle me in this fight," should probably have warned potential opponents that the Kirkby man could still be dangerous at the top level.

The backers of Birmingham's unbeaten Hugh Forde certainly seemed to have focused on Kevin's recent paper record rather than his performances or the calibre of his opponents, when they matched their man with Kevin for the British super-featherweight title at Dudley Town Hall in October 1990. With every winner of the title since it's re-introduction in 1986 losing the title in their first defence, perhaps they also felt that Kevin was an easy touch for Forde to break the 'jinx'. The Birmingham southpaw had won the title just five weeks previously when stopping Manchester's Joey Jacobs in the eleventh round at Wolverhampton but true to recent form Kevin sensationally stopped Forde in the fourth round to win the title. To say Kevin was overjoyed would be an understatement.

"I was so excited at winning the British title. I could hardly believe it. It was a great achievement for me, like climbing Everest. It had taken so long and I'd fought a lot of hard fights to win it. I was elated, relieved, overjoyed. Even thinking about it now is bringing it all back! I'd never been a champion, even as an amateur, so to win the British title? It was a tremendous feeling. Overwhelming. As soon as the fight was over I remember telling my manager in the dressing room that I didn't care if I died the next day because I'd already achieved my dream!"

Kevin was unable to break the 'jinx' either however, and he held the title for just five months, losing it in his first defence against Carmarthen's Robert Dickie in Cardiff. *[Dickie couldn't break it either, losing to Liverpool's Sugar Gibiliru who also subsequently lost it in his first defence eds.]* There may however, be a reason for Kevin's loss. "A superstition of mine was that I always wore something brand new for each fight, either a new gumshield, socks or shorts. Travelling down to Wales for this fight however, I realised that I didn't have anything new to wear so I went to a market and bought a pair of socks. During the fight however, my feet were killing me and it really distracted me. It turned out that the reason was a four inch blister on the soles of my feet - I'd only gone and bought nylon socks! Completely the wrong ones for exercise of any kind let alone a British title fight!"

With 46 contests in nine years, Kevin's career was coming to an end but the calibre of his remaining two opponents remained top class. Two months after his loss to Dickie Kevin travelled to Copenhagen to take on unbeaten prospect Jimmi Bredahl. Kevin was stopped in the third but so good was Bredahl that just two fights later he would win the European title and in 1994 he would lose to the legendary Oscar De la Hoya in a WBO world title challenge.

In his career Kevin had fought at as many as six different weight divisions and had met the leading domestic and European stars of the day. His last contest was no different. Able to make featherweight yet again, Kevin challenged for the British title held by future WBO world champion Colin McMillan. The contest, at the York Hall in September 1991 was to be Kevin's last. He was stopped in the seventh and then retired. "Colin was a tremendous fighter. Young, hungry and very slick, very sharp. I knew my career was coming to an end, that I was past my peak and was grateful for the chance he gave me. He was just too good for me in the end."

Kevin is rightly proud of the career he had. "Taking up boxing was the best thing I ever did. It taught me discipline and respect. I had some great times and met some great people." Although he agrees that it may have been tougher to succeed in his day, Kevin remains philosophical about comparisons between the two eras. "It would have been nice to get the money the fighters of today get but good luck to them. Some fight for the purse and others fight for the glory. I fought for the glory and am proud to say that I was a British champion."

Kevin currently lives in Preston and works as a carpenter, and has two children, "my lovely daughter Leah, who is a European salsa champion and son Ruben, who just wants to play football for England."

A top amateur with the Golden Gloves ABC, just a stone's throw from his home in the Dingle, Robbie Robinson now lives thousands of miles away on the other side of the world in Sydney, Australia – a place he has called his home for almost 15 years. A tall, classy, good-looking lightweight, Robbie turned pro in 1978 with George Francis and in a five-year career he won 19 out of 29 contests, losing nine, including two final eliminators for the British title. A first round KO loss in Africa in April 1982 still rankles with Robbie however, as the fight never finished because he and trainer Franny Hands were escaping a riot at the time! This article was compiled through interviews with Robbie in 2007.

ROBBIE ROBINSON

Lost two British title eliminators – but first round KO 'loss' in Benin still hurts!

"I first started boxing at the age of 10 when I joined 'the Florrie' – the old Florence Institute in Dingle. I don't think I was that good initially, but once I joined the Golden Gloves when I was 14 I came on leaps and bounds. Tommy Bache was the trainer then and the club had so many top class boxers they could have fielded virtually an entire England team at the time." With the likes of Terry Wenton, Joe Lally, Robbie Davies, Carl Speare, Greg Evans, Andy Palmer and Ronnie Gibbons, the club certainly had its fair share of talented fighters, whilst in Ray Gilbody and John Hyland they also had outstanding schoolboys and internationals of the future. Robbie recalls that, "Ronnie Gibbons later turned pro and won about 25 fights in New York under Gil Clancy." Suffice to say that with such a line up Robbie wasn't short of quality sparring. "I sparred every day with truly world class amateurs. George Turpin and George Gilbody were also there at the time. They were both top class. I have the greatest admiration for them as they were already established international stars and they never took liberties with youngsters like myself and clubmate Brian Snagg."

From being, in his own words, "a mediocre schoolboy," Robbie turned senior at 17 and duly won 25 out of 27 amateur contests. "I entered the ABA's for the first time when I was 17 and beat three England internationals; Terry Wenton, Paul Fletcher and Johnny Chesters, on the way to the 1975 finals at Wembley." Robbie was unlucky in the final however, "I lost a close decision, as did Robbie Davies the same night." Luck plays a not insignificant part in amateur boxing but Robbie views a reverse many saw as unlucky at the time as entirely justified. "I lost on a cut eye with 12 seconds to go in the Northern Counties finals at bantamweight. This was against the eventual ABA champion Jim Norman from Birkenhead. I was streets ahead on points at the time but the ref was correct to stop the fight as the cut was a bad one." As a senior Robbie also represented England on 11 occasions – winning all of them.

Like many fighters boxing played a role in Robbie's family history. "My uncle Barney Hughes was a top Liverpool fly and bantamweight before the Second World War and was a close friend of both Jimmy Molloy and Gus Foran. My Dad Bobby also boxed as a schoolboy with 'the Florrie'. I came from a rough area in the Dingle and was fighting in the street almost every day. My Dad took my brother Shaun and me to 'the Florrie' to straighten us out. I was 10 and Shaun was eight. He was a tough kid. He's now the Managing Director of the Beverly Hills Hotel in California, where he has presented the Golden Globes on six occasions. So my Dad was probably right to take us 'the Florrie' to keep us out of trouble!"

Robbie turned pro in 1978 when he was 20. "My first manager was George Francis who managed John Conteh at the time and later took Frank Bruno to a world title. He was a great man George. It was a great shock when I learnt he had passed away a few years ago." As in his amateur days, Robbie's training regime with George also saw him take part in class sparring. "I sparred daily with the likes of Cornelius Boza-Edwards, Clinton McKenzie, Frankie Lucas, and my good mate to this day, Chris Sanigar from Bristol. He was hard as nails Chris. He's now a top promoter in the West Country.

"My first fight at the Liverpool Stadium as a pro was in March 1979, a third round stoppage win over Najib Daho. I followed up with Stadium wins over former ABA champion Tommy Wright, local lad George Scholfield, and a very good win over Mickey Duff's fighter Lance Williams. Williams had just outpointed Ken Buchanan on his comeback. I was then managed by Blackpool's Manny Goodall and was coached by Franny Hands. He too had a great local team at the time and I sparred regularly with good lads such as Joey Frost, Tony Sinnott, Sammy Brennan and Brian Snagg."

Robbie can remember several tough contests. "One was against George Metcalf in the chief support to John Conteh's last ever fight (v James Dixon) at the Stadium in May 1980. I hit him with so many hard shots but he just wouldn't budge! Coming out for the sixth of a scheduled ten rounder I was cut under both eyes and I could see referee Ron Hackett hovering and having a good look at me ready to stop the fight. I pulled a big left hook out which caught George flush on the chin and dropped him at long last. I didn't think he'd get up from that but he did – and twice more in the same round, before the referee stopped it in my favour. Harry Mullan later picked it as one of *Boxing News* top ten fights of the year." Robbie had another tough one when he outpointed British light-welter champion Lloyd Christie in 1982. "Although the referee Brian Hogg scored me a wide points winner, each round was close and I had to work extremely hard for the win. Lloyd showed his class in his next bout just two weeks later when he inflicted the only blot on world champion Terry Marsh's record, when Marsh climbed of the canvas to salvage a draw".

Robbie also had several eliminators for the British lightweight title. "The first was at Liverpool Stadium in January 1981 against George Feeney. I had followed up the Metcalf win with a hard fought points win over another Liverpool lad, Tony Carroll. I had boxed in the same England team as Feeney and knew him quite well. I had rewarded myself with a good Christmas following the Metcalf and Carroll victories and I must say I spent more time in the old *She* club than the gym! I totally underestimated George, who was a strong, fit, determined fighter and I was floored for the first time ever as an amateur or pro before being stopped in the fourth round. To make matters worse the fight was live on national TV!"

It must have seemed like déjà vu for another 'scouser' Tony Willis a year later as not only did he meet Feeney – this time for the vacant title, but despite also being the favourite he was stopped early after, according to Robbie, similarly underestimating the Hartlepool man. "Like myself I believe Tony also sold George short. He carried his hands low and was tagged with a cracking shot before being stopped in the first."

Robbie then spent six months away from the game, before getting in shape to return with points wins over Eric Wood and Lloyd Christie, and solid stoppage wins over Dai Davies, Welsh champion Ray Price, Colin Wake and Gerry Beard. "I was then matched with Scottish lightweight champion Willie Booth at Kirkby in another 10 round British title eliminator. I was mad fit and won by a wide margin. I remember celebrating later with Franny and actor Bernard Hill who was in Liverpool filming the classic *Boys From the Blackstuff*! I'd won so easily against Booth that people thought he was lucky to get the eliminator but he returned to Liverpool shortly after to defeat one of my sparring partners Tony Sinnott at the Stadium – and Tony was a good, hard punching box-fighter."

Robbie Robinson c. 1982   *Source: Robbie Robinson*

Robbie's final contest was against Tony Willis in a final eliminator for the British title, again at Liverpool Stadium on the eve of the 1983 Grand National. "I had married and become a father for the first time in that year. I had no other income apart from boxing and after several bouts fell through I'd only had one fight in nine months so things were pretty grim! I loved boxing and would never have contemplated giving it up but given the circumstances at the time I really had to consider getting a proper job! I found it difficult to train properly and against quality fighters like Tony even 90% was never going to be enough. I was extremely disappointed in my lacklustre performance to say the least. I sustained a bad cut under my eye after the fourth and as it wouldn't stop bleeding Franny pulled me out. I announced my retirement from the ring that night and the crowd showered it with 'nobbins' - I was only 25 but my desire had gone."

Despite his, by boxing standards early retirement, Robbie looks back on his career with fondness, and quite often with a chuckle or two. "In 1982 I took a fight in Benin, between Nigeria and Ghana, against former world amateur champion Davidson Andeh. It was held in an old football stadium, a bit like South Liverpool's old ground, and they managed to cram around 20,000 people in there. I was the only white fighter on the bill – with a white trainer in Franny – and straight from the start the crowd were hostile towards us to say the least.

"Towards the end of the first round a few missiles started to get thrown in our general direction and although Franny kept shouting at me 'to get off', I refused as I still wanted to fight. All of a sudden however, a bottle flew past my eyes, missing me by inches! I decided to take Franny's advice and we did a 'runner' from the ring. We were ushered into a police car and kept telling the driver to get us both out of there. The crowd had followed us however, and were trying to turn the car over – with us inside it! Two of the policeman immediately jumped out of the car and went to work with their batons. They must have cracked a dozen heads apiece. The crowd duly dispersed and we were able to drive away. It was only then I realised that I still had my boxing gloves and shorts on! In fact my clothes might still be in the dressing room over there! The next day I read in the paper that I'd been stopped in the first round – and that's what my record still says if you look it up today. I don't suppose it's nothing you wouldn't see down Scottie Road on a Saturday night though."

In retrospect Robbie believes he lacked discipline as a boxer. "I think that was the difference in me not progressing further. I beat several British champions but never won the title myself even though I had all the physical attributes. I was very tall for a lightweight, almost 6', and had sparred with heavier guys for years so I was always strong for my weight. Syd Dye described me as a stylist, a hurtful puncher who was difficult to hit. I was tempremental though and often let events outside the ring distract me. I loved it all though. I'd gladly do it all again."

Robbie recognises that boxing today is vastly different from the sport he knew in his day. "There is a lot of talent about these days but there doesn't seem to be that much strength in depth. There is no doubt that it's a totally different game than it was in the 1980s – and earlier. I think that the likes of Alan Rudkin, Jimmy Molloy and lots of other Liverpool lads could easily have been world champions today. I don't envy today's fighters though. If I had to choose to give up all the great experiences I had at the Liverpool Stadium to earn the enormous purses even very ordinary fighters seem to pick up today it would be no contest!"

Like many ex-Merseyside fighters Robbie laments the passing of Liverpool Stadium. "It was a very sad day for me when they pulled it down. It should have been a listed building really. No matter what amount of money they spend on a new venue they'll never be able to replicate the uniqueness that was the Stadium. I still reckon that after it was gone it was much easier for me to leave Liverpool. I had the great honour of boxing at the Stadium on numerous occasions both as an amateur and a pro. The atmosphere was always electric. People used to wait for weeks in anticipation of the West Lancs and Cheshire championships held there in February each year.

"I remember fighting last on the bill in the prelims there in 1977. I won in the first round against a lad from Barrow, and Syd Dye wrote in the *Echo* the next day that I'd sent the crowd home early. It was 1am when I won and there were still over 2,000 people there. The Stadium crowd were always very knowledgeable, and fair. I never attended an arena that could compare to the Stadium.

"When I was working on the QE2 in February 1990 the ship was berthed in Tokyo, Japan and we had laid on a coach to take people to the Tyson v Douglas world heavyweight title fight at the Tokyo Dome. It turned out of course to be a fantastic fight – one of the greatest upsets in boxing history but the atmosphere that night was nothing compared to the Stadium. I watched the American TV replay of the fight and I can tell you they must have dubbed the noise of a roaring crowd over the actual sound from the night!"

After retiring from boxing, Robbie managed to gain work at sea and it wasn't long after that he left Liverpool for the warmer, sunnier climate of Australia. "I broke up with my first wife and eventually left Liverpool in the mid-80s but I was fortunate enough to get a job on the QE2 in 1987 and had three great years there before leaving to join P&O for another three years. I met my wife Laura on TV's original '*Love Boat*' in 1991. We both loved Australia, married in Brisbane in 1993 before moving to Sydney. After five years there we moved to Queensland's Gold Coast near the beach and we've been here now for almost eight years. We've no intention of moving from here – it's just so good – sunny almost all the time. We have two children, Emily and Patrick. They're typical Australian kids – energetic and on the beach almost every day. I often look at them and think ' What a life they have – a far cry from the Dingle all those years ago!'"

Few boxers win a version of a world title within 10 pro fights, but that's just what Kirkby light-welterweight Gary Ryder managed to do when he beat Manchester's Wayne Rigby for the WBF crown in his tenth pro contest. A successful amateur with the famous Kirkby ABC before turning pro in 1996, Gary had just one contest in his first three years as a professional but managed to chalk up nine wins from nine before getting his crack at the title. He beat the likes of Kevin Bennett and Glenn McClarnon, the latter in a terrific contest at Everton Park Sports Centre, in an eleven fight career that ended in March 2003. Still living in Kirkby, this article was compiled through interviews with Gary in 2007.

GARY RYDER

'World' champion in just tenth pro fight!

Although Kirkby's Gary Ryder is perhaps remembered best as a tough, hard-hitting professional at the light-welterweight limit, it is often overlooked just how good his amateur record was. Gary boxed for the famous Kirkby ABC, joining the club when he was 15 mainly, "to keep myself out of trouble." He won 53 of 62 amateur contests, winning two North West Counties featherweight titles, and two at light-welter, before turning pro with local managers Munro-Hyland in 1996 when he was 24.

Gary's all-action style proved too much for Salford's Andy Davidson, a former victim of Gary's in the amateur ranks, who was stopped inside two minutes on his pro debut in February 1996 at Everton Park Sports Centre. Due to a bout of glandular fever that kept Gary out of the ring for almost three years, his next professional outing was delayed until March 1999 – a dominant four rounds points win over Lincoln's Trevor Tacy. Six weeks later St Helens' Stuart Rimmer felt the full force of Gary's power as he succumbed to a first round KO. The inactivity continued for Gary however, and he had just one fight in the next 18 months, albeit another points win over Birmingham's experienced (John) Benny Jones. A first round KO over Tunisia's Mohammed Helel followed before Scottish promoter Tommy Gilmour stepped in to take charge of Gary's career.

Just as he had done with Alex Moon, the Scotsman seemed to relaunch a career that, at one time, had threatened to fade away. Gilmour had seen enough to know that Gary could mix it with better company than he had been used to and for his next outing, in June 2006, he matched Gary with unbeaten local prospect Kevin Bennett at Hartlepool

Borough Hall. Bennett came into the contest with seven straight wins so like Gary he was unbeaten as a pro. It was the Hartlepool boxer who lost his proud unbeaten record however, as Gary forced a stoppage in the sixth round to finally make his mark in the domestic rankings.

Three months later, Gary brilliantly outpointed Lurgan's Glen McClarnon at Everton Park Sports Centre on the Richard Williams v Andrew Murray Commonwealth light-middleweight title show. The Northern Ireland man had lost only four of 17 contests to date and was high in the British rankings. Indeed, Gilmour had worked hard to make the contest an official final eliminator for the then vacant British title but it wasn't to be, the contest instead being made part of an eliminating series for the championship. Gilmour knew however, that should Gary win, he would be, "just one fight away," from a shot at the domestic crown and a possible Lonsdale belt. In a toe-to-toe battle, one of the best seen in the city for a long time, both boxers threw a myriad of excellent body shots, with Gary winning 78-76 on referee Keith Garner's scorecard, sending his fervent home support delirious.

Although a contest for the British light-welterweight title never materialised, Gilmore did manage to secure Gary a crack at the fringe WBF world title, then held by Manchester's former British lightweight champion Wayne Rigby. In a twist of fate that perhaps only boxing can provide, Gary's first title fight was to be for a 'world' title! Wins over Birstall's David Smales and Cardiff's David White kept Gary ticking over until November 2001 when he faced Rigby in front of the Mancunian's home supporters at Altrincham Leisure Centre.

Few in the boxing press gave Gary much hope. Although Rigby had lost eight of his 28 contests to date, he was a former British lightweight champion and had met fighters of the calibre of Tanveer Ahmed and Bobby Vanzie. Such experience counted for nothing against the Kirkby fighter however, as Gary boxed almost to perfection to secure a unanimous points victory. Straight from the opening bell Gary was the busier of the two fighters, settling behind his jab and refusing to allow Rigby to dictate matters. A huge right hand by Gary rocked the champion early in the second but although he managed to survive it was only to receive more of the same in the following rounds. A right hook from Gary in the fifth almost floored Rigby but although appearing out on his feet he managed to last till the bell. Such was Gary's dominance that in the ninth round he even adopted a southpaw stance to protect two small cuts above and below his left eye. The result was a formality with Gary winning by a wide margin on all three judges' cards. After just ten professional contests Merseyside had yet another 'world' champion. After the contest Gary stated that he was prepared to meet anyone at the 10st. limit, including Junior Witter and another Mancunian who held a version of the 'world' title, the WBU champion at the time, Ricky Hatton. "I work hard. It's my heart. I keep going. Now I've just got to get used to 12 rounds and I'll go in with anyone," said Gary at the time.

Despite the best efforts of his management team however, neither contest came off and four months later Gary defended his title against Pablo Daniel Sarmiento, an Argentinian with a wealth of experience who also held the IBO 'world' title. Although Gary acknowledges that Sarmiento was his hardest opponent. "He was very, very tough - and awkward," he says that, such was his training regime for the Rigby fight, when, "I had not seen my daughter for months," to fight again a few months later was not good for him. "Not seeing Libby again for so long affected my mental state at the time and I was probably not as well prepared as I should have been." Even then however, "Sarmiento was definitely on top for the earlier part of the fight but I felt that I was starting to get to him just before the fight was stopped due to a cut in the eighth round." Not long after this, "personal problems outside the ring," forced Gary to retire. "If it wasn't for them I would have won more titles."

Looking back on his career today, Gary wishes he could start over. "I think it's a bit easier than it was in my day. Although I still think the money is poor for the amount of work you have to do to get to the top." One contest that Gary remembers vividly was as an amateur in Jersey. "Just as we were getting introduced my opponent laughed at me. This really upset me and I went at him from the start eventually knocking him out in the second."

One of Gary's most memorable contests came in the 1993 ABA championships when he lost a majority verdict by the smallest of margins to Scarborough's established England international, Peter Richardson at Everton Park Sports Centre. It was a performance that convinced the England selectors to give Gary his first international vest against Ulster at Portstewart in June the same year. Gary rewarded them with a points win over C McFarland, whilst clubmate Alex Moon was also successful in a match the ABA won 4-3.

"I didn't fight at the Stadium but Everton Park was a great venue for me. I had one of my best performances as an amateur there when I boxed Peter Richardson in the ABA quarter-finals. He had won the ABA featherweight title in 1989. It was a great fight, non-stop all the way and Syd Dye said it was the best boxing action he'd seen for years. I remember the atmosphere was fantastic, as it was when I beat Glenn McClarnon as a pro."

Born in Liverpool but resident in Australia for many years, Kenny Salisbury was an accomplished amateur, firstly with the Mayfair ABC, then with Halewood, and finally the Salisbury and Knowsley Vale. His amateur career took in around 100 contests and he was good enough to represent England on three occasions. Kenny never boxed professionally in this country but after emigrating to Australia, he turned pro and went on to win both the Australian and the British Commonwealth light-middleweight titles, eventually retiring in 1985 with a fantastic record of 30 wins from 32 contests. This article was compiled through interviews with Kenny during September 2006.

KENNY SALISBURY

Kenny was a real hit 'down under'

"I was about nine years old when I first became interested in boxing," remembers Kenny. "I suppose coming from a city like Liverpool and subsequently living in Kirkby, not far from John Conteh, you couldn't fail to catch the boxing bug. I was I believe, Jackie Cunningham and Gordon Ashun's first pupil when they started up the Mayfair ABC and my Dad took me down and introduced me to them. They were really great with me but I mustn't forget the other people who helped me so much whilst I was boxing, particularly Johnny Regan, Eddie Pugh, Ritchie King and the late Billy McDonald and 'Tucker' Hetherington. I couldn't have gone as far as I did without their continued support. It was through the help and guidance that these people gave me over the years that I was able to reach the levels I did."

Kenny certainly reached a high level - winning the majority of around 100 amateur contests and being deemed good enough to represent the ABA three times. "Robbie Davies, Joe Lally and myself all made our International debuts together against France.

"There was no previous history of boxing in our family," recalls Kenny, "and I really took up the sport as a way of training and keeping myself in shape. I always took pride in keeping myself fit and boxing training allowed me to do that. I found that it also taught you discipline and self-control. My father also encouraged me because it would stop me from getting myself into trouble when I was growing up. I'll always be grateful to him for his support.

In his early twenties, Kenny emigrated to Australia where, "I felt I could make a better life for myself. I did in fact have a few amateur bouts in Australia – although I boxed under my mother's maiden name of Nelson. They put me in with one of their top amateurs and I destroyed him so I had to admit that I had a bit of 'previous' as far as the ring was concerned."

When he was 25 years old Kenny decided, "I'd give the professional sport a go. I thought it was a great way of keeping myself fit and maybe earning a few pounds at the same time. I was living in Sydney at the time and I signed with Australian manager Bernie Hall. I found that I hadn't lost my affection for the game and I soon got myself a good following over there."

Billed as 'Kenny Salisbury of Australia', Kenny had a total of 32 bouts as a pro, winning 30 with one draw and one defeat. "I soon fought my way through the light-middleweight rankings and in April 1981 I challenged Phil Davies for the New South Wales light-middleweight title and earned a draw." Just over 12 months later Kenny met Alex Temelkov for the Australian title - a fight that has since entered ring folk-lore. The contest took place at the Sydney Opera House, that magnificent building on the front at Sydney Harbour. It was the first time professional boxing had been held there but, because of what happened during and after the fight, it would also be the last!

"Temelkov and I didn't like each other at all," explains Kenny, "and I suppose this may have lit the fuse for what followed. Charkey Ramon, the former Commonwealth light-middleweight champion from Australia was referee. The fight hadn't long started when Temelkov started rabbit punching me. The referee stepped in to deal with it and then all hell broke loose. My manager leaned over the ropes and tried to pull Temelkov off me. Someone then flew across the ring like a cruise missile about three feet in the air trying to karate kick my manager! It finished up with about twenty people in the ring knocking seven bells out of each other!"

Known as 'World War Three' in Australia, "you can probably understand why there has been no further professional boxing allowed at the Sydney Opera House. Someone said to me, 'trust a scouser to spoil a good thing', but it really wasn't my fault!" Temelkov was disqualified as a result of his actions and Kenny found himself the Australian light-middleweight champion. He defended the title four months later against Dave Edwards, "who I knocked out in the sixth round," and had two more successful title defenses, the first in

December 1982 when he outpointed Billy Johnstone over 12 rounds. "That was a hard battle! I have no hesitation in saying that the hardest fight I had was against Johnstone. He was an awesome fighter and he pushed me all the way. He's a football coach now." In May 1984, Kenny beat Eugene Eades in Sydney, again over 12 rounds, in another defence of his title. This was his 27th pro contest and he was still unbeaten.

Kenny Salisbury (right) c. 1984   *Source: Kenny Salisbury*

Three months after his successful defence against Eades, Kenny was nominated to challenge Zimbabwe's Nelson Bosso for the vacant British Commonwealth light-middleweight title in Sydney. "Again I had to go the distance but it was worth it because at the end I was declared the winner, the new Commonwealth champion! I was so proud! Everything had gone so well for me since I arrived in Australia." In a strange twist of fate Kenny points out that he was the second Liverpool fighter to win the title, "Pat Dwyer had held it previously and he had lost it to Charkey Ramon who was the referee in my contest with Temelkov."

Another ten rounds points win kept Kenny's unbeaten record intact, but in June 1985 he was then matched with Bristol's talented southpaw Nick Wilshire at the Royal Albert Hall. It wasn't to be a glorious home-coming however, as the referee stopped the contest in Wilshire's favour in the second round. "I also lost my Australian light-middleweight title, but not in the ring. I was stripped of the title for not being able to defend it. I was involved in a serious car accident which kept me out of the ring for many months and, as it was obvious that I was never going to be able to return to full fitness, I called a halt to my ring career."

Today Kenny has, "a thriving scaffolding business and a lovely home in Bondi. I married a lovely Australian girl and we have two beautiful daughters. I enjoyed my boxing career and I have no regrets whatsoever. I would do it all again, although I feel that it is much easier today because there are so many titles around. When I say that I would do it all again, I mean if I had my time again – but not today! Although I enjoyed my time in boxing, I must admit that if I had a young son who came home and told me that he wanted to take up a ring career, I would find it difficult to encourage him."

Kenny boxed many times at the Liverpool Stadium as an amateur and was, "sad that they demolished it. I suppose that you could call it the equivalent of playing at Wembley as a footballer. The Stadium had a truly great atmosphere and the crowds were always great. It's so sad that it's no longer there."

A popular lightweight of the late-1970s and early-1980s, George Scholfield (who fought professionally under the name Schofield) boxed for the old Wavertree ABC before turning pro with Les Ratcliffe in October 1978. In a fine eight-year career George managed 26 pro bouts, winning 13 and losing ten, meeting the likes of Tony Caroll, Robbie Robinson, Brian Snagg and George Metcalf, the latter for the Central Area title, before retiring in 1986. Still living and working in Liverpool, where he runs a pub and trains local pros with Shea Neary, this article was obtained through interviews with George in 2006/07.

GEORGE SCHOLFIELD

Six-rounder took over an hour!

Inspired by a father who literally 'punched for pay' it was no surprise that a young George Scholfield jnr. became interested in boxing at a young age."My Dad, George Scholfield snr. was my main inspiration," says George. "He had boxed as a young lad and then travelled the country on the boxing booths that used to go around from fairground to fairground. He would take on all comers for £1 a round. I first went to Wavertree ABC with Tony Darby when I was 10 years old and I had my first contest for them when I was 11. Altogether I had around 72 amateur fights. I won most of them but as far as championships go I only won local junior titles."

There were other reasons behind George's decision to take up boxing as a sport besides his father's background however. "I was the only son with two sisters," he explains, "and I was sometimes picked on for being the only boy. My Dad found out and taught me how to defend myself and my sisters at an early age though. Through his tuition I can tell you we weren't picked on for long!"

Deciding that it would perhaps be more beneficial to actually get paid for boxing, George turned pro when he was only 18 with local manager and ex-pro Les Ratcliffe, "the same manager as my old friend Brian Snagg." He made his pro debut, a fourth round stoppage over Nottingham's Kevin Sheehan, in Manchester in October 1978. Further wins over Joe Mills and Shaun Stewart ensured George ended the year with three wins from three. His fourth contest saw him matched against Manchester's Lance Williams in Burslem in February 1979 and it was here that George's unbeaten record came to an end, eventually losing on points over six rounds. A month later however, he was back on track stopping fellow Liverpudlian and ex-Golden Gloves junior

ABA champion Stan Atherton inside six minutes. "I had some fantastic KOs at the Liverpool Stadium. In all my career, amateur and pro, I was only on the floor once."

A fine points win over Brighton's experienced Barry Price in Birmingham followed before George was matched with rising Liverpool light-welterweight Tony Carroll. Despite trying his best Carroll, who had lost only two of 13 at the time, proved too strong for George and, in his first eight-rounder, he lost on points.

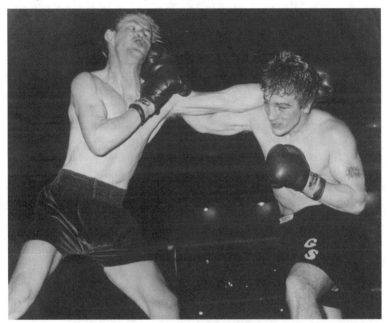

George Scholfield (right) v Barry Winter, 30 October 1980, Liverpool Stadium
Source: George Scholfield

Three losses followed, one against the talented Dingle southpaw Robbie Robinson, before a draw with Glasgow's Barry Winter in October 1980 stopped the rot. Three straight wins later and there was talk George may be in line for a shot at the Central Area title against another local lightweight, Brian Snagg. However, George was then matched with the highly rated Welsh lightweight Ceri (Kerry) Collins This was his toughest contest. "My hardest fight was in Morecambe Bay against Kerry Collins," says George. "He was ranked No. 4 in the country at the time and was very good, very clever. I tried my best but lost on points over eight rounds. Before I boxed him Kerry had had the reigning British champion Brian Cattouse on the floor in a non-title bout that many thought he had won."

Despite this loss the match for the Central Area title was close to being made, but as George explains however, it didn't turn out that way. "Brian Snagg and myself should have boxed for the Area lightweight title in September 1981 but Brian came in overweight. We fought anyway, and I won an eight round contest on points. The fight was broadcast on ITV and near £170 in 'nobbins' were thrown into the ring after the fight." Such a good performance meant George's next fight was for the Area title, but he was stopped in five by yet another local man, George Metcalf, at the Stadium.

Down-hearted though not despondent, George returned five months later with a win and then a loss to Jamaica's Winston McKenzie. These, his only contests of 1982, were followed by one of his most memorable bouts. "I remember boxing a Northern Irish lad, Ray Ross, in Liverpool on a Pat Dwyer show at the old Rotters night club in St Johns Precinct. I was boxing well and then, in the middle of the fourth round, the fire alarm went off and everyone had to evacuate, including the boxers. We all stood outside the building waiting for the all-clear, Ray and me with our boxing gowns on, still wearing our gloves, boots and shorts. Anyway, it was a while before we could go back inside but when we did we simply carried on from where we'd left off! I won over six rounds."

Two further wins rounded off a good year for George, but there were to be no more victories. Three fights later, following a draw with Manchester's Peter Flanagan, he all but retired. This was in March 1984 but just over two years later George returned one last time to meet Paisley's future Scottish light-welterweight champion Dave Haggerty. Haggerty won their eight-rounder in Glasgow on points however, and George retired for good soon after.

Looking back on his career, George is full of praise for his old trainers, and those who inspired him to take up the sport in the first place. "My biggest inspirations were my father, George, who passed away in August 2005, and my old trainer and mentor, Tony Darby, who died in May 2006. They were both a massive influence on me." Those who watched regular shows at the Liverpool Stadium are also worthy of mention for George. "I fought at the Liverpool Stadium on many occasions. It was a great venue for atmosphere, especially if you were from Liverpool yourself, but I always found it to be a very cold place." Like the old Liverpool Stadium in Pudsey Street, the St Paul's Square arena was called 'the Graveyard of Champions' because lots of champions lost their titles there but George reckons there was another reason for its nickname. "It was also built on an old graveyard, perhaps that's why it was so cold in there, even in the summer!"

George acknowledges that boxers today may find their paths to the top less difficult to travel than he and his contemporaries found it. However, he also knows that in order to become a champion sacrifices still have to be made. "There are more titles these days and less boxers so I suppose you could argue that it is easier to succeed, but boxing will always be just like it was in my day – a tough, hard sport. In order to be good you still have to work damn hard. I'm glad I boxed when I did though as I don't think I could have boxed wearing a head-guard like they do in the amateurs now."

George retained an interest in the sport after retiring by training local pros with Jimmy 'Shea' Neary in Old Swan. "I've been with Jimmy ever since his amateur days and throughout his pro career," says George. "I did a few labouring jobs whilst I boxed, but in the end I made a decent living out of boxing. I also ran a few pubs, but I never lost my interest in the sport and in later years I worked with a number of Liverpool boxers, many of whom went on to win national and international titles." In short for George then, there really is no comparison as far as boxing is concerned. "Boxing is the best thing I ever did. I wouldn't change a thing."

Born just two days before Christmas 1938, Ray Shiel first boxed for his local club Lowe House Boys, when he was nine years old. Just six losses out of around 360 bouts followed before Ray turned professional in 1960. A big punching heavyweight who met most of the leading domestic fighters of his day, Ray had a total of 45 pro contests, winning 22 with two draws and 21 losses. Still living in St Helens with his family, this chapter was obtained through interview with Ray in 2006.

RAY SHIEL

First round KO win in Germany - now a third round TKO loss!

Despite there being no history of boxing in his family, Ray Shiel's amateur record with Lowe House Boys' Club in St Helens was an outstanding one. He had a total of 360 contests over 12 years and lost only six. He was ISBA Army cadet champion on three separate occasions, won two NABC titles and a National Schoolboy championship. He also represented England a total of 11 times, and was captain for four of those before turning professional in 1959 when he was 19.

To say that Ray had a tremendous start to his professional career would also be an understatement. His pro debut was a second round KO against Nigeria's Johnny Barday in Manchester in June 1960. A run of eight victories followed, five by KO, including a fine eight round points win over the top ten rated Tony Smith, before he drew with Peter Bates in Manchester. This was in February 1961 but less than a month later they met again at Liverpool Stadium where the St Helens man won a close points decision.

Ray ended 1960 in the top ten British heavyweights himself (No. 7) with the likes of Joe Eskine, Dick Richardson, Brian London and Jim Cooper above him, but his eleven fight unbeaten run was ended in April 1960 when Tonga's Johnny Halafihi edged an eight round decision at the Stadium.

Following a win over Jack Whittaker in Manchester five months later Ray was matched with Jim Cooper, twin brother of Henry Cooper, in his first ten-rounder. Whilst his brother had been British champion for the past three years, Jim Cooper had been ranked in the top five

British heavyweights himself throughout the same period, and it was a step up in class for Ray. After 10 tough rounds however, Cooper was adjudged the winner.

A fine ten round points win over Bootle's Dave Rent, a former amateur colleague of Ray's with both England and the ABA, in November 1961, was followed just 17 days later by another ten round points win over Philadelphia's Don Warner. Ray had lost just two of his 16 pro fights to date and was beginning to get himself noticed on a national level. His next contest confirmed this as he was matched with Germany's Gerhard Zech for his first contest outside England.

Ray remembers his January 1962 contest with Zech in Dortmund in some detail, and rightly so for it saw the German emerge victorious in one of those home-town decisions that all boxers dread when fighting outside their own country. "I knocked out Zech in the first round with a solid right hand," says Ray. "After the ref had counted to 10 I went back to my corner and had almost taken of one of my gloves when he called me back to the centre of the ring to tell me to box on. I couldn't believe it and neither could my trainer! I'd just seen Zech counted out but the referee was adamant we continue. We carried on until the third round when the referee stopped the contest due to a cut above my eye – a cut that had been caused by a blatant headbutt by Zech earlier in the round. So what should have been a first round KO victory on my record actually reads as a third round TKO loss!"

A rematch with Jim Cooper followed and this time Ray gained his revenge courtesy of a fourth round stoppage. A fine win over Peter Bates in Nottingham in October 1962 was Ray's only other win in 1962 (nine contests), but two of these losses were against local boxers in Bologna Italy, whilst a draw with Birmingham's Johnny Prescott in November 1962, when Prescott was undefeated and on his way to challenging for the British title himself, was no disgrace.

Losses against Tommy Fields, Chic Calderwood and Johnny Prescott followed before Ray achieved arguably the best win of his career, a fifth round disqualification win over Birkenhead based Jamaican Joe Bygraves. Bygraves had been British Empire Champion 1956-57 and had met a host of top class heavyweights in his prime; Paddy Slavin, Frank Bell, Henry Cooper, Peter Bates, Dick Richardson, Joe Erskine, Kitione Lave and Heinz Neuhaus and despite being past his prime he was still a tough opponent.

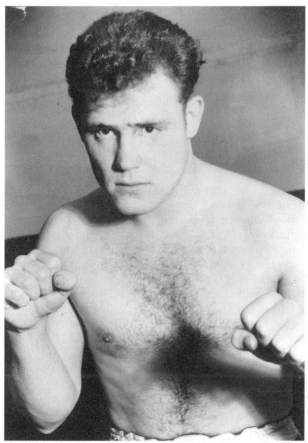

Ray Shiel c. 1964   *Source: Gary Shaw*

Ray met Bygraves at the Liverpool Stadium in August 1963. Bygraves
had long been a favourite at the venue but Ray, no stranger to the
Liverpool boxing public himself recalls, "I fought at the old Liverpool
Stadium many times. I had ten fights there and lost four – three on
points. I filled the Stadium to the rafters the night I met Bygraves.
There were only half a dozen people who fancied me against him –
and one of those was my wife!"

Despite beating a local favourite Ray recalls the Liverpool fight fans
with affection, "I remember what a great reception I got afterwards."

Only six wins out of his next 17 contests (losses to Carl Gizzi, Jack Bodell and, in Stockholm, the tough American Thad Spencer – "the toughest man I ever fought") persuaded Ray to retire in October 1966. This was despite his last contest being a sixth round KO of Joe Buck – again at the Stadium. Looking back on his career today, Ray acknowledges that there were times when he, "listened to the wrong people," although he has no regrets - "I would gladly do it all again."

When asked his opinion of Britain's current boxing stars Ray says, "I think that compared to today's fighters, boxers in my day had to fight a lot harder for a lot less money. However, I do believe the fight game is a lot straighter than it was then. It's for these reasons that I sometimes wish I could start my career over again today!" Ray still lives in St. Helens with his wife of 47 years Betty. "We have five children; Karen 46, Kim 44, Kay, who we sadly lost two years ago, Kieron 32 and young Ray who is 37. Thinking of them all I can say that I am a very proud man."

Born Owen Thomas Jones in 1911, Birkenhead welterweight Billy Simpson turned pro with Jim Turner in 1931 but had only one fight under his real name before changing it after a win as a substitute to the name of the man he replaced. At one stage talked about as a potential challenger for both British and European honours, Billy retired in 1943 and became a referee in the mid-1950s and died some years ago. This chapter is based on an article by Frank Johnson that was first published in 1972.

BILLY SIMPSON

Nearly 250 fights but Billy never took a count

Born in 1911 and christened Owen Thomas Jones, Billy Simpson was educated at Laird Street and Brassey Street Schools and was brought up in Patten Street, Birkenhead. Following a conversation with Gerry Byrne, who mentioned that former schoolmate Charlie Smith was making a name for himself as a boxer, Billy decided to give the game a go himself and he duly joined Gerry's club. After some intensive training, he climbed through the ropes just six weeks later to make his professional debut at Bebington Stadium. In the opposite corner was a tough docker by the name of Danny Clarke and although he was out-pointed, Billy put up such a good show that the promoter added an extra shilling to his purse - thereby making it up to 11 shillings.

A few weeks later Billy had his second pro contest at the Victoria Stadium, Birkenhead, when he deputised for a lad by the name of Billy Simpson. After winning on points, Owen Thomas Jones adopted the name and he used it for the remainder of his career. 'Billy' signed a pro contract with well-known Northern manager, Jim Turner, soon after and the partnership thrived. He boxed all over the country and at one time recalled having seven fights in 15 days. He met all the top welterweights and middleweights in the North even though he never scaled much more than 10st 8lbs. He even went in with the odd light-heavyweight if the money was good enough.

As Billy improved, talk of a clash with local hero Charlie Smith became inevitable. The pair eventually met over 15 rounds before almost 3,000 spectators at the Birkenhead Drill Hall, the winner to meet another rising star from the other side of the Mersey in Ernie Roderick. After a terrific fight, Billy got the nod over Charlie, but the proposed fight with Roderick never materialised as Jim Turner wanted £15 for the contest. Charlie Smith asked for £10 but another local fighter, Bob Nelson, took the contest for £7 and caused a sensation by beating Roderick and becoming the only Merseyside fighter to do so.

On the outbreak of the Second World War Billy joined the RAF as an Air Gunner. In 1943 he became a Parachute Jumping Instructor, taking part in no fewer than 67 jumps. His last contest came in 1943 at the Royal Albert Hall when he boxed for the RAF professionals against a similar from the Army. During the war, Billy organised numerous boxing tournaments for the boys, and he recalled featuring the great Joe Louis on one of them. He travelled extensively in the company of great fighters such as Peter Kane, Tommy Farr, Freddie Miller, Ernie Roderick, Jack London snr., and a host of others.

At the end of the war, Billy was invited to re-enlist. He did so and in 1952 he left Birkenhead with his wife and two sons and settled in Blackpool, near to his RAF base at Weeton. He left the Air Force in 1959 and took up employment with the Atomic Energy Commission as a process supervisor. In 1955 Billy had become a professional boxing referee and at one time he was the only professional 'third man' in the three armed services.

Billy had lasting memories of the hard times in the boxing game in pre-war days. "Once I fought 12 rounds on Tuesday night and I had another 15-rounder on the Friday." They were hungry fighters in the 1930s and in the holiday season they would flock to the fairgrounds to take on all-comers in the boxing booths. "I must have fought in every hall and market place in Lancashire, and I can vouch for the punches and moves which we daren't try out in a pro fight. In the booths, I've had as many as 40 or 50 fights in a week". A 12-hour day was not uncommon and Billy remembers that one of his fellow battlers on the booth at a Newcastle race meeting, was none other than the great Benny Lynch, who went on to win the world flyweight championship.

Although retiring to live in Blackpool, Billy remained a Birkenhead man. Whenever boxing is talked about in the town, Billy's clashes with Jack Clive, Jimmy Dean, George Massey, Jim Beswick, Jimmy Baird, Larry Hamill, George Davies, Jim Martin and that bone cracking puncher, Young Ash, are always to the fore. Billy reckoned he had around 247 pro fights and he was never knocked down long enough to take a count.

With a professional fight career lasting a staggering 17 years (1929 - 1946) Birkenhead's Charlie Smith was one of the most dedicated and popular 'old time' fighters Merseyside has produced. The type of rugged, all-action, fight anyone, anywhere type of boxer whom the sport can't do without, Charlie was a value for money fighter with a terrific right hook and he gave his all whenever and wherever he appeared.

CHARLIE SMITH

Seventeen years a pro!

Born in January 1912, Charlie Smith grew up in the Laird Street district of Birkenhead. A book by former French world champion Georges Carpentier first got Charlie interested in the sport and his ring idol throughout his career was the great Jack Dempsey. His first experience with gloves took place at a fairground boxing booth in Hoylake when he was 14. Charlie recalls that after he had KO'd Holywell's 'Battling' Kehoe he had to walk home as he had missed his bus. Upon arriving late however, he received a hiding from his father who had no idea his son had taken the first steps towards becoming a boxer. The purse money Charlie received for this fight, a total of 7/6d, took some of the pain away but it also gave him a lifelong love of the game.

Charlie joined the Conway Athletic Club in the late-1920s and, with little amateur experience, he made his proper paid debut at Liverpool's Pudsey Street Stadium in December 1929 when he was just 17 years old. His relative lack of amateur and professional experience didn't hinder Charlie however, and he managed to force Taffy Jones of Shotton to retire in the third of a scheduled six round contest.

Charlie fought regularly, sometimes every other week, at Pudsey Street where he quickly established himself as a firm crowd favourite due to his non-stop style and commitment. He beat Liverpool's Jimmy Dean and Les Douglas, Jim Belcher, George Green and Larry Bonner amongst others. He would also suffer defeats against such devastating punchers as 'Cyclone' Charlie Ovey of Oldham – who stopped Charlie twice in successive bouts, 'One of the hardest punchers I met', and fellow townsman Bob Nelson, the only Merseyside fighter to defeat Ernie Roderick.

Charlie often sparred with Roderick and he had no hesitation in saying that Ernie was the cleverest fighter he ever faced. Another who Charlie rated highly was Londoner Harry 'Kid' Brooks. When they met at Pudsey Street in June 1933 however, Charlie was on his way to the ring when he overheard Brooks' manager saying to a friend, 'This won't last long.' He was right too, as Charlie forced the referee to stop the contest in the third of a scheduled 15 round contest.

Perhaps Charlie's toughest contest came against Harry Evans of Pendleton at Morecambe in July 1935. In the second round Pendleton landed a tremendous punch to Charlie's jaw and from that moment on the Birkenhead man was fighting on pure instinct. The fight was scheduled for 12 rounds and at the start of the last Charlie had to ask his manager what round it was as he couldn't remember anything from the previous nine rounds! His instinct must have been good however, as he was declared the winner on points.

Charlie suffered from brittle hands throughout his career. Following a fifth round stoppage of Liverpool's Martin Shinnick at the Stadium Charlie remembered taking off his gloves and discovering that his bandaging had simply disintegrated. Although broken bones were a regular occurrence for him however, Charlie never changed his fighting style.

Charlie fought throughout the 1930s and into the early-1940s. Like many his career was disrupted by the Second World War although the lack of younger fighters around in the early days of the war meant that he managed to top a few bills at the Liverpool Stadium during this time - one just days after the death of his father.

Charlie did his duty by joining the RAF but his biggest war-time shock came not when he was on active service, but when he was home on leave. On 12 March 1941 Charlie was at home when the air-raid siren signalled yet another raid by German bombers. His wife and two children found a shelter quickly enough but Charlie was in the house when a landmine exploded nearby in Nelson Street. The house was completely destroyed and with Charlie still inside, buried in the rubble, people feared the worst. Whilst Charlie survived however, all his boxing records, awards and memorabilia were gone forever.

The experience affected Charlie so much that he was discharged from the RAF and he returned to his pre-war employment with the local cooperative dairy in Woodchurch Road. He attempted to resume his boxing career but had only two contests in 1943, both at Liverpool Stadium; a third round retirement to a then young but up-and-coming Alex Buxton (later British light-heavyweight champion) in July and, in what turned out to be his final contest on 5 August, a second round KO of Jim McConnell.

Charlie later worked at Vauxhall's and he remained a popular figure in Birkenhead until his death in January 1988 aged 75. He never fought for a title but was always popular wherever he appeared.

Charlie Smith c. 1939   *Source: Jim Jenkinson*

Born in March 1913, Jerry Smith soon established a reputation for terrific punching power and earned the ring name of "The Rock Ferry Assassin". In a 60 fight professional career, and many fights in the travelling boxing booths, Jerry became a man to be feared among his fellow professionals. This story was obtained from an article written by former boxing writer, Frank Johnson, and was first published in 1973.

JERRY SMITH

The 'Rock Ferry Assassin'

An attraction of any sport is the appeal of a gifted performer. The ability for one man or woman to draw the crowds simply because of their seemingly magic ability. This could be a great batsman treating a quality bowling attack with disdain, dispatching ball after ball for fours or sixes. It could be a gifted footballer blessed with speed, grace and the ability to score goals from all angles, with both feet and head. Boxing is similar in the sense that spectators and commentators alike share a passion for a gifted performer. There is a subtle difference however, as besides expecting a great boxer to show skill, speed and courage, the one thing that draws the crowds to ringside more than any other is the man who has the ability to put other men on the canvas with devastating punches. One such man was Jerry Smith - a boxer from the 1930s who, because of his KO record, soon earned the nickname, the *Rock Ferry Assassin*.

Jerry's father John, a useful amateur in his younger days, managed Jerry during his 60 fight career, and they formed a partnership which set local boxing halls alight. His first introduction to boxing in a serious manner came when Jerry was working in Edge's butchers in New Ferry. The owner, a true boxing fanatic, would travel far and wide in order to watch a tournament and it was he who informed his young helper that a boxing booth at a fair in Beaconsfield Road, New Ferry was offering anyone ten shillings if they could stay three rounds with one of the booth fighters. After considerable persuasion, Jerry went down one evening and while the booth barker was shouting the odds, Mr. Edge shouted that he had a lad with him, a lad who was good enough to take on any of the booth fighters.

Resplendent in his working gear of breeches and Russian field boots, and after being pushed into the makeshift dressing area, 17-year old

Jerry tied his braces around his breeches and clambered through the ropes to 'do battle' with Nipper Brown. Jerry dispatched Brown in two rounds with a jaw breaking left hook - the punch that would become his main weapon in the years to come. Although pleased at the win, Jerry informed his boss that he had only entered the ring to prove that he wasn't afraid.

Fear was a commodity that Jerry didn't seem to have and, after further persuasion, booth promoter Sam Barton coaxed Jerry back the following night, where he KO'd 'Slogger' in equally devastating style. Jerry received £1 for his efforts and when he accepted a third scrap with another tough booth fighter, he saw himself billed on a blackboard outside the tent as 'The New Ferry Wonder Boy.' With another KO win Jerry soon found himself the focus of attention of local promoters and managers and he turned pro soon after.

In his first proper contest, Jerry met George 'Kid' Stephens. Stephens was regularly boxing 15 rounders and having his fair share of success, so it was a tall order for Jerry. Billed for six rounds for 30/- however, Jerry had Stephens down in every round and won handsomely. Based in Johnny Howlett's *[who boxed as Jack Howlett eds.]* stable at Brougham Street, Rock Ferry as a featherweight, Jerry mixed in the gym with Charlie Tonner, Charlie Cole and a host of other top-rated local fighters.

Jerry's main attribute was his terrific left hook, but this was not the only weapon in his armoury that other boxers came to fear as he was also a southpaw and, as many boxers have found, his right foot forward stance puzzled many of his opponents. This two edged sword took Jerry firmly along the pathway to stardom, and he recalled boxing at Little Ness at the Oddfellows Hall and KOing Frank Whelan (Higher Bebington) in two rounds. He strung together a tremendous run of 43 wins, including 36 KOs and the national, as well as the local press, hailed the arrival of a new discovery almost certain to gain a title shot before too long.

With a run of sensational KO wins, Jerry certainly seemed to be living up to his new billing as 'The Rock Ferry Assassin.' He boxed regularly at St. Helens, Hoylake Central Hall, Birkenhead Drill Hall, St. Martins Hall in the tough Scotland Road district of Liverpool and the Majestic Ring in Preston. It was at St. Helens that Jerry accepted a fight against the local Lancashire hero Mick Kehoe - known as, 'the man with the iron jaw' - as he had never been on the floor in over 100 contests. Jerry KO's him in one round however, and then had a harder fight battling his way through the hoard of angry miners who had seen not only their hero toppled, but a large slice of their hard earnings go to the bookmakers. Jerry tasted defeat for the first time when future British welterweight and middleweight champion, and world title challenger, Ernie Roderick stopped him in the seventh round at the Liverpool Stadium. It should be remembered however, that Jerry was only a featherweight at the time and probably gave Roderick over a stone in weight.

Another top class featherweight at the time was Tommy Dexter, who had just taken the great Nel Tarleton the distance. In agreeing to take Dexter on many believed that Jerry was over-stepping his mark. Jerry thought otherwise however, and blasted Dexter out inside five rounds at the Birkenhead Drill Hall. Jerry also met Roderick at the same venue but, after receiving a severe cut after a clash of heads in the first round he simply couldn't see by the seventh and the fight was stopped in the Liverpool man's favour.

Roderick was one of only three men to defeat Jerry, the others being hard-hitting Jimmy Stewart - later Northern Area lightweight champion, and tough Scottish champ Jake Kilrain. Prior to the Stewart contest Jerry was having a Sunday morning spar with local fighter Jim Falone and, in an accidental clash, Jerry received a nasty eye injury. It would perhaps have been wiser to have pulled out of the Stewart clash but Jerry went through with it and it ultimately cost him the fight. Against Kilrain, Jerry mis-timed the count after taking a big right hand and the referee counted, "eight, nine, OUT!" instead of, "eight, nine, ten, OUT!" The rule had just been changed and, as Jerry was not used to being on the canvas, he rose too late.

The hardest hitter and toughest man Jerry ever met was the Liverpool scrapper, Paddy McGrath, in a fight at St. Martin's Hall, Scotland Road. It was a terrific bout with the crowd in uproar throughout, as the hot local favourite McGrath dropped the decision over 12 of the fiercest rounds ever contested on Merseyside. Both fighters took counts on several occasions, and so exciting an atmosphere was it that the timekeeper got carried away and made the 11th round six minutes long! Although Jerry got the verdict, and the applause of both Nel Tarleton and Dom Volante afterwards, 12 rounds was enough at that pace but 13 was perhaps a bit too much! Prior to this contest, McGrath had beaten the rugged Italian champion Aldo Spaldi, and it was a shock when the Rock Ferry man beat McGrath over the full course.

Jerry also recalled sparring with another great southpaw, world featherweight champion, Freddie Miller, who had just beaten Tarleton for the first time. Jerry sparred at Dom Vairo's Gym in Islington, Liverpool, prior to Miller dropping a sensational disqualification defeat against the Liverpool banger, Billy Gannon.

Jerry retired from boxing in 1933, although he did box on several occasions whilst in the RAF during the war. He married in 1939 but sadly lost his wife in 1947. They had a daughter and three sons. Jerry passed away some years ago.

One of Liverpool and Merseyside's most respected boxers and trainers, John Smith boxed for a variety of local amateur clubs, winning the majority of his 61 contests and earning selection for England on a number of occasions. Although turning pro at 28 John went on to have almost a century of contests in a fine eleven-year career, meeting the likes of Mark Winters, Bobby Vanzie, Michael Carruth, Paul Ryan, Jonathan Thaxton, Shea Neary and Robert McRacken. Always popular due to his fight anyone, anytime attitude, John often fought up-and-coming prospects in their own backyard, being selected for both his durability and ring-savvy. Still living and working in Liverpool, where he has become a fine pro trainer, working with the likes of Alex Moon, Gary Ryder and Tony Moran, this article was compiled through interviews with John in 2007.

JOHN SMITH

A tough test for anyone

Being good friends with two local amateur boxing stars it didn't take John Smith long to become involved in the sport. "I followed my mates Tony and Kenny Willis into boxing when I was about 11 years old," recalls John. "They were both great talents, world class amateurs. I used to watch them all the time and through this they would teach me things. I only had one junior contest, the rest were all as a senior, although I remember it well; it was against Steven Hussy from Huyton ABC.

"My first club was the Furs but after a while I left there and boxed for the old Kensington ABC, and then the Rotunda with Jimmy 'Albo' Albertina. Once I was trained by Jimmy things started to happen for me as an amateur. He was a great man."

With a total of 61 amateur fights, 45 wins and only 16 losses, John soon caught the attention of the England selectors. "I was good enough to box for England a few times and won a bronze at the Copenhagen Cup, a tournament in which I also won best boxer. I boxed for the North West Counties loads of times, losing only once, the Army - where I won a BAOR title, and my Regiment - the Kings. I never lost a fight for them."

John turned pro at the relatively old age of 28, "with the Lynch brothers from Birmingham who had managed Tony Willis." In a remarkable eleven-year career, John went on to have almost 100 contests, a phenomenal record in the modern game. He would meet countless former or future champions, many of whom were matched with him in the early stages of their career in order to gain valuable experience. Lasting four, six or eight rounds with John was seen by many as evidence that their rising star had what it took to reach the top. "Despite what *BoxRec* says *[the internet boxing record site lists John as having 92 contests eds.]* I had 97 contests, winning 15, drawing 10 and losing the rest. Some of these losses were stoppages by the referee but I have only ever been KO'd twice in my career. Once by Wayne Greene as an amateur in an Army v Navy match, and once by Ross Hale as a pro."

John's pro debut came in June 1986, a six rounds points win over Alfreton's Ray Golding at Edgbaston's Tower Ballroom. This was followed by a similar victory over Scotland's John Townsley at the same venue three months later. Despite winning his first two pro bouts, John wouldn't win again until March 1988. "My third fight was against Glasgow's Robert Harkin in Glasgow. He had lost only one of nine and was being talked of as a future British title challenger. *[Harkin later won the Scottish Area light-welterweight title and challenged for the Commonwealth crown eds.]* Despite taking the fight at short notice I gave a good account of myself but lost by just half a point over eight rounds. After that it was difficult for me to get matches with lads at the same sort of level as me. I didn't win any titles, I just boxed all-comers. If the money was right I boxed. It didn't matter who, or where or when. I loved it though. They were great times!"

John had five bouts in his first year as a pro, winning two and drawing with Birmingham's Gary Somerville, who was just coming back after his first loss in eleven. In 1987 John had three contests, the least number he would have in a calendar year in his career. In 1988 he again won two and drew one of five contests, including a points loss and a revenge stoppage victory over Somerville.

In March 1989, John had his 15th pro contest at Solihull Conference Centre. It was an experience he will never forget. Despite meeting fighters of the calibre of Robert McCracken, Ross Hale, Paul Ryan and Shea Neary, men who would floor you if they caught you right, this was John's hardest fight. "The toughest man I fought was Welshman John Davies. Every shot he hit me with hurt. Like many of my fights I gave weight away in this contest but managed to last the eight rounds only to lose on points. To look at me the next day you would have thought a lorry had ran over me."

258

It was four months before John fought again, a third round stoppage win over Londoner Richard Adams and he followed this with another rare victory, an easy points win over Manchester's Muhammad Lovelock. Six losses on the bounce followed however, although these mirrored how the rest of John's career would pan out; - distance losses against rising names in their own backyard.

Two wins from eight contests in 1990 included a stoppage loss to Newcastle's Paul Charters in Hartlepool. A future Area champion Charters would challenge for the European lightweight title in Italy just a year later. In 1991 John had 13 contests, drawing one and losing the rest. Amongst these however, were two fights against names that would become familiar to boxing fans in the coming years; a second round stoppage loss due to cuts against Billy Schwer at Watford. Schwer would win both the British and Commonwealth titles the following year, the European title in 1997 and challenged for versions of world titles on four occasions; and Robert McCracken, British light-middleweight champion 1994 and Commonwealth champion 1995. He too would challenge for a world title later in his career.

Two draws and five losses from seven fights was John's record in 1992. Again however, a first round KO to future British and Commonwealth light-welter champ Ross Hale was no disgrace, as was another cuts stoppage to Sweden's George Scott in Birmingham in February 1992. Scott is probably not a name many would recognise now but as John explains, he certainly had a good pedigree. "Scott's real name was Cranme, and although born in Liberia he was adopted and represented Sweden in the 1988 Olympics, where he won a silver. He was trained by none other than Angelo Dundee and was on his way to a 22-fight unbeaten start to his career when I met him at the NEC. I'd only just got going in the third round when referee Terry O'Connor stopped it due to a cut. Technically Scott was very good and he later challenged for the WBC and IBF light-welterweight titles."

If John didn't lose on points, having taken a younger prospect the distance, he would invariably lose as a result of a cut. "I was always bad for cuts," recalls John. "After one fight I got caught using plastic skin on my eyes. One of the doctors reported it and next thing the Boxing Board representatives were involved. They were all looking at my eyes wondering what to do when Pat Dwyer told them that I suffered badly from cirrhosis, and with that they all just walked off and left me."

Despite celebrating his 34th birthday in 1993 John was still as keen as ever to fight and he had six contests this year, drawing one and losing on points to future world champion Shea Neary, future British champions Jason Rowland and Jonathan Thaxton, and West Bromwich's talented Mark McCreath. All of course were a lot younger than John. Fellow Liverpudlian Neary was 'only' nine years his junior, with Rowland two years younger still and Thaxton giving John a full 15 years head start!

From left, George Scholfield, Shea Neary, John Smith and Pat Dwyer c. 1998
Source: John Smith

John enjoyed just one win from nine in 1994, including a stoppage loss on cuts to unbeaten Hackney prospect Paul 'Scrap Iron' Ryan, later British and Commonwealth champion. Showing no signs of slowing down however, John averaged a fight a month in 1995 were he lost to the likes of Andreas Panayi, Shea Neary again, Ireland's 1992 Olympic gold medallist Michael Carruth and another future British champion in the shape of Bobby Vanzie. John's third round KO win over Manchester's Wahid Fats in Manchester in June this year was to be his last victory however. Eleven more fights followed in 1996, including losses to Mark Winters and Chris Barnett, before John finally called it a day, aged 37 and after eleven years as a solid pro, in June 1997.

Looking back on his career today John would hardly change a thing. "I've no regrets at all and I would gladly do it all again. I loved it. I would have liked to have turned pro a bit sooner however, if only to make it to 100 fights." With such a long and distinguished amateur and pro career, John knows most of the city's boxing personalities well but is keen to thank those who helped him the most during his time in the sport. "I'd like to thank all the trainers I've had and worked with over the years. Jimmy West and Tony Salovon at the Furs; Reg Gadd and Terry Quinn at Kensington; Jimmy Albo at the Rotunda; and both Pat Dwyer, he was my last manager, and Georgie Vaughan in the pros." John also acknowledges the help and support his family gave him during his long career. "I have a great wife, Sheila, and three lads Mark, Shaun and Joseph. Shaun boxed for Stockbridge ABC for a while, doing really well to win a Schoolboy title in his first year."

Boxing for so long also meant that John saw action at a number of different venues, although few compare to his hometown. "I loved boxing at the Stadium," recalls John. "It was a great venue. Proper, true boxing fans turned up to watch, even old-time gangsters. You name them and they were all there. All old fighters, different gangs, but there was never any trouble. They just came to watch as fans."

Today John retains an active interest in the sport through his role as a pro trainer, a role he has filled with distinction since he retired. "I work in a gym for Knowsley Council but also train fighters for Matchroom. I've trained fighters for years and have had some good boxers; Alex Moon, Tony Moran, Gary Ryder, Steve Mullins, Dave Keir, Andreas Panayi and so on. There are some good young kids coming up too."

Being so involved in the sport today means that John's views on the modern game are especially interesting. "I don't think there is more money around today. In fact there is probably less for the average boxer, but if you manage to hit the big-time then the money is good. Saying that, too many boxers on the way up today think they've made it before they really have and that they're some sort of superstar. There are fewer shows today than there was even 15 or 20 years ago so maybe that's why, but rather than fight the best they avoid them to build up a good record. That is until its crunch time and they come unstuck."

Born in January 1959, Brian Snagg enjoyed a successful amateur career with first the Phoenix ABC in Childwall and then the famous Golden Gloves in Park Road. It was with the Dingle club that he won National Schoolboys titles in 1972 and 73 whilst the following year he made the quarter-finals of the Junior ABAs. A regular Lancs. and England Schoolboys representative 1972-75 he also won the West Lancs. lightweight titles in 1976 and 77. He turned pro soon after and in a seven-year career amassed 26 fights, including a contest for the Central Area title. A manager and boxing promoter after retiring, Brian then became a publican, and now runs The Fusilier in Prescot. This article was compiled through interviews with Brian during 2006.

BRIAN SNAGG

Boxer, manager, promoter - Brian has no regrets

Tough lightweight Brian Snagg enjoyed a successful amateur career with the famous Dingle Golden Gloves ABC, before turning professional in 1977. The highlight of his pro career was arguably a 10 round points defeat to the Manchester based Moroccan, Najib Daho for the Central Area Lightweight title in June 1979.

"My Dad Barnie had boxed a little in his time and I mainly became interested in the sport because of him. I started with the Phoenix in Childwall when I was 10 but then moved to the Gloves and it was here that I had most of my amateur success. I had 46 amateur bouts in total, winning 34 and losing just 12. I represented England at Schoolboy level quite a few times and managed to win National Schoolboy titles in 1972 and 73."

Just four years later, not long after becoming West Lancs amateur champion and aged only 18 Brian turned professional with Les Ratcliffe. "As a pro I was trained at first by Johnny Cooke, then Charlie Atkinson. Altogether I had 26 fights, winning 13 and losing 12." Despite having such illustrious trainers, Brian's pro debut was a losing one, a six round points defeat to fellow scouser Tony Carroll at the Liverpool Stadium on 10 November 1977. Undeterred however, Brian quickly put this loss behind him and just 19 days later was in the ring again, this time in Birkenhead, to score a fine points win over Selvin Bell.

Two defeats in his next four contests meant that Brian had had a mixed start to his paid career but a fine run of six wins followed before he was held to a draw by Birkenhead's Dave Taylor. "The fight against Dave Taylor was definitely my hardest," recalls Brian. "It was toe-to-toe for eight rounds but there was no stopping him. He just kept coming forward." A couple of defeats followed before Brian was matched with the Manchester based Moroccan Najib Daho for the Central Area title in 1979. It was Brian's biggest test to date and the first time he had fought at the championship distance of 10 rounds. Brian remembers, "the fight was held in Manchester and although I lost I felt it was a close decision. I received my biggest purse for this fight - £500. Daho was a good boxer though, remember he later fought for the British, European and Commonwealth titles and scored a good win over Pat Cowdell. It was a shock when I heard he'd died in a motorbike accident in 1993. He was only 34."

Brian Snagg (left) v Jimmy Bunclark, 22 April 1982, Liverpool Stadium
Source: Brian Snagg

A return with Daho three months later, though this time not for the title, saw Brian outscored again over eight rounds. He had nine more contests before retiring in 1982 including a fine win over the talented, tall and tough Sheffield star Glyn Rhodes, as well as two stoppages over local boxer Jimmy Bunclark and a points defeat against another Liverpool fighter - George Scholfield. It was whilst sharing a bill with George that Brian recalls one particular amusing incident from his career. "When George boxed on the same bill as me at the Stadium I remember he KO'd a kid in the first round. I was in the dressing room with the kid when he came back and I remember him asking his trainer what time he was boxing. He was stunned when the trainer replied that he'd just been knocked out and to get his gloves off!"*[probably Braford-based Jamaican John Lindo, who was KO'd in one round at the Stadium on 22 October 1981. eds.]*

Another great memory for the young boxer was travelling to the USA to train. "I remember going to the States for seven months in 1981. It was a great experience, the highlight being the time I was sparring with Bruce Finch whilst he was in training for his fight with Sugar Ray Leonard."At the time Finch was NABF champion and had 29 victories from 34 contests. Besides his loss to Leonard he also met the likes of Don Curry and Al Kareem Mohammad.

"One day I only did seven or so rounds with Finch rather than the usual ten," recalls Brian. "One of the trainers threw a kid in with me for my last three rounds and we circled each other a bit - I was going easy on him. As I moved to him though, he dipped and brought up a great left hook to the body that really hurt. I thought you little bleeder! I'm not letting you get away with that! I went after him then but bang, he did it again, then again. I got his name after and it turned out to be Juan Laporte!" Laporte would later win the WBC world featherweight title.

Despite the plan being that Brian's time in America would result in a few contests, they never materialised. "I was due to fight on a big Mike Weaver show in Vegas but it was scrapped after he pulled out. Another proposed fight fell through and by then I was frustrated and wanted to come home. I didn't train as I should have for my proposed third fight, came in overweight and that was it."

Looking back on his career today, Brian makes some interesting observations. "I have no regrets at all about my career and would gladly do it all again. However, although I loved the game as it was then, I don't think I would want to start it again today. A few things have changed and I think headguards spoil the amateurs - not as many kids want to really fight as they did in my day. Also, I think the money they get – both amateur and pro – is better than in my day and this makes it a lot easier to succeed in that sense compared to when I was boxing." Like many ex-boxers from his time and before, Brian also holds great affection for the Liverpool Stadium. "It was a great place to box - in front of your own fans and family you can't beat it. They certainly knew their stuff there."

Brian's interest in boxing continued once he had retired from the ring, as he managed a number of boxers and promoted numerous shows, whilst his interest in Everton remains as big as it ever was. Together with fellow Evertonian Tommy Birch and ex-Everton player Roger Kenyon, Brian set up Bluenose Productions and they arrange team reunions, events and popular sportsman's dinners, often with ex-Liverpool players in attendance as well, all over Merseyside. "Before boxing I worked as a scaffolder, then after retiring I was a publican but also managed a few fighters and promoted a few shows. I run the pubs with my wife Carole. We have three kids – all grown up now; Kerry, Tony and Angela."

A top amateur with the famous Lowe House ABC in St Helens, Gary Stretch turned pro in 1985 and went on to record 23 wins (13 early) out of 25 contests in the paid ranks, the highlight being his reign as British light-middleweight champion (1988-89), and his challenge for the WBO world middleweight title in 1991. In his eight-year career he met the likes of Lenny Gloster, Sammy Sampson, Denys Cronin, Gary Cooper and Chris Eubank, although he is arguably more famous today than when he boxed. After retiring Gary moved to the United States, took acting lessons, and has since appeared in a number of top British and Hollywood movies. Although work commitments mean he spends most of his time travelling between the USA and UK, Gary lives in Los Angeles, California and this article was compiled through email interviews with Gary in 2006/07.

GARY STRETCH

British champion turned Hollywood star

When Gary Stretch beat Bracknell's George Collins in the National Association of Boys' Clubs welterweight final at London's Grosvenor House in January 1985, the tall, classy southpaw caused one of the biggest upsets in English boxing for many years. Collins, a top amateur with the Pinewood Star ABC, had won National Schoolboys titles (1981-84), NABC titles (1983-84) and was a two-time junior ABA champion (1983-84). In compiling his fantastic junior record, Collins had run up a sequence of 73 straight wins, all by stoppage or unanimous decision. One more victory for the Londoner would create a then world record so the contest was screened live for BBC TV's *Record Breakers*. Unfazed with such a daunting task however, Gary KO'd Collins in the first round so making the first of what would turn out to be many headlines over the coming years.

Gary's father, Ronnie, had raised him and his two brothers since their mother left the family home when Gary was just 10. "It left its mark on me obviously," recalls Gary, "and I got into fights at school. They were going to expel me and I went to a boxing gym as a last resort. I guess it gave me the attention I thought I should have been getting and I took to it, and the discipline it offered, straight away. Next thing you know I'm in the National championships, I'm fighting Collins and I'm on TV. Then I beat him and I turn pro!"

Mike Barrett snapped Gary up soon after his win over Collins and his paid debut came in April 1985 when he tackled Leicester's Steve Tempro, a veteran of 44 fights at the York Hall, Bethnal Green. It was a useful start for Gary as he floored Tempro three times and was well on top when referee Tony Walker called it off with just 15 seconds of the sixth and final round remaining. The following month he made it two wins out of two by stopping another opponent with plenty of experience, Hull's Bobby Welburn. Welburn was decked by a Stretch right hand in the third only to regain his feet and come under intense pressure before the referee stepped in soon after.

Barrett remarked at the time that although it was early days yet, there were signs of potential in the young St Helens boxer. "He's definitely a future British champion," Barrett said, "and I rate him as one of the most promising young prospects around at the moment." Such rave reviews were not without substance. None other than *Boxing News* wrote that Gary's matador style, fast accurate combinations and ability to evade punches boded well for the future noting that he, "has the ability to slip shots and survive. He does this better than anyone in boxing in this country at the moment." It was no wonder Gary had 'The Gifted One' written on the back of his satin gown!

A further three wins from four contests followed in 1985, one an eye catching third round stoppage *[a scheduled 8 x 2 minute rounds contest, eds.]* over the capable Peterborough based West Indian Lenny Gloster, a fighter who had taken talented stars like Tony McKenzie and Chris Blake the distance previously. Wishaw's Jim Kelly, a former Scottish welterweight champion, was dropped in the first round of their October 1985 contest, before being outpointed over six rounds – the first of Gary's opponents to take him the distance. In his last fight of 1985 however, Gary tasted defeat for the first time. An accidental clash of heads resulting in a cut eye and a second round TKO loss against Hackney's Julian Monville.

1986 was a highly successful year for Gary. In winning seven out of seven contests, including fine wins over the top ten rated pair of Darwin Brewster and Terry Magee, Gary rose up the British rankings, finally getting a taste of championship honours himself when he stopped Preston's hard-hitting Sammy Sampson at Sutton Sports Centre, St Helens in February 1987 to win the Central Area title. "This was my time to shine." Victory here assured Gary, together with up-and-coming Liverpool featherweight Paul Hodkinson, a share of the BBC *Grandstand* Young Prospect of the Year Award.

Due to managerial problems with Mike Barrett, Gary did not appear in the ring for another nine months and when he did, for new manager Frank Warren, it was arguably his toughest test to date. A contender for one of the fights of the year, Gary gave 8lbs to Welsh middleweight champion Denys Cronin at the Royal Albert Hall in December 1987. With the Welshman never taking a backward step and the crowd on their feet for almost the entire eight rounds, Gary dug deep to get the verdict to maintain his march towards a British title shot.

The win was not without its price however, and Gary suffered numerous small cuts all over his face and badly bruised knuckles through having to snap out his jab to keep Cronin at bay. Cuts are of course an occupational hazard for boxers but for Gary, whose tall, dark good looks meant he was always open to modelling offers – he was sponsored by a fashion company at the time – they could have cost him dear. Indeed, some even said that Gary earned more from modelling than he did boxing!

A serious contender for Lymington Romany Gary Cooper's British title, the pair were due to meet following Gary's victory over Cronin but promoter Mike Barrett cancelled the show. Gary kept in shape with two easy wins over Tommy McCallum and Robin Smith respectively, before the title fight was finally confirmed for September 1988 at Rivermead Leisure Centre, Reading.

Cooper was a fair few years older than Gary, indeed he had turned pro just as Gary was entering a gym for the first time – way back in 1978, and the younger boxer was favoured to prove too much for the veteran. Like his Hollywood namesake however, Cooper went down all guns blazing and Gary won a gruelling battle over 12 rounds having decked the champion in the second and fifth rounds. Like his contest over Cronin Gary had some wounds to show for his victory – a broken nose, and a busted left hand. Although pleased at the outcome, Gary admits to mixed feelings about this fight. "Gary Cooper was the only man I didn't want to beat ," says Gary. "He loved the game and he loved being the champion. I hated beating him but I had to do it."

Gary's injuries kept him out of the ring until May 1989 when he met Argentina's Rafael Sena. Obviously being groomed for a shot at one of the then world title holders at light-middle, three of Gary's next opponents were all South American and this, at the newly opened Docklands Arena, was his toughest. The Argentine fought like a bar-room brawler and Gary was relieved to hear the bell after ten tough rounds. Bleeding from his left eye and with a deep cut to his scalp, Gary took the decision. "Senna was my hardest fight," says Gary. He was just so awkward."

Gary Stretch c. 1986   *Source: Gary Shaw*

A sensational first round KO over Derek Wormald in defence of his British title in October 1989 put a second notch on a Lonsdale belt but, with few domestic challengers keen to take him on and with a world title fight seemingly as far away as ever, Gary was thinking about moving up a weight to get a crack at the big money and big name British middleweights of the day; Benn, Eubank and Watson. Winning the WBC International light-middleweight title by stopping Argentine champion Ramon Alegre in a brawl of a contest at Docklands on Valentine's day 1990 didn't bring a genuine world title fight any closer and Gary immediately relinquished this belt so stablemate Tony Collins could win it.

An easy but laboured points win over Argentine veteran Eduardo Contreras followed three months later but time was fast running out for Gary. The Contreras fight was only his tenth outing in four years and, thinking his best days were perhaps behind him Gary took some time off, "I learned a lot during this time," eventually moving up a weight and, some 11 months after his last contest, agreeing to a big pay day against the WBO middleweight champion, Chris Eubank. Despite holding his own as far as the judges were concerned - there was only a round or so in it at the end - Gary was stopped in the sixth.

After the loss to Eubank Gary invited Michael Watson to study the 'Beauty v the Beast' video, to help devise a strategy for Watson to beat Eubank as they were due to meet next. Watson lost controversially to the flamboyant Brighton boxer before going on to challenge Nigel Benn for the WBC version of the world title. Watson is still recovering from brain surgery following that September 1991 contest. The dangers in choosing boxing as a career couldn't be more vividly expressed. "A different life was just one punch away for me," says Gary, "I don't dare think about it. Just march forward."

After his retirement Gary still found time for modelling - and making the headlines. He strutted his stuff on the catwalk for Versace and Calvin Klein, and dated a long-line of glamourous women, including Raquel Welch, before marrying Puerto Rican model/actress Roselyn Sanchez in 1999 (they divorced two years later). By then Gary had already appeared in a number of movies. In 1994 director Nigel Dick gave him his first role when he cast Gary opposite Michael Madsen in the thriller *Dead Connection*. Gary's boxing career helping him overcome any nerves he may have had about his change of career. "This was my first real film. I played a serial killer called 'Lights Out'. It went well. I was never terrified. That's the good thing about the fight game. Once you've had 5,000 people screaming your name and a guy trying to kill you, you're sure not going to worry about something as simple as turning up in a movie studio!"

The story behind Gary's change from ex-boxer to actor is an interesting one. On holiday in New York Gary was walking through

Manhattan when he saw an argument over a parking space. An elderly lady had claimed the space first but two men were trying to steal it before her. Most passers-by ignored the altercation, but Gary's interest was peaked when, "One of the men got out of the car, walked over and punched her car with his fist. It was at this point that I went over."

As any visitor to New York, or any large city these days will tell you, total strangers rarely back each other up this way. Even fewer would stand firm if confronted with a knife. "The guy pulled a blade on me but it was a tiny one. I said to him, 'What are you going to do with that? You're going to stab me over a parking space?' He said, 'Yer, I'm gonna kill you!' So I walked right up to him and said, 'Get on with it then. Stick it right here big guy, because you're only going to make a tiny little hole and then…I'm going to rip your head off!" At which point Gary laughingly points out that the guy ran away.

The old lady in question turned out to be none other than famous New York acting coach, Janet Alhanti. Janet invited Gary to her studio, where he saw Sydney Poitier reading poetry, "It was the most extraordinary thing I'd ever seen." She then took him for lunch, where he informed her that he wanted to be an actor. He started classes the very next week.

Gary learnt well and has since appeared in a number of varied productions. In 2001 he co-starred with Sarah Graham Hayes, Tommy Flanagan and Peter Greene in director Craig Singer's *Dead Dogs Lie*, playing one of three hit-people, 'Duck'. For his work in the film Gary jointly won a Copper Wing for Best Ensemble Acting from the 2002 Phoenix Film Festival. In 2004 Gary landed the role that many see as his best to date, that of psychotic small-town gangster 'Sonny' in Shane Meadow's cult thriller *Dead Man's Shoes*, opposite the talented Paddy Considine. This role finally gave Gary the respect he desired and he was nominated for a Best Supporting Actor award at the British Independent Film Awards.

Gary then landed his two biggest roles to date; a supporting role as Cleitus in Oliver Stone's 2004 historical epic *Alexander*, played by Colin Farrell and also starring Anthony Hopkins, Val Kilmer, and Angelina Jolie; and in 2006 he was reunited with Stone as John McGloughlin's paramedic in *world Trade Centre*, this time appearing opposite Nicholas Cage, who played McGloughlin, and Michael Pena.

Looking back on his career to date, Gary's faith in hard-work above all other attributes is plain to see. "Janet Alhanti once said to me that the greatest thing you need for your new acting career is a vast and vivid imagination and you'll only get this from reading. So I started to read. Something I hadn't done for years. I did this exercise where I read the *New York Times* cover to cover, every day, for a year. Five, six, or seven hours reading a day. It was tough but she made me do it. Building any career takes a great deal of work and effort, but I always believed I would make something of myself, even as a boy. I believe you can do anything if you want to so long as you work hard enough."

As if to emphasise this last point Gary remembers, "watching Sugar Ray Leonard when I was about 12 and saying to my brother, 'I'm going to do that one day.' Years later I did it. I fought for a world title. I don't think modern boxing is as good as it was in my day. I've got lots of regrets sure, but I never dwell on them." Asked about boxing at the Liverpool Stadium, Gary believes that, "Merseyside loves its fighters, to fight there and at other local venues, in front of your own supporters, was always an honour."

With such a varied and interesting post-fight career Gary recalls many amusing moments, although the time he, "paid $300 to get tape off a guy to hide my recently broken nose because I was going on a date with Lucy Blair!" ranks as one of the best.

Like his great friend Billy Aird, Pat Thompson is another Liverpudlian now domiciled in London. As an amateur with the Liverpool Transport ABC, Pat won a North West Counties title, silver in a multi-nations tournament in Denmark and represented England. As a professional he won the Central Area light-heavyweight title, just one of his 72 paid contests. A keen runner and keep fit fanatic (he has completed over a dozen marathons for charity over the years) Pat was born in Liverpool in March 1948 and this article was obtained through personal interviews during 2004-05.

PAT THOMPSON

London-based pro won
Central Area title in his own city

"There wasn't any previous history of boxing in my family, however this didn't stop me from starting at 12 years of age. Even then I was always keen on physical fitness and I found that boxing training suited me down to the ground. I liked the discipline involved in boxing and like many before me, I found that it also kept me out of trouble. I used to train with the Maple Leaf ABC but never represented them. Instead I boxed for the famous Transport ABC and it was whilst with them that I won a North West Counties title. I was good enough to box for England as well and was lucky to win silver at a big multi-nations tournament in Denmark."

Like many young Liverpool men before him, Pat joined the Merchant Navy and went to sea on '*The Empress of Canada*'. This didn't stop him from boxing however. "I had three fights on the ship," says Pat. "All of which I won." When he decided to turn professional Pat did what a few local boxers did at the time and went to London. His journey South wasn't without incident or humour however. "I called at my manager-to-be Ernie Fossey's home on the Saturday I arrived. Ernie wasn't home but his son John informed me that he wouldn't be long, 20 minutes or so, and invited me in to wait. I walked through to the kitchen and John and I began a conversation. Whilst talking I noticed a lovely plate of meat on top of the fridge and, being a hungry 'scouser' I began to pick at it.

"We continued our conversation and shortly thereafter Ernie and his wife, Pat, returned home. When they saw what I had done however, they burst out laughing for it turned out I had started to eat the cat's dinner! It wasn't the most appropriate way to go about introducing yourself to your new manager I suppose but we all had a good laugh about it!

"I thoroughly enjoyed my professional career. I had 72 contests – all at light-heavyweight, and I fought all over the country. There were much more fight arenas and venues back then and it seemed like I fought at them all. Being based there I obviously boxed all over London, but I also fought in Bradford, Birmingham, Sheffield, Blackpool, Wolverhampton, Southampton. In fact if you name it I probably fought there!"

One of Pat's favourite venues was the Liverpool Stadium. "I loved boxing there. There was a great atmosphere, especially for the big fights, but what I liked best was the crowd. The Liverpool fight crowd certainly knew their boxing. Even if you were a local favourite, if they felt that you had been given a dodgy decision, they would soon let you know their feelings. I don't think you'll ever get the same atmosphere at some of the new arenas they use today. I was sorry when they knocked it down as it was part of the city's great boxing tradition."

Pat fought for the Central Area title twice. "The first time I fought for it I lost to Phil Martin of Manchester in London. But the next time I had a go it was at the Adelphi Hotel in Liverpool and I beat Terry Armstrong. It felt great winning a title in your home city. I also felt the downside though for I lost the title in my home city as well," - a ten rounds points loss to Alfreton's Alex Panarski at the Stadium in March 1977. "I wouldn't have minded but I'd beat Alex three times already, once over eight rounds just two months before!

"The hardest opponent I met was easily Barry Clough. We fought each other twice, winning one apiece. I beat him on points at the NSC and he beat me on points in Stoke. He was the most awkward opponent I ever met – amateur or professional. He would do everything he could to spoil your style. He would grab you, pull you, push you, and turn you, lean on you – as awkward as anything. He's a great guy out of the ring though and you'll never guess what he does now. He's a vicar in Stoke-on-Trent!" Pat has no regrets over his chosen career. "I loved every minute of it and met some great people. Boxing people are great to be amongst and whenever I can I love coming back to Liverpool and meeting up with old friends at the MFBA. We always have a great time."

A top amateur with Higherside, St. Helens Star, and finally the famous Transport ABC, hard punching Gary Thornhill turned pro in 1993, quickly establishing himself as one of the country's leading featherweights. In an exhilarating 11-year career, Gary never ducked anyone and met most of the leading 9st men of the day including Justin Juuko, Dean Pithie, Benny Jones, Michael Gomez, Ritchie Wenton, Scott Harrison and Stephen Foster, winning the Central Area and British title in the process. Still living and working in Liverpool this article was compiled through interviews with Gary in 2007.

GARY THORNHILL

'Tornado' blasted his way to British title

"I was 12 years old when I first became interested in boxing. I joined Higherside ABC with coaches Dave Mulchay and John Clotworthy. I then went to St Helens Star with Tony Smart, before going to the Transport where Georgie Vaughan was the coach. I loved boxing from the first time I went. It was like a drug. I couldn't get enough of the buzz, the excitement of getting in the ring, of sparring and fighting."

Gary enjoyed the buzz of the ring so much that he amassed 81 contests as an amateur, winning around 60. He was good enough to win four England U19 vests too, and although he lost on each occasion he met some of the top European stars of the day, including East Germany's D Drumm twice inside four days in December 1986. Drumm was the reigning European U19 bantamweight champion at the time, but Gary took him to the judges in each contest.

Having built up such a good rapport with Georgie Vaughan whilst at the Transport ABC, both boxer and coach stayed together when Gary decided to turn pro with local managers Steven Vaughan and Lee Moloney in 1993 when he was 25. Their good relationship reaped instant rewards when, on his paid debut, Gary stopped Sheffield's Brian Hickey at Ellesmere Port Leisure Centre in February the same year. In a sign of the style that was to become his trademark in the future, Gary's non-stop, all-action approach saw the Sheffield man down four times before the referee came to his rescue in the fourth session.

Five months later Worksop's Dougie Fox was blasted out inside a round at Everton Park. Fast and destructive, Gary wasn't nicknamed 'The Tornado' for nothing. After just two fights of his pro career it was clear Gary was too strong for some of the country's more inexperienced featherweights. His next three opponents therefore, were selected with one thing in mind, their ring knowledge. Gary won his next two contests on points, being taken the distance by awkward Welsh veteran Miguel Matthews in October 1993 and Sheffield's Wayne Windle two months later. Rhyl lightweight Ed Lloyd then halted Gary's run of victories, holding him to a draw at Chester's Northgate Arena. Despite the result it was an indication of how much Gary had improved as a professional. Lloyd had met some dangerous and experienced boxers himself, including the likes of Najib Daho, Kevin Pritchard, Sugar Gibiliru, Steve Robinson and Nigel Haddock.

Five more wins set Gary up for a December 1995 meeting with Manchester's 110-fight veteran Des Gargano for the Central Area super-featherweight title. Despite his vast experience, the Mancunian southpaw was stopped in the second round and Gary had won his first championship belt. Two victories later and Gary was finally matched for the British title he had coveted since his amateur days. Unfortunately however, the December 1996 fight fell through and, not wanting to waste the time he had spent in the gym, Gary was matched with Ugandan Justin Juuko for the Commonwealth title at London's Elephant and Castle on the same date.

Gary admits that the Juuko fight was a step up in class. "We took the fight too early in my career really, but we knew what we were doing. Juuko was a world-class fighter in his prime whereas I was just an up-and-coming fighter. Georgie and myself took the fight mainly to learn, to see what I was capable of at the time but he was just too good for me. He had everything;- power, speed, variety, footwork. Everything."

For Gary, this was the toughest fight of his career. "Juuko was definitely the toughest fight for me. He hit me that hard I could have sworn he had bricks in his gloves." Looking back on the contest however, Gary is proud he took the champion eight rounds. "I think I shocked some people. I gave him a tough time and I walked away with my head held high. I made him earn his money that night."

If Juuko earned his money then Gary almost certainly did, especially considering the lengths his trainer made him go to in the lead-up to the fight. "On the train on our way to London to fight Juuko there were about ten of us, my team and George, and a few friends. As I hadn't been weighed that day George was worrying about my weight but I kept telling him there would be no problem as I was rarely over 9st 4lbs at any time.

"When we got off the train George was still going on about the weight and he said I should use the weighing machine at Euston Station. I kept saying no but he talked me into it. The next thing I'm standing at the machine with my team around me. George said I should strip off and get on but I was worried about there being so many people around, but George said that he and the rest of the team would all stand round so no-one could see me. I stripped off, got on the scales and turned to George to see what he thought – only to find they'd all moved away and I was standing there with nothing on, in the middle of Euston, on a weighing machine. I laugh about it now but I could have killed them at the time!"

It was a year before Gary boxed again, this time easing back gently with a six rounds points win over the experienced Peter Buckley in Sheffield. This was to be Gary's only contest of 1996. In June 1997 he was matched for the WBO super-featherweight intercontinental title against the unbeaten Coventry prospect Dean Pithie. Before a packed partisan crowd at Everton Park however, the Midlander had no answers to Gary's pressure boxing and he was finally worn down after nine rounds thus securing Gary's second belt. A tremendous ninth round stoppage over Hartlepool's talented and much lauded Steve Conway followed six months later. Conway would later win the IBO light-middleweight title and meet the likes of Steve Robinson, Junior Witter, Alex Arthur and Yuri Romanov.

Gary had four contests in 1999, winning three but losing the one that mattered the most. In September he was matched with the Dublin born, Mancunian Michael Gomez for the vacant British title. Gary was a strong favourite but, despite dominating the first round, Gomez rolled underneath a jab in the second and in textbook style, stepped to his left, pivoted and crashed a hook to Gary's jaw. Gary went down but rose too quickly, immediately realised his mistake and went back down again on one knee to take an eight count. He weathered the storm for the next 30 seconds or so but was forced to drop to his knees again with barely a minute of the round to go. Hoping to wait for the count to reach eight before rising again, Gary took his eyes off referee Larry O'Connell during the count and, despite getting to his feet, "ready to carry on," was amazed to see the contest waved over.

Although disappointed with his performance against Gomez, "who is still a good mate," Gary was just as determined to succeed and three wins from three contests later he was matched with fellow Liverpudlian Ritchie Wenton for the vacant British featherweight title in Warrington. Despite concerns that he could make the 9st. limit for only the second time in his pro career (he eventually scaled 8st 13lbs) Gary managed to retain both his strength and power and, after decking his opponent in the first and having to endure a cut in the second, he forced Ritchie to retire at the start of the ninth.

Speaking about the contest, Gary is full of praise for his opponent. "I'd known Ritchie for a long time, twenty years or so, since we were

Gary Thornhillc. 1998   *Source: Terry Churchill*

amateurs. He was a good fighter. If he had been a bit heavier it might have been different, but really I won it at the scales. Ritchie was used to fighting super-bantams, whereas, despite a lot of people thinking I would struggle down at featherweight, I had actually been giving weight away to super-feathers for most of my career." In winning the title at the grand age of 32, Gary became the third 'scouser' to lift the title after Nel Tarleton and Paul Hodkinson. Although the highlight of his career so far, Gary didn't get a chance to defend the title. Indeed, he didn't fight again for over a year, courtesy of a failed drug test after the Wenton fight.

At the start of 2001 Gary was 33 years of age and had enjoyed a highly successful seven-year career, fighting for a Commonwealth and two British titles. Having averaged only three fights a year in that time however, he was far from ring weary. Indeed, Gary was still good enough to mix it at the top level of a division which, at the time, was one of the most competitive in Britain. So much so that in September 2001 he was matched with an up-and-coming featherweight from Glasgow for the British and Commonwealth titles. Whereas Gary had been the bigger featherweight in his battle with Ritchie Wenton, the tables were turned for his meeting with rugged Scotsman Scott Harrison. "At the weigh-in Harrison looked very drawn, very pale. It was clear he had struggled to make the weight. When I saw him across the ring from me the night of the fight however, he looked massive, like the Incredible Hulk!"

Such disparity in size, and age – Harrison was seven years younger than Gary – proved too much of an obstacle to overcome and, despite Gary boxing superbly in the early stages, he was stopped in the fifth with one of the most vicious body shots seen in a British ring for a long time. Gary remembers, "I had won every round easy but hadn't really troubled him. Although I was scoring well Scott seemed to walk through my shots. I hit him with a good right uppercut early on, a shot that probably would have hurt lots of fighters, but he just looked at me and carried on.

"When he caught me with that body shot the pain was unbelievable but I didn't go down straight away. I remember just pausing for a split second and thinking 'God, that was a good shot!' Harrison must have thought the same as he seemed to pause for a bit as well. In fact he looked at me in a puzzled sort of way, as if to say, 'Why haven't you gone down yet?' I just slowly lowered myself to the floor, on one knee, and pushed my gum shield out to try and breathe. It was then I remember Scott looking at me and asking if I was OK. He knew I wasn't going to get up. I just nodded and he turned to his corner to ask them to get me some water!

"A few months later I was up there sparring him as he prepared for his European title shot and his Dad told me that I'd boxed his head off in the first five rounds. That I'd given him a boxing lesson and it was one of the toughest fights he'd had so far." Harrison would go on to win the WBO world featherweight title.

Just over a year later Gary came back again to challenge another up-and-coming prospect in the shape of Dagenham's Nicky Cook, this time for the WBF intercontinental super-featherweight title. As in the Harrison fight Gary gave away years in age, though this time the Londoner was a full 11 years younger as opposed to 'only' nine. Despite boxing well however, Gary was stopped in the seventh round by the soon to be European champion.

Gary thought seriously about retiring at this point but decided he still had something to offer the sport and he returned in August 2003 with a first round stoppage win over Birmingham welterweight Jason Nesbitt at Everton Park. A year later another win set him up for a tilt at the recently reintroduced English title against Salford's Stephen Foster at the MEN. Again however, despite out-boxing his younger opponent (12 years younger this time) Gary succumbed to a body shot in the ninth and he retired soon after. "I was 36 by then and it was time to get out. Not long after I was offered good money to meet Phillip N'dou but, after watching a few tapes of him, George and I decided it was too much of a risk."

Listening to Gary speak about boxing, and his career in particular, it's clear he still loves the sport. "I'd love to do it all again. I had a great time, both as an amateur and a pro. I just loved to box. It's a tough sport but one you should really enjoy while you can." Whilst many boxing commentators criticise the proliferation of titles Gary, himself rewarded with a couple of 'fringe' belts in his career, is dismissive of such misgivings. "Boxing will never change. Talent comes around in different stages. Anyone who gets through ropes to fight deserves a medal. They're putting their lives on the line. Just because there are more titles around doesn't make them any easier to win. I say good on those lads who do win a title, whatever it is. They've earned it."

Although he never boxed at the Liverpool Stadium, Gary gives credit to other local venues for creating their own special character. "There's nothing like fighting in front of your home crowd and Everton Park has a great atmosphere. Liverpool boxing fans always back their own of course but they know good fighters when they see them, wherever they're from."

Always one to acknowledge those who helped him achieve what he did in his 11-year career, Gary credits his family and trainer in particular. "My grandmother, Nanny Brown, and my children Liam (14) and Katie (11) were a big inspiration to me. Also, Georgie Vaughan who as a coach is unbelievably talented in what he does, and as a person was a great friend. He is one of the best coaches around. He made me into a champion."

Unknown to all but the most knowledgeable local boxing fans today, Birkenhead's Arthur Townley was one of the top heavyweights of his day in the 1910s and 20s. Exceptionally tall for his time, Arthur was spotted by fellow townsman and famous boxing trainer Alex Powell whilst they both served in the Army and before long, courtesy of a 15-fight winning start to his pro career, he was being talked of as a future champion. In a career that lasted at least ten years, Arthur met all of leading European heavyweights of the day, including the likes of Frank Goddard, Fred Fulton, Tom Gummer, Dick Smith, Bombardier Billy Wells, Victor McLaglen, Frank Moody, Gypsy Daniels, Paolino Uzcudun and Georges Carpentier.

ARTHUR TOWNLEY

Birkenhead heavyweight met Bombardier Billy Wells, Carpentier and McLaglen!

Already a member of the Royal Naval Volunteer Reserve at the start of the First World War, Birkenhead's Arthur Townley was one of the first men to be called up for active service. Sent to a training camp in Deal, Arthur quickly made friends with another of his townsmen, tough lightweight Alex Powell. At 6'2" tall, Arthur was exceptionally tall for the time and, after learning that Alex had an eye for a talented boxer, he asked him if he could show him the ropes. It didn't take long for Alex to see that Arthur showed more than promise and, with an eye on having a go in the paid ranks after a war everyone thought would be over by Christmas, they stepped up their training.

Boxing was put on hold for a while however, as it became clear that the war would last. Alex and Arthur soon found themselves involved in Gallipoli, scene of some of the most intense fighting of the war. Despite Alex losing an eye, both men survived and Arthur returned home keen for Alex to train him for his shot at the top. After training at Nolan's gym in the town, everyone could see that Arthur had potential but he didn't remain in Birkenhead however, and set off for London where he was trained by the renowned Arthur Goodwin.

Arthur won his first 15 contests, one a ten rounds points victory over future British middleweight champion Tom Gummer. A ninth round KO over London's Dick Smith at Pudsey Street in April 1918, when Smith was the reigning British light-heavyweight champion showed that Arthur could mix it at the highest level. Two months later however, Arthur suffered his first defeat when future British heavyweight champion Frank Goddard stopped him in nine rounds.

1919 saw further inside the distance wins for Arthur over Dan McGoldrick (twice), the highly rated Harry Curzon and Harold Hardwick before he returned to fight before his home supporters at New Brighton. A tenth round KO win over Poplar's Tom Berry in June 1919 sent the partisan crowd home happy and showed that Arthur was still improving as a boxer. Berry was a dangerous opponent and would later win both the British and the British Empire light-heavyweight titles.

Three months later Arthur was back in London at Olympia. His opponent on this occasion was the American Fred Fulton who, just 12 months earlier, had met Jack Dempsey. Promoter CB Cochran later wrote that for the Fulton contest, he paid Arthur £500 and, "agreed to give him a match against Bombardier Wells, and the French heavyweight Balzac, for each of which he was to get £250." There had been a lot of talk about the formidable stature of Fulton, and all the boxing experts were keen to see what he could do. Although not much heavier than Arthur, the American made short work of the Englishman however, Arthur rushing in at the sound of the first bell like a novice. There was a minutes in-fighting, then a break-away. Arthur again rushed in only to be met with a hard left. This happened once more and then Fulton, with a grim smile, put the Englishman out with a left to the jaw and a heavy right-handed punch.

True to his word, Cochran put Townley in with the Frenchman, Billy Balzac, five weeks after the Fulton contest. This time however, Arthur made no mistake and he KO'd Balzac in three rounds. One month later, Arthur faced Nutty Curran at Plymouth and forced him to retire in the seventh round.

It was then time for Cochran to make good his promise and put Arthur in with Bombardier Billy Wells. Although Wells was no longer the British and British Empire heavyweight champion when the pair met in November 1919, he was still a formidable opponent. Cochran wrote that Arthur, "had made a good impression a few weeks earlier at the Stadium by knocking out Balzac in three rounds and the tremendous enthusiasm which greeted Wells indicated that, in general opinion, the Bombardier was on the road to regain his lost honours...Townley was game all the way through but in the sixth round, it was apparent to everybody except, perhaps, Wells that Townley had 'shot his bolt', yet

Wells remained cautious. In the eighth round, Townley was sent down for a count of eight and a beautifully timed right to the chin dropped him for a count of nine and when he rose, he could only lean back on the ropes with his gloves to his face but the Bombardier held off in inexplicable fashion, and in the ninth round, Townley actually got home several jabs to the face. Finally, Wells sent his man down twice for a count of nine, the referee intervening, and the towel was thrown in. This was a fight that went far to keep alive the interest in the 'big men.' Wells fought on percentage and he received £610, Townley was paid £250".

Arthur Townley c. 1918   *Source: Gary Shaw*

Arthur took a few months rest after the Wells defeat but came back in great style with another five wins on the trot. He was then matched at the NSC against a certain Victor McLaglen. Arthur KO'd the future film star in the seventh round. Arthur would later relate that following the contest, McLaglen walked into his dressing room accompanied by his brothers, who were equally as big as Victor. Arthur immediately feared that some family retribution was about to take place but he needn't have feared as McLaglen told him that he was about to leave for Hollywood for a career in movie pictures and he invited Arthur to accompany him.

Arthur declined but later wondered what would have happened if he had accepted the offer. He also said that the money he made on a side bet on this contest paid for his house in Higher Tranmere. A further 18 contests with varying degrees of success followed. Although he lost the last seven contests of his career among his opponents in that losing streak were men of the calibre of Frank Moody, Gypsy Daniels, Paulino Uzcudun and perhaps the most famous name of all, Georges Carpentier.

The Frenchman had his first professional contest when only 14 years old and would go on to win titles at almost every weight, the first being the French lightweight title, which he won when he was only 15. Carpentier went on to win the French welterweight title and added the European title when still under the age of 18. He would go on to become the scourge of British heavyweights, recording wins over Billy Wells, Dick Smith and Joe Beckett, and is also remembered for his challenge for the world heavyweight title against the fearsome Jack Dempsey in July 1921. The first $1 million gate.

Townley travelled to Vienna to fight Carpentier with one of the judges - referee Joe Palmer, later describing the contest and both fighters preparations in some detail. "Carpentier was accommodated in a sumptuous hotel along with his usual retinue. Georges was taking no risks about this contest. I saw that very quickly," said Palmer. As for Arthur, Palmer interviewed him at his palatial hotel training quarters and put it to the Birkenhead man that there was a rumour he would throw the fight. "'As for lying down in this contest,' said Townley, 'the idea is preposterous – look at my condition.' I did, and I must say that I never saw Townley in better fettle. He must have worked hard. 'I was offered this match at a fee that would take me several contests to earn in England,' said Townley. 'I promptly accepted it knowing that if I did not, then someone else would – win or lose, I'm going to do my best as always.' Subsequent events proved the truth of every word Townley uttered."

A downpour of rain meant that the outdoor contest was postponed however, until May Day, but none of the participants complained. When the fight did take place over 20,000 people were in attendance. They didn't get much for their money however, as Carpentier floored Arthur in the second round. Palmer described the chaotic scenes that followed, "Townley was soon in a daze. He tried to rally but couldn't. First his legs went as he was knocked from pillar to post, then a stinging right cross dropped him. He came back after a count, thoroughly dazed from that punch to the jaw only to receive another one. The ringmaster began to count while Carpentier stood over the prostrate Townley. The French boxer should have been ordered to stand back but this was not done. Townley rose before the "out" and neither his hands nor any part of his body except his feet were touching the floor but before he could stagger into an upright position, Carpentier, who was on top of him all the while, dropped the Britisher for keeps. There was immediately a wild outburst of dissent and cries of "foul" from the crowd..."

A decision on the result of the fight was held over until the judges and referee had reviewed the movie of the fight the next day. The result remained unaltered however, and Arthur had no complaints. Indeed, both his camp and Carpentier's later visited one of Vienna's famous cabarets.

A month later Arthur travelled to Paris to meet the Basque, Paolino Uzcudun, but was KO'd in the first round. In his last contest on 28 May 1925 at Pudsey Street Stadium he was outpointed over 15 rounds by Gypsy Daniels.

The heavyweight champion of the North of England Arthur fought most of the leading European cruiser and heavyweights of the day. After retiring he went to work on the docks and was famous for exhibiting feats of strength among his fellow workers. In the 1950s however, he fell from the staging whilst working and was killed – he was just 52 years of age.

A highly skilled flyweight with St Helens Star ABC, Keith Wallace won two senior ABA titles as an amateur, was an England regular and favourite for a Commonwealth Games gold medal before switching to the pro ranks with Frank Warren in 1982. Keith went on to win the Commonwealth flyweight title in only his eighth pro fight and also challenged unsuccessfully for the European crown. Following a loss in an eliminator for the British bantamweight title in 1985 he retired with a fine record of 15 wins from 19 contests aged 24. The boxing world was shocked when he died from cancer in January 2000 aged just 39.

KEITH WALLACE

Top amateur and Commonwealth champion who died tragically young

Like his contemporaries and fellow townsmen, Ray and George Gilbody, to say that Keith Wallace enjoyed a successful amateur career would be something of an understatement. In 1974 he won his first national title - a junior A class Schoolboy crown. He never looked back. In 1977 he won a further Schoolboy title, this time in the senior class, before adding an NABC title two years later. Keith had already represented his country at Young England level but in February 1979 the young flyweight also made a winning debut for the ABA U19 squad when they beat their Irish counterparts 5-3 in London. A run of classy performances ensured his participation in a four-man ABA team sent to the world U19 tournament in Yokohama, Japan whilst he was also part of a five-man team to enter a similar European event in Rimini, Italy. On each occasion however, Keith returned home without a medal, but he was gaining valuable international experience.

Keith's move up to full England honours came in January 1980 when he travelled to Herning in Denmark to win his bout in a 7-5 England loss. Just 10 days later he outpointed Scotland's D. Flynn in London as the ABA team, which also included George Gilbody, Jim McDonnell, Tony Willis and Lloyd Honeyghan, ran out comfortable 10-1 winners. With such good performances internationally it was no surprise that Keith won his first senior ABA title this year, stopping the same opponent from his ABA v Scotland appearance, D. Flynn from Meadowbank, in the third round.

1980 of course was an Olympic year, but despite the ban by some nations Great Britain sent a full team to Moscow and, as he had won the ABA title earlier in the year, Keith was selected to go to the Soviet Union. Despite sending a strong nine-man team however, that also included Ray and George Gilbody, only Tony Willis returned with a medal, although Keith did manage to make the second round where he was beaten by Romania's Daniel Radu. The ABA also celebrated its centenary in 1980 and a multi-nations tournament featuring boxers from nine countries was held in London in October. Keith boxed brilliantly to make his final by outpointing the East German R. Marx, before stopping fellow Englishman T. Kennard in the final itself to win one of five gold medals for England.

1981 was Keith's last year in the amateur ranks, but he ensured it was a good one by winning his second senior ABA title and gold at the Acropolis Cup multi-nations tournament in Athens, Greece. This was a fabulous tournament for Merseyside boxers as John Lyon, John Farrell, Steve Johnson and Tony Willis also won gold. Keith's only representative bout of 1981 however, was a rare stoppage loss against the talented American A Pruitt in Gloucester in November. This was no disgrace however, as John Lyon also suffered a rare stoppage loss in this fixture as a strong USA team eventually ran out 8-3 winners. Still aged only 20, Keith was considered favourite for the following year's Commonwealth Games in Brisbane, but the temptations of the pro game proved too good to resist and, with a host of top promoters clamouring for his signature, he signed for Frank Warren in January 1982.

Extremely tall for a flyweight, with a classy, solid jab, honed in the amateur ranks, and a fiery mop of red hair, Keith had a sensational start to his pro career. After stopping the experienced Norwich-based Scotsman Robert Hepburn in the second round on his debut at the Bloomsbury Hotel in February 1982, Keith won a further 11 on the spin, with eight of these ending before the final bell had sounded.

Less than four weeks after his debut Keith stopped Newport's Steve King inside three rounds, and just six days later he stopped another Welshman, Steve Reilly, a round earlier. Four more early victories in the next six months, including his first appearance in Liverpool since his amateur days – a sixth round stoppage win over Jimmy Bott – paved the way for Keith's first serious test. Gutsy Yank bantamweight Steve Whestone, in some quarters on the fringes of the world's top 20, was drafted in for Keith's first 10 rounder, and his first televised contest.

Despite never hitting the canvas, the first of Keith's professional opponents to make that boast, the American was outclassed by a man who boxed close to perfection and was saved from further punishment by the referee in the eighth round. It was voted one of the best contests of the year and proved beyond doubt that Keith had what it takes to compete at the highest level. A match had already been made for Keith to challenge British champion Kelvin Smart but the Welshman was injured in training and although the fight was ultimately cancelled, Frank Warren was confident enough to match Keith with Kenya's Steve Muchoki for the Commonwealth title.

Muchoki, a former world amateur champion, had won a Commonwealth Games gold in 1978 and had turned pro a year later, amassing a fine record of ten wins from 11 contests from his Copenhagen base. Warren had certainly thrown Keith in at the deep end, especially when you consider that Muckoki had gone 13 rounds with Argentina's Santos Laciar for the WBA title in his previous contest – his only loss as a pro to date *[Muchoki had only lost one fight as an amateur – against Cuba's 1974 world champion Jose Hernandez. eds.]* Training as he had never done before however, Keith was confident he could not only beat the Kenyan but also, as he had done with nine of his 12 opponents to date, stop him early.

Keith's confidence was well placed. Despite the champion's jab appearing to have him ahead by the eighth round the Merseysider was never in serious trouble. Early on in the eighth Keith caught Muchoki with a tremendous uppercut and the Kenyan did well to last to the bell. The ninth started almost exactly the same way and, courtesy of another uppercut, and the roar of the Bloomsbury Hotel crowd, where he had become a firm favourite, Keith piled on the pressure before the referee came to the champion's aid with just seconds of the round remaining. A champion at last, Keith kept busy by outpointing Croydon's future Commonwealth *lightweight* champion, Pat Doherty in Belfast barely a month after his title win, with North American champion Henry Brent also being outpointed just three weeks after this.

Ranked at No. 2 in the world by the WBA, it seemed only a matter of time before Keith would find himself in title action again. As all boxing fans know however, such logic rarely applies in the sport, and few would hazard a guess as to whether a world, European or Commonwealth title defence would be next. Prior to his win over

Muchoki, Keith's manager Frank Warren had clamoured for a European title fight with Charlie Magri, who had held the crown since 1979. Despite his best efforts however, Warren's words fell on deaf ears and Keith could only watch as Magri won the WBC version of the world title just days after his win over Doherty.

Keith Wallace (centre) with Ray and George Gilbody c. 1980   Source: George Gilbody

In all such stories however, there is often a silver lining and, at first glance at least, it seems that this was no exception. In order to fight for the world title Magri had had to vacate his European crown and Keith, together with France's Antoine Montero, was nominated to contest the vacancy. However, just as Keith thought it could hardly get any better, it was revealed that Montero's backers had managed to get enough money together to win the purse bidding and force Keith to travel to Switzerland in June.

Shortly before the fight was due to take place however, Keith was injured and had to pull out. In his absence the EBU practically handed the title to Montero, naming Spain's 37 year old Mariano Garcia as a replacement. Unsurprisingly he hammered the outclassed Spaniard inside the distance. While Keith convalesced, Montero earned well with an easy defence against Italian Giovanni Camputaro in Nimes. Warren did manage to secure purse bids for Keith's delayed challenge but fate dealt the Prescot man an even crueller blow than before -

Keith's father Andy died suddenly and the fight was postponed again. By the time he had his next fight, a 10 round points win over Mexico's experienced Juan Diaz in September 1983, Keith hadn't fought for almost six months. He was still only 22 and, for a flyweight, this combination can have severe consequences. Keith, for whom weight was always an issue, was still growing and if he wanted to meet Montero he would have to do it before his body simply gave in trying to make the eight stone flyweight limit.

Montero's career was uncannily similar to Keith's. He had won his countries amateur flyweight title twice (1979 and 1980 – Keith had won in 1980 and 1981); he won the French title in his 12th pro contest (Keith had won the Commonwealth crown in his ninth), and he too was undefeated with 19 wins from 19 as opposed to Keith's 12 from 12. A short southpaw with some pedigree yes, but Keith was certainly not overawed. Indeed, he was a slight favourite to add the European belt to his Commonwealth one.

Keith's preparations however, had not gone well. He was finding it increasingly difficult to make the weight; he had lost his father suddenly; and he was frustrated at his lack of action in the recent months. Even world-class fighters could be forgiven for finding these problems too much, and so it proved for Keith. Lacking the sparkle that had seen him establish himself as a legitimate world title contender Keith, despite a standing count in the seventh, was ahead on points by the start of the eighth round, but a body shot from Montero, who was cut above the eye, in the next round saw Keith stopped for the first time in his pro career.

Keith could perhaps have been excused requesting an easy opponent on his return to the ring some four months later. Instead however, he picked a national champion two weight classes above flyweight – Esteban Eguia, the featherweight champion of Spain. Keith outpointed the Spaniard over ten rounds to give himself a much needed confidence boost. Boxing outside of the flyweight class for the first time Keith felt that he could challenge the top British bantamweights just as he had with the flyweights, but a points loss to Swansea's Peter Harris in June 1984 put the brakes on such aspirations - for the time being at least.

Eight months later Keith returned with quick wins over the Mexican pair of Felipe Morales and Juan Castellanos to get his title ambitions back on track. Again however, another setback followed this time in the shape of a fourth round stoppage loss to Ray Minus of the Bahamas. Despite this latest blow however, Keith was ranked No. 3 in the domestic ratings and he was keen for another crack at titular honours.

Dealt yet another cruel hand by fate however, Keith was matched with another top ten-rated bantamweight in the shape of former amateur star, Sunderland's Billy Hardy, in a final eliminator for the British title. In one of the fights of the year however, Hardy, despite being floored in the third round, was on his way to winning British, European and world titles, and stopped Keith, who was down a total of three times himself, in the seventh round. The third reverse in his last five contests Keith, aged just 24, almost decided to call it a day but he returned a year later with a third round stoppage win over Birmingham's Rocky Lawlor.

Keith then retired but in April 1989, almost two and a half years after his last contest, he returned again with a win over Manchester featherweight Henry Armstrong. Three further wins in the year set him up for a March 1990 meeting with Glasgow's highly-rated and future European and British bantamweight challenger, Donnie Hood. Keith lost by stoppage in the eighth round and, just three days short of his 29th birthday, he called it quits for good. Less than 10 years later he would tragically die of cancer.

Born Charles Anchowitz in Liverpool in 1891 and unknown to all but the most knowledgeable local boxing fans today, Charlie White was one of the world's most outstanding lightweights of the 1910s and 20s, with a renowned and devastating left-hook. As well as meeting all the best boxers of the day, including Hall of Famers Jack Britton, Johnny Dundee, Abe Attell, Ted 'Kid' Lewis and Matt Wells, he also fought twice for the world title, losing to both Freddie Welsh and Benny Leonard. In an amazing 24-year career (although he had only one fight after 1923) Charlie won at least 90 bouts (60 KOs) and lost less than 20 from almost 170 pro fights - with at least 50 'Newspaper Decision' contests. He died on 24 July 1959.

CHARLIE WHITE

They called him 'left hook Charlie'

Ask any Liverpool fight fan who was the first local boxer to contest a world title and a few would correctly name Ike Bradley, the battling bantamweight who fought for the world title in 1906 and 1911. Even fewer however, would be able to name the second local boxer to fight for a world crown, even if they were given the names and dates of the man's opponents on the two occasions he did just that - famous Welsh lightweight Freddie Welsh in 1916, and American boxing legend Benny Leonard in 1920.

Voted the 99th hardest-hitting boxer of all time in a recent *Ring* magazine poll, Charles Anchowitz was born in Liverpool on 25 March 1891. His family moved to America when he was young, eventually settling in Chicago. A frail, sick boy with one lung affected by Tuberculosis, Charlie was ordered to a sanatorium by the Chicago TB Institute when he was 13 but, as his family could not afford such a placement at the time, he was instead put in the care of a physical culture instructor.

Within two years Charlie was almost completely cured and his strength and weight were above the average for his age. It was at the physical training school that Charlie first became interested in boxing and, after deciding there was no place for him in the Anchowitz family clothing business and in light of his tremendous punching power, especially in his left-hook, he turned professional at the age of 15.

A long run of KO victories saw Charlie rise up the featherweight rankings with rapidity and the newspaper men of the day were not slow in calling him 'Left-Hook Charlie'. His first fight of note was an eight rounds points loss to Abe Atell, the reigning world featherweight champion at the time, in Memphis in December 1909.

Boxing was illegal in many of the American States at this time, and even in those that permitted contests to be fought, decisions were prohibited. It was therefore customary for many of the leading sports writers of the day to give their decision on who they felt was the winner of a certain contest, these being called 'Newspaper Decisions'. Such a decision saw Atell 'win' a return with Charlie over ten rounds in Milwaukee in September 1910. Despite this loss, Charlie was now ranked as one of the world's leading featherweights and a quick look at the names on his record over the next ten years show exactly why this was. Charlie went in with some of the world's best known fighters. As well as Atell, Wells, Welsh, Lewis and Britton he also met such men as Pal Moran, Ad Wolgast, Willie Ritchie, Johnny Kilbane, Ritchie Mitchell and Johnny Dundee. If Charlie had been as quick in his thinking as he was in the way he wielded his famous left-hook, then he would have easily been champion of the world. He had two fantastic chances to win world titles but just failed on each occasion.

The first time he fought for the world crown was on 4 September 1916 when he met Freddie Welsh over 20 rounds at Colorado Springs. Fighting in the fair grounds before the largest crowd in Colorado boxing history, Liverpool-born Charlie had a slow start but he enjoyed a terrific ninth round. After a barrage of punches he had Welsh reeling around the ring, the Welshman on the point of going down when the bell came to his rescue. Charlie should have calmed himself at the start of the tenth, and cut down the shaken champion. Instead however, his wild efforts to land a winning punch came to nothing until the twelfth round, his left-hook doing the business as usual. The punch caught Welsh flush on the chin and he staggered across the ring, his hands down open to further attack. Inexplicably however, Charlie hesitated and Welsh's renowned recuperative powers enabled him to see the round out.

In the 13th round the champion endured another torrid time when Charlie connected again with his left-hook, but just as it seemed there would be a new champion, part of the grandstand collapsed. Prior to the contest a similar incident had occurred and two people were later found to have died. During the chaos that followed Charlie's chance was gone. Welsh boxed his way out of trouble to such an extent over

294

the next seven rounds that he was adjudged the winner on points by referee Billy Roche. So incensed were the crowd at the decision - many thought Charlie had been the aggressor throughout and all Welsh had done was back-pedal - a riot broke out and both fighters, referee, sports writers and others were forced to seek cover under a wooden platform.

Although disappointed Charlie was adamant he would get a chance to prove himself again and he battled away for four more years until, on 5 July at Menton Harbour in Michigan, he got another chance, this time against Benny Leonard. In the sixth round Leonard felt the full force of Charlie's left-hook and was sent clean though the ropes. Indeed, if his brother hadn't pushed him back into the ring he would have fell off the canvas altogether. Again, had Charlie been a quicker thinker he could have claimed the title by a foul - as receiving help in returning to the ring was strictly prohibited. Charlie kept his silence however, and the referee allowed the incident to pass.

Charlie compounded matters by waiting for Leonard to regain his composure and then the round was over. All through the next round, and the eighth Charlie, instead of taking his time and measuring his shots against the still groggy champion, threw haymaker after haymaker, hoping to floor the champion once more. By the ninth, Charlie was shattered and Leonard had recovered. After a terrific onslaught, Charlie was floored for the fifth time in the round by a short right and failed to beat the count. For the second time he had let the world title slip from his fingertips.

Charlie continued to box for another three years after losing to Leonard, but he never got another shot at the title. In 1921 and 1922 he fought Johnny Dundee four times, each fighter winning once with one draw and one 'Newspaper Decision'. He also fought future world lightweight champion Rocky Kansas in 1923, losing a 15 rounds decision, whilst his last serious contest came in Philadelphia in December the same year when he outpointed local man Bobby Barrett over 15 rounds. He made one ill fated come-back attempt in 1930, but was stopped by Henry Perlick, a non-descript fighter who wouldn't have stood a chance against Charlie in his prime.

Nat Fleischer, the famous editor of *Ring* magazine, wrote of Charlie, "He had a hook that was marvellous. It was one of the best of all time." When Ted 'Kid' Lewis KO'd Jimmy Duffy in one round at Boston in

November 1915, he was amused to receive a telegram from Charlie which read, "One rounders my copyright – don't infringe." Lewis replied with a telegram to White which read, "Copyright? I've been carrying it about for six weeks waiting to slip it to you." Charlie's lack of a killer instinct when it mattered the most moved the famous sportswriter of the day, Hype Igoe, to write, "White is like the artist who can't resist the temptation of stepping back and admiring his incompleted work."

Charlie White c. 1918   *Source: Gary Shaw*

After retiring from the ring, Charlie opened a gymnasium in Chicago teaching physical fitness to local businessmen and women, and he later moved to Hollywood where he took charge of the fitness of many of the leading stars of the screen of that era. He passed away in hospital in Napa, California on 24 July 1959. He was 69 years of age.

Charlie however, was not the only member of the Anchowitz family to take to the roped square, for he had two brothers, Jack who boxed under the name of Jack White, and William, who boxed under the name of Billy Wagner. Born in Liverpool on 25 May 1890 Jack had a total of 73 professional fights against the likes of Patsy Cline, Johnny Dundee, Owen Moran, Mexican Joe Rivers, Rocky Kansas, Johnny Kilbane, Abe Attell and Charlie Goldman. He also used the names Kid White, Young White and Jack Ankover. Reports at the time stated that he traded on his brother Charlie's name and got fights that he had no business being involved in, although his record shows that he only suffered 26 losses and 9 draws. William was also born in Liverpool and he had around 66 bouts, also featuring against the likes of Freddie Welsh, Ad Wolgast, Charlie Goldman and Monte Attell.

A talented amateur in the late-1930s/early-1940s, Birkenhead's Frankie Williams was one of the country's most talented feather/bantamweights of his day, meeting all the leading contenders including Cliff Curvis, Kid Tanner, Jim Brady, Johnny Cusick, Johnny Molloy, Ray Famechon, Al Phillips and Peter Keenan. In a nine-year career Frankie won 29 of 41 contests and despite being ranked in the top 10 in Britain for most of his career he had only one contest, albeit unsuccessful, for a British title. He died in 2005 aged 80.

FRANKIE WILLIAMS

Two pro debuts led to British title shot

So keen was Birkenhead's Frankie Williams to start a boxing career as a boy that he lied about his age in order to compete in the Northern Counties 5st Schoolboy Championships. Although he added a year to his age, the scam seemed to pay off as Frankie enjoyed a highly successful amateur career, winning at least one title a year between 1936-1942. Indeed, in 1942 Frankie won a Youth Championship of Great Britain.

Frankie may have gone even further as an amateur if, at the age of 19 he hadn't turned professional. His pro debut couldn't have started any better either, as he stopped Leicester's Billy Barnes in the first round at Blackpool in January 1944. It seemed that a fine pro career was on the cards for the Birkenhead man but Frankie decided otherwise and he applied to be reinstated as an amateur. His sensational first round stoppage victory turned out to be his only professional fight of the year. After some deliberation, the Northern Counties decided to honour Frankie's request and he was duly re-instated as an amateur. He was only 19 afterall, and they must have felt, as Frankie and his friends did (many of whom had urged him to go back to the amateur status where he had enjoyed so much previous success) that he could achieve only better things wearing a vest - perhaps even a coveted ABA title.

Barely a year later however, the lure of the professional ring once again proved too strong for Frankie and he 'turned over' once more – this time for good. His second 'debut' was at the Liverpool Stadium in August 1945 and again it was a victorious one, albeit not as sensational as his first - a fine six round points win over George Green of Warrington. A similar win over Birmingham's Al Benton followed a month later.

It was a solid, if unspectacular, start to his second pro career. However, all that changed in Frankie's next contest. In November 1945 Frankie dispatched the rugged Liverpool battler Len Wiseman in the first round with a tremendous punch. It wasn't just the local fight crowd who were forced to take notice of this new featherweight sensation and local promoter Johnny Best realised that in Frankie he had found yet another local star in the making.

Wales also had another rising star at this time. He too was a former amateur star who had made a decent start to his pro career. Former Welsh Schoolboy Champion and Welsh ABA finalist Cliff Curvis was two years younger than Frankie. The son of a former Army bantamweight champion of India, Dai Davies, Cliff had begun his career with a second round KO of Bryn Collins in Swansea in January 1945 and had won all seven of his pro fights to date. It promised to be a great contest and the Liverpool fight crowd certainly thought so as the Stadium was full to capacity for their January 1946 meeting.

Unfazed by the southpaw style of Curvis, Frankie tore into the Welshman from the opening bell knocking him all around the ring. Curvis had no answer to Frankie's power and as early as the fourth round he was reduced to holding in an attempt to thwart Frankie's attacks. A warning from the referee in the fifth had no effect and, continuing to hold, Curvis was disqualified soon after. It was a tremendous scalp for the Birkenhead man.

Just a fortnight later Frankie was back at the Stadium to face the reigning Irish 9st champion, Jim McCann. It was a significant step-up in class for Frankie but although boxing brilliantly behind his classic straight left, and appearing to keep the Irishman at long range to pick up points easily, McCann caught Frankie with a sweeping right hand in the sixth round. The punch opened up a small cut Frankie had received in the Curvis fight. Two weeks rest had obviously not been enough and with the cut refusing all attempts to stop bleeding upon his return to the corner, Frankie was retired on his stool.

Undeterred by his first professional loss, Frankie took a well-earned six-week rest and returned to the ring with a KO win over George Thomas of Aberfan at Blackpool. April 1946 saw a return to Liverpool Stadium for his next contest, to face the man who had inflicted his first defeat, Jim McCann. This time he made no mistake and he KO'd the Irishman in the third.

By now Frankie was topping the bill regularly and he beat Jackie Hughes – a Welsh featherweight contender, over ten rounds at the Stadium and was then offered an eight round return against Curvis in Swansea. Had the talented Welshman learnt enough from their first contest? To the dismay of Liverpool fans it appeared that he had for Curvis won on points. A quick knockdown in the first - when Frankie was caught by a smart counter after throwing a sloppy right straight from the bell – and a further knockdown undoubtedly cost him the fight.

1947 started with a fine win over the former world top 10 ranked Guinean Kid Tanner. Frankie would beat Tanner again in 1948 but he would also suffer losses to such talented boxers as Ben Duffy, Jim Brady, St. Helens' Johnny Molloy and that great little Frenchman and scourge of Liverpool fighters, Ray Famechon. Although adjudged a loser over ten rounds against Famechon however, this was one of Frankie's best fights. There was little in it at the end and Famechon later said it was one of the hardest fights of his career. The Frenchman was cut as early as the second round and he had to box supremely well to avoid further punishment from the hard-hitting Birkenhead man.

Frankie's punching power was much in evidence in the fight immediately prior to his meeting with Famechon. An appearance in Manchester against local hero and former British champion Johnny Cusick proved that he could box and punch with the best of them. In the fifth round Frankie produced a peach of a right hand that sent Cusick crashing to the floor. Cusick grabbed hold of Frankie's legs and refused to let go until his head had cleared. Cusick was decked twice more and each time the former champion was loathe to release his hold on Frankie. The Manchester man was duly disqualified for holding in the fifth.

Frankie produced another fine performance in Manchester in February 1948, this time against the man who had given featherweight champion Nel Tarleton such a difficult challenge for the title a few months previously – the 'Aldgate Tiger' – Al Phillips. The Williams v Phillips contest was described later as one of the best fights of the year. It was non-stop for ten pulsating rounds, with the Londoner getting the verdict by the narrowest of margins. By now Frankie had met almost all the leading contenders in the featherweight division and he felt, like many observers, that he was close to securing a fight for the Central Area title at least. However, in June 1948 Frankie lost a close decision to Tony Lombard in Manchester. He became disillusioned with the fight game and retired.

Frankie Williams c. 1947   *Source: Gary Shaw*

Just like the start of his career however, Frankie came back again – this time after nearly two years out of the ring. In August 1950 he suffered a sixth round loss to Johnny Molloy and decided to call it a day again. The lure proved too much again however, and Frankie returned a third time, this time beating Tommy Higgins on points at Liverpool Stadium in September 1951. This victory seemed to galvanise Frankie and he went on a great winning streak. He beat Al Young, Tommy

Proffitt, Billy Taylor, Reuben Carl, Peter Fay, Theo Nolten, Al Young again, Ron Johnson, Gaeten Annaloro, and last, but by no means least, future world champion Hogan 'Kid' Bassey. Five of these wins came inside the distance.

In January 1953, Frankie finally got his chance to fight for the British title, a full nine years after turning pro. It wasn't the featherweight title he contested however, but the bantamweight crown as, when he made his third comeback in 1951 he had returned in the lower division. Frankie's one and only shot at a title, at Paisley Ice Rink, Scotland, ended in disappointment however, for the referee was forced to stop the contest in local man Peter Keenan's favour in the seventh round.

Perhaps Frankie should have been called 'Hokey Cokey' Williams, for he was certainly in and out of the fight game. One thing was certain however;- when he was 'in' Frankie was a match for anyone. He did not enjoy the greatest of times in later life and passed away in September 2005 aged 80. He was one of the top bantam and featherweights of his day, winning 30 out of 40 contests, with 17 stoppages.

Kenny Williams' first club was the old St James' ABC. When this closed he joined the famous Maple Leaf under Dave Rent's guidance and went on to have around 250 contests, losing less than 25 and winning a host of local Schoolboy titles in the process. He had his last fight in 1966, the same year he was selected to box for England for the first time, and he then turned to coaching, staying with the Maple Leaf until 1973. A committed member and regular at the MFBA, this article was compiled through interview with Kenny in 2007.

KENNY WILLIAMS

England rep became Maple Leaf coach

Kenny Williams first started boxing when he was around 12 years old. "I joined St. James ABC in Hooton Place in 1950," recalls Kenny, "where the trainers were Mick Gosling and Bill Murphy. When this closed down I joined the Maple Leaf ABC where the trainer was Mr Rent." Kenny had around 250 contests, losing only 23. "I was Lancashire Schoolboy champion at 6st 8lb in 1951 and National champion at 7st 4lbs in 1952." West Lancs championships at flyweight in 1954, 55 and 56 were followed some ten years later by Kenny's first senior titles. He was crowned West Lancs bantamweight champion 1965 and 66, adding the Northern Counties titles the same years. In October 1965 Kenny also won international recognition, being selected by England in a match against Poland in Lodz. "Pat Dwyer also made the team," remembers Kenny. "I was stopped in the second round against their top bantamweight Radikowski. I had the flu and was in hospital for three days afterwards." Liverpool light-middleweight Dwyer was one of only two England victors in this match, as Poland ran out comfortable 8-2 winners. Kenny also remembers, "boxing for the Northern Counties against an Ireland select, beating Christy Rafter on points."

Kenny has many fond memories of his time as one of the region's top amateurs. "I boxed Tommy Edge a few times and the first time I fought him was in Ellesmere Port. He was a good southpaw Tommy." After their fight, the decision was so long in coming that Kenny, despite eventually being declared the winner on points, was physically sick afterwards. In a Schoolboy final at Wembley I also remember a flash bulb from a camera going off in the second round. I thought the bell had gone and dropped my hands, only to get caught cold. I recovered though and went on to win. The last time I fought Frankie Morgan I left the ring suffering from double vision and lost." Kenny has no regrets about choosing boxing above other pastimes. "I loved boxing as a sport. It taught me discipline and self-respect and I'd gladly do it all again."

Kenny Williams c. 1964   *Source: Keny Williams*

Although never turning pro, Kenny's time as a coach means his views on today's game are worthy of consideration. "I can't speak for the pros but I do think it's easier to succeed today, even for an amateur. This is because the championships are stretched a bit more than they were in my day. Now they have the semi-finals and finals on different days, whereas in my era you often boxed all on the same day."

Liverpool Stadium holds particularly god memories for Kenny. "I boxed at the Stadium quite a few times and each time the atmosphere was electric. Few places have that sense of history about them and nowhere compares with it today." Kenny had his last fight in May 1966, "but stayed with the Maple Leaf where I trained and coached until 1973." After serving his time as an apprentice joiner, Kenny worked for Liverpool University, "where I met and became good friends with the late Sandy Manuel." Kenny married ex-Vernons Girl Carmel in September 1959 and, "we have four daughters, Leonie, Carmel, Margaret and Jacqueline, and seven grandchildren; four grandsons and three grand-daughters."

A talented middleweight with the Salisbury ABC, Paul Wright won the vast majority of his

100 amateur contests, boxed for England on a number of occasions and made the ABA semi-finals in 1989 before turning professional with Barry Hearn soon after. In an eight-year pro career Paul lost just three of his 22 contests, with two draws. In addition to winning the Central Area middleweight title in 1996, Paul twice fought in eliminators for the British super-middleweight title, and challenged for the WBO Intercontinental title in his last contest. The older brother of Carl Wright, who was included in the first volume of The Mersey Fighters, this article was compiled through interviews with Paul in 2006 and 2007.

PAUL WRIGHT

Middleweight contender once led to the ring by 'Bart Simpson'

With a father, Tony Wright, who was one of the founding members of the famous Salisbury ABC, and a younger brother who also graced the sport with distinction, it is little wonder that Paul Wright would box at some stage. "My father took me to the Salisbury when I was eight years old," explains Paul, "and I liked it as it kept me fit, kept me off the streets and stopped me from getting up to any mischief."

Boxing certainly kept Paul busy and he went on to have 100 amateur contests, winning 72, and was good enough to make the National Schoolboy finals in 1982, the NABC finals in 1985 and the ABA semi-final in 1989. He also represented England at various international tournaments, most notably perhaps when he lost to East Germany's Willie Schmidt when representing the ABA U19s in October 1984. Shmidt was the reigning European U19 light-welterweight at the time so this loss was no disgrace.

Paul turned pro with Barry Hearn's Matchroom team not long after his senior ABA semi-final defeat in 1989 and took on the moniker of Paul 'Do It' Wright. "Carl always said that my nickname was wrong," says Paul, "and that as he was called 'the Wildcat' I should be called 'the Pussycat!'"

Paul made his debut at Preston Guild Hall on 13 October the same year, forcing a first round stoppage win over Swindon's Andy Balfe. Two weeks later Rochdale's John Tipping likewise never heard the bell for the end of the first round as he too was stopped inside three minutes at Bowlers Club in Manchester. Two months later Paul rounded off the year with a six rounds draw against Wolverhampton's Nigel Rafferty.

Contractual disputes meant that Paul didn't box again for over two years but, now managed by Colin Moorcroft, he picked up where he left off with two points wins in April and May 1992. A fifth round disqualification win over Swansea light-heavy John Kaighin in September soon followed before another early stoppage win, this time over Jason McNeil.

In November 1992 Paul met Swansea's experienced and durable Russell Washer on the undercard of the Chris Eubank v Juan Carlos Jimenez world super-middleweight title fight at Manchester's G-Mex Centre. Paul admits that this was his toughest fight. "It was my first eight-rounder, and I wasn't sure if I would be able to last the distance. I prepared really well though and in the end the distance wasn't a problem – I sailed through it – but Washer was unbelievably strong and tough. He was the hardest opponent I faced."

For this contest Paul was led to the ring by a friend dressed up as Bart Simpson. "I used to fight with Disney badges on my shorts; Donald Duck, Mickey Mouse, that sort of thing. It was just for a laugh really. Something to make people notice me and smile. One of the lads from the Powerhaus gym who sponsored me at the time, Neil Fitzmaurice, jumped in the ring after one of my wins at Everton Park dressed up in a Pink Panther suit. The referee wasn't impressed though and pushed him out of the ring! For the Washer fight on the Chris Eubank bill at the G-Mex the same lad got dressed up as Bart Simpson and he led me to the ring. In his review of the fight Reg Gutteridge mentioned it in the *Boxing News* saying that boxing was getting like a circus - but everyone seems to be doing something like that now, coming to the ring on a flying carpet, or dressed as a gladiator."

With another early stoppage victory Paul's record now read eight wins from nine contests, and he was beginning to move up the British rankings. So much so that for his next contest he was matched with Bury's Glen 'the Bomber' Campbell for the Central Area super-middleweight title. A tough, hard-hitting super-middleweight, Campbell had held the title since 1990 and was unbeaten as a professional. Despite the added incentive of the contest also being an eliminator for the British title, Campbell stopped Paul in the fourth. Despite his first loss as a pro, Paul was as determined as ever to be a success in the ring. Three wins from three contests later, including two over the experienced pair of Alan Baptiste and Seamus Casey, meant that Paul found himself in another eliminator for the domestic crown, this time against tough Scotsman Stephen Wilson. Just as in the Campbell fight however, Paul had to travel to his opponent's back yard for this October 1994 contest and although he gave it his best shot, he was outpointed in Glasgow over ten rounds.

Paul remembers that, "Wilson was probably overweight for this fight. I saw him jump on the scales and it kept going up and up and up. It didn't look like it was going to stop at the right weight! I just wanted

Paul Wright c. 1993   *Source: Paul Wright*

the fight to go-ahead so I let it go. I gave it a good go. In the seventh Wilson completely turned his back on me but the ref never said anything to him. By the end of the fight he had two bad cuts over both his eyes but the ref never even looked at it, let alone stopped the fight. They were that bad that if the fight had been in Liverpool it would probably have been stopped in my favour." Two fights later Wilson lost to Joe Calzaghe for the vacant British title.

"I was supposed to fight Joe for the British title but although we verbally agreed to meet his management never made the fight. He's a good lad. A few years ago my sister met him on holiday in Florida and mentioned to him that he was meant to fight her brother. He asked who it was and when she said me his first reaction was to ask after Carl and how he was doing following his accident."

A draw and five wins from his next six contests showed that Paul still had the attributes to win a title of some description however, and this he did in August 1996 when he outpointed Leeds' Colin Manners for the Central Area middleweight title at the Adelphi Hotel. A lack of fights ensured Paul never defended the title however, and it was a full seven months before his next contest, against Hackney's Jason Matthews for the WBO Intercontinental middleweight title in Norwich.

Matthews was unbeaten in 13 contests and would later win the WBO middleweight title so it was no disgrace when Paul was stopped in the third. It turned out to be his last contest. Seven months later, on 11 October 1997, younger brother Carl lost on points to Antrim's Mark Winters for the British light-welterweight title in Sheffield. Driving home from the contest Carl fell unconscious and trainer Colin Moorcroft rushed him to hospital where surgeons removed a blood clot from his brain. To his family's, and older brother Paul's relief, Carl made a miraculous recovery. Paul announced his retirement soon after.

Despite what happened to his brother Paul has no regrets about his chosen career however, "I would gladly do it all again. In fact I think I would do even better. There are more titles around now and this gives fighters more of a chance to win one and therefore earn a bit more money."

Paul adds that although he never boxed at the Stadium he would have loved to have done so. "My Dad used to take me and Carl there when we were kids. We saw quite a few shows there and, watching the fights and knowing the history of the place, I remember the hairs used to stand up on the back of my neck. The first year I boxed in the ABAs at Everton Park was a similar experience. It was a brilliant atmosphere. There's nothing like boxing in front of your home crowd with family and friends all cheering you on to win." Married to Gillian for two years, Paul continues to work and live in Liverpool, where he is now a scaffolder.